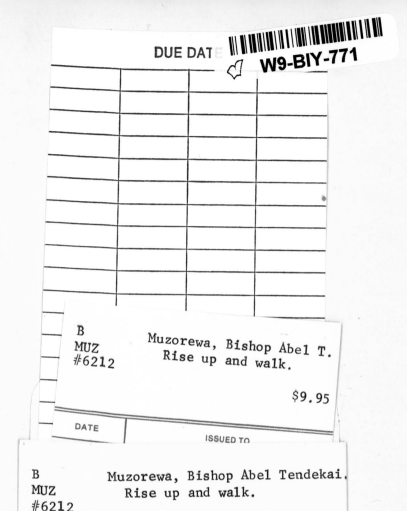

B
MUZ
#6212

Muzorewa, Bishop Abel T.
Rise up and walk.

$9.95

DATE

ISSUED TO

B
MUZ
#6212

Muzorewa, Bishop Abel Tendekai.
Rise up and walk.

$9.95

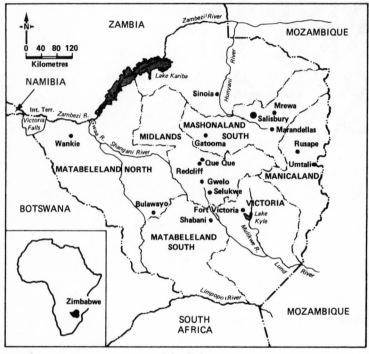

Rhodesia

RISE UP & WALK

The Autobiography of
Bishop Abel Tendekai Muzorewa

Edited by
Norman E. Thomas

Abingdon
Nashville

Rise Up and Walk

First Published in Britain in 1978
by Evans Brothers Limited.
United States edition by Abingdon, 1978.

Library of Congress Cataloging No. 78-19546

ISBN 0-687-36450-7

MANUFACTURED BY THE PARTHENON PRESS AT
NASHVILLE, TENNESSEE, UNITED STATES OF AMERICA

to
MAGGIE MUZOREWA
my life partner
whose courage and sacrifice
made this adventure possible.

Contents

Foreword

Authentic revolutions begin in the minds and hearts of people when their circumstances dictate that the mere act of living is at the same time an act of self-degradation. When a society determines that one is to be consciously forced through the essential social processes for survival to practise and participate in their own oppression, there is one predictable response—radical fundamental Change.

Revolutions and true revolutionaries are born indigenously. They are not imported. They bear the patent of the oppressed people, they are rooted in the soil of their lands. They are a part of the history of the culture and the religion that has suffered through oppression. To attribute their will to change their powerless state or their demands for full human dignity to 'foreign devils' is to support the system which oppresses them and to make the conflict for liberation and justice more violent.

Abel Muzorewa presents here an anthology of true revolutionary African personality. The story of the struggle for an independent Zimbabwe must be told now. It must be told by an African who has been intimately involved in the process. Historians, politicians and sociologists will have their day. When they write they will lack the authenticity which is evident on each page of this book unless they draw on fundamental sources like this one prepared by Bishop Muzorewa.

There are many things that I could say about this very readable historical autobiography. You will be impressed by its authenticity, sincerity and simplicity. Its unencumbered style permits the reader to participate in the life of the writer with an intimacy of his person and involvement to significant contemporary history that will fascinate you.

Any person who understands the task which the Bishop has done should share his credentials. This he has done very well.

He shares deeply and honestly his early life beginnings and his pilgrimage. With selfless candour he gives credit to many people, friends and enemies alike, who have contributed to his life. There is of course recognition for the patterned western credentials; his academic degrees, honours and citations. But his essential credentials are revealed in his profound Africanness; specifically his very conscious awareness of being a son of Zimbabwe.

This is most important to keep in mind as this book is read. This book is more than the life story of a man and his family. It is a vital romance story where his life has been inextricably united with the struggle of his people for liberation. He breathes when his people breathe. He suffers with them, shares their fears and longs for total liberation. There is no part of the struggle which he does not share. There are times when the reader can sing and dance with Sithole, Nkomo, Muzorewa, and Mugabe in unity. At other times you will fear, for the depth and hostility of the intrigue which suggests a neutralizing futility of the African efforts. Ian Smith's role as a brilliant tormentor and a tyrant is revealed in a documented chronicle. It should help many to understand why the negotiations with the white minority government have failed, leaving the armed struggle as the Africans' only alternative.

As a churchman and political leader the Bishop has had to play two major roles in his country. Some people have difficulty considering the two. He does not. As church leader he remains free to appreciate the values which have come through the Church. He is also free to criticize it for its shortcomings.

'It is not surprising that political leaders emerged from among these trained by the churches. Not only did the Church provide the schooling for future Zimbabwean nationalists, but also it gave significant opportunities for leadership.'

Speaking about the brutal detention of Didymus Mutasa, deportation of Clutton-Brocks and the Tangwena people, the Bishop laments the silence of the churches.

'Where are the voices of these churchmen who had so vehemently opposed violence. Is this not violence too? But the church leaders were conspicuously silent.'

He is equally clear and candid on the role of violence in the overall struggle. One can sense his own development as one who is basically a pacifist, he reveals the painful road to a world of reality where violence of every nature must be dealt with. He breaks with the giants of non-violence, Gandhi and Martin Luther King, Jr. Yet he sees a valid place for negotiation till people are forced to other alternatives.

'I do not subscribe to the romantic and unhistoric view that the liberation struggle is won by armed clashes between the forces of liberation and the colonial army. Important as they are, such acts of war form only sporadic episodes in the total process of liberation. Liberation embraces the whole process of opposition to all forms of the colonial oppression. This opposition is at various times moral, spiritual, mental, economic, political, and physical, as appropriate. The Church's contributions are manifold, including its attack on the very rationale and philosophy of racism. In the future it must continue in the struggle for liberation even after the overthrow of the Smith regime. At that moment the struggle for liberation will not end but will enter a new and perhaps more difficult phase.'

There are tender sensitive moments in the book. Insights into the human moments of historical drama are shared. He is in Mozambique perhaps under house arrest. Utter frustration reigns. He longs to see the 'boys'. He even thinks of hitch-hiking to a camp whose location he does not know. He shares the horror of the massacre at Nhazonia where over 600 Rhodesian civilian refugees were wantonly killed.

Events have their impact on the Bishop. His health calls him to task at one critical period. His resilience is evidenced again and again as he and colleagues are disappointed by defections within the ranks, intrigue by Smith, and the failure of the British to show courage to meet their responsibility in the negotiations.

Of the British he says, 'We felt used and abused.' He defends ANC's position without appearing to be defensive in relation to talks with Smith. For he says at one point, 'The Zimbabwe war of liberation is not an aggression against white people. It is a last response, taken in self-defence, when all non-violent methods have been tried and spurned by our oppressors. This is why I am a freedom fighter. This is why I support the armed struggle. I cannot sit smugly and passively in the comfort of my home while my people are being tortured to death, shot down, or bombed.'

Another important issue raised by the Bishop is the role of external forces that are at work in their own interest and on behalf of foreign investment. The role of Henry Kissinger was of little aid. His support of South Africa's *détente* was seen by Africans as being of greater assistance to the oppressors in Southern Africa than to the blacks. Muzorewa is open and courageous in condemning the role of the so-called Frontline Presidents. He shares his frustration with them as he views them making decisions for Zimbabwe. His phrase after one of the meetings with the five Frontline leaders, 'It is a terrible thing not to have a country of one's own,' expresses the depth of his agony.

Here then is an authentic story of a man seeking to be an instrument of liberation and history. It is a story well told. It is a history of a people and one of their leaders going through the birth pains to be born a free nation.

Read it well. For this may be the autobiography of the first president of an independent Zimbabwe. The man stands out for what he is: a person of strong opinions, self-directed, people oriented and Christian. He is one of the last Zimbabwe leaders to surface in the struggle. He is far from the least. Already he has his footstep indelibly etched on the historical scroll of Zimbabwe history.

Isaac H. Bivens
Assistant General Secretary
Africa Affairs
Board of Global Ministries
United Methodist Church

Acknowledgements

My grateful thanks go to many persons who have helped in the preparation of this volume. Much of it has been written in strange places during periods of self-exile from my homeland and amidst the intense activities of Zimbabwean politics.

I am grateful to the Rev. Webster Mutamba, my personal assistant, who both inspired me to write during my peripatetic existence, and turned my rough notes into well-ordered sentences. Upon his departure for further studies in 1976 Solomon Nenguwo gave the same talent and devotion to this task.

I also wish to express my gratitude to Dr. Norman E. Thomas, my editor. His own knowledge and experience of Zimbabwe, and personal sympathy with our liberation struggle, enabled him to reorganize the material to cover the major events with which my life story is intertwined.

Many secretaries in several countries deserve thanks for their labours in typing the manuscript: Panna and Mandakini Patel, Evelyn Kawonza, Mrs. A. Jampies, Anna Morford, and Jamie Gray.

Many persons helped in recalling past events, and in developing the basic content of speeches, addresses and sermons which, although quoted here, will be the content of future volumes. I am grateful to Aeneus Chigwedere who assisted with oral traditions and to Ezekiel Makunike and Farai David Muzorewa who assisted in the revision of various chapters of the autobiography.

Finally, I am grateful to all leaders of the United Methodist Church in Zimbabwe who have borne extra responsibilities during my intense involvement in politics and in the writing of this book. Among them is Pat Fulmer, my personal secretary, whose faithful attention to administrative details freed me for creative writing.

I and my publishers would like to thank the following for the use of their photographs: Camera Press; Associated Press; Ernest Sells. Other photographs are my own.

Abel T. Muzorewa

Chapter 1

Between Two Worlds

In the eastern highlands of Zimbabwe, ten miles north-east of the city of Umtali, lies Old Umtali Methodist Centre. During the early days of colonization of Rhodesia, Old Umtali was ideally sited for a town. A later survey for the railway resulted in moving the town across a chain of hills. It was then that Bishop Hartzell, the early United Methodist missionary, secured from Cecil J. Rhodes and the British South Africa Company a grant of the abandoned town area for mission work. In the ensuing years, Old Umtali grew into what United Methodists call their 'Jerusalem', because all the Church's work in that country started at Old Umtali, later spreading from there to different parts of Zimbabwe.

This was the place where I was born prematurely on April 14, 1925. I owe my survival to an exceptionally efficient Swedish nurse, Ellen E. Bjorklund. She was the only nursing sister around who knew how to care for premature babies.

When only a few weeks old, my frail little body was attacked by a bout of pneumonia. Seeing me weaken, the medical orderly at Old Umtali advised my parents to take me to a renowned African herbalist, Muchemwa Mafarachisi. He was my maternal uncle (*sekuru*)—one of a long line of traditional healer/diviners in our family. In panic my parents bundled me up and took me to his home in the Nyakatsapa area twenty miles north of Old Umtali. It was a dark night—so dark that an unidentified wild animal came close to us and then disappeared into the night, either because it was hesitant to attack us or because my parents paid little or no attention to anything except their sick baby.

I am told that I nearly died that night. Upon arrival, Sekuru Mafarachisi wasted no time. He prepared thin porridge from millet (*rapoko*) flour mixed with herb juices. To my worried parents that medicine porridge must have appeared to be my last meal before death, for they had lost all hope for my survival.

1

After several hours of hard bargaining for life, however, I slowly regained strength. My eyes began to brighten like those of a healthy child. That early incident was the first of a series of episodes in which my life hung in the balance.

Upon reflection it does not surprise me that my parents took me for healing both to a missionary nurse and to an African healer. Like others who had been exposed to hospitals and clinics, they went there for healing of those diseases which they thought the white men knew best how to handle. They retained the belief, however, that certain disorders little known to the Europeans could best be healed through traditional medicine. Living between two worlds, they tried to hold on to what was worth while in both cultures.

A Precious Pair

My father, Haadi Philemon Muzorewa, was the only son of Mapisaunga and Nhambura (Chipunza) Muzorewa. My paternal grandfather was the son of Zvekuomba of the Makombe clan. I am, therefore, in the traditional sense, a Makombe, with neighbouring Mozambique as the historic homeland of our clan.

It was my ancestors of the Makombe tribe who fought courageously against Portuguese rule in the early years of this century until beaten into submission or forced into exile. They were the earliest 'freedom fighters'. The tradition is still told of the time when a swarm of bees attacked the Portuguese soldiers when they were fighting with the Makombe, forcing the Portuguese to flee in haste. Even today some persons remember my ancestry and address me, saying, 'Wamurwa ne nuchi ('You fought with bees').

My father's mother was of the Chipunza family, one of the royal houses of the Makoni tribe, with the same totem, Shonga, as those named Makoni. They were among the first to be evicted by the Europeans from their rich farmlands of the Headlands area, halfway between the present cities of Salisbury and Umtali. Today as one travels between those towns following the rail line across the high plateau, one passes for one hundred miles through the historic homeland of the Makoni people. Gradually family after family was evicted to make way for white farmers, usually without compensation and with perhaps six months' notice. My relatives chose to resettle at a place called Murango, about five miles from Inyazura. Today that place is also a European farm. In the 1920s a European farmer wanted that good land and they were evicted once again. In fact, the history of my father's family mirrors the saga of so many thousands of Zimbabweans under white rule in Southern Rhodesia who became displaced persons in the land of their birth. This helps to explain my own father's drive in life to have land to call his own.

The history of my mother's family is also deeply affected by the land-grabbing of the Europeans. My mother's father was Munangatire Mukundu, a member of one of the royal families of the Wajindwi or Zimunya people. Their family totem is *Soko* (monkey), following the customary African way of naming each clan. Historically, they lived in the area south of Umtali, until they too were displaced by white farmers.

My mother's mother was named Maitirwa at birth, and later was given the name Dorcas at her baptism. She was a *Warozvi* by birth—the people whom we honour in Shona history as the builders of ancient Zimbabwe. Her clan of the *Mwoyo Muturikwa* totem lived, in earlier times, about fifty miles north-east of the present city of Salisbury.

My parents were among the first in their respective families to become Christians. The experience of their parents in regard to Christianity was a common one at that time. Both my grandfathers were polygamists. As such, they were not eligible for church membership. In addition my maternal grandfather's practice of healing and divination as a *nganga* must have been condemned as evil by the early missionaries. In each family, however, the first wife became a Christian and was baptized. As for the second wife, she was not accepted by the Church for baptism and membership until either the first wife or her husband died, although she could and did attend church services.

Christianity was one of the common denominators which brought my parents together. In those days it was not easy to meet a young person of the opposite sex. In traditional society one had to wait for some kind of gathering, perhaps a wedding or funeral. There, while the elders were attending to the solemnities of the occasion, young people were usually left to meet and mix. Acquaintances were made and marriage plans hatched. My parents took advantage, however, of the more regular weekly meetings of Christians for worship at the Muziti Methodist Church which they attended. In due course they became the first couple to be married in that church building. How proud must be the now-aged pastors who presided at that wedding, Rev. H. I. James and Rev. Samuel Chieza, to know that the union they helped to cement has lasted for over fifty years.

My father is about 5 feet 2 inches tall, and light in complexion. His bright eyes reflect a sense of humour and also a philosophical attitude to suffering. He has always been a disciplinarian, a quality supported by a quick temper. This temper, however, is moderated by his never-failing sense of humour.

Discipline, sharp temper, humour—those words summarize my upbringing. Add regular Bible lessons plus church-going, and you have the ingredients which have moulded my character and that of my five brothers and three sisters.

I bear a marked physical resemblance to my father. Laughingly, my father likes to relate the story of the church gathering which he attended when I acted as interpreter for a senior missionary, the late Dr. M. J. Murphree. At the end of the meeting many people gathered around my father to congratulate him on his brilliant performance as an interpreter!

From grandfather Mapisaunga my father inherited the nick-name 'Benengu'. The family story is told of how it originated with my grandfather's rich humour. One evening the old man came into the house and found his daughters-in-law shelling nuts by hand. With inevitable tongue in cheek, grandfather thereupon declared that nobody in the house really knew how to shell nuts properly. He then proceeded to give a verbal demonstration of how to shell them properly, saying 'Benengu, benengu, benengu, benengu' over and over again. Each 'benengu' was accompanied by a nut-shelling motion. From that day he became known as 'Benengu', thanks to his equally good-humoured daughters-in-law. The name became a family name, for my father used it for a long time. In fact, in the official Journal of the Church my father is listed as 'Pastor-teacher Benengu'! In a sense, I too am a 'Benengu'.

When I was a year old, my parents moved from Old Umtali Centre to Mwandiambira, a small community near by just behind Chiremba (Hartzell) Mountain. There my father served the Church as a pastor-teacher. He was one of that stalwart group of Christian leaders who served both as mission teachers in the village schools and as Christian shepherds in the same community. The first Africans to be ordained as ministers in the United Methodist Church came from among these remarkable Christian workers. My father's deep religious convictions, and the irreproachable life in which he lived out what he preached on Sundays, left an indelible impression upon me.

Like father, my mother is a devout person. Hers, however, was a faith which taught more through persuasion, compassion and example than through formal teaching and discipline. This was effective and long-lasting.

One striking feature about my mother is her voice. Although she is soft-spoken, when she sings her voice assumes a golden tone, melodious and beautiful. For that reason she has always been a valued member of church choirs. She taught us, her children, the joy of hymn-singing as well.

At 5 feet 4 inches my mother stands taller than my father. Dark in complexion, she has always been my standard of African womanhood in poise, in culture, and in industry.

At birth, mother was named *Takaruda*, a beautiful traditional Shona name meaning 'we loved it'. Like so many African names, it tells a story—in this instance of the joy which her parents experienced upon her birth.

There was always significance to one's African name. For instance, *Chenzira* ('something of the path') is a name given to a child born while the mother was on a journey. Similarly, a child whose mother passed away at the birth was almost always named *Masiyiwa* ('the one who was left behind'). How foolish were the early missionaries who considered such African names to be 'heathen', insisting that a person be given a so-called 'Christian' name upon baptism! At baptism my mother acquired a new name, Hilda. To this day no one has been able to tell us of any depth of meaning in that word apart from the fact that it was used at my mother's baptism.

My parents tell how about the age of four I became an accomplished mimic, imitating their actions and those of others with hilarious accuracy. Dr. Murphree, the missionary preacher, was one whom I loved to imitate. My congregation would be dried twigs stuck in rows in the sand. The double-bladed leaves of the *musekesa* tree served as my Bible. Remembering his sermon about the parable of Dives and Lazarus, I would stand before my 'congregation', and my childish voice would ring out in Shona in the characteristic tone of Dr. Murphree, 'Are you rich up there, Dives?' When other children came near the scene, I would immediately insist that they join my 'congregation'—

5

grateful for a live audience! Others marvelled at how I could remember and repeat every syllable of the preacher's words over and over again.

Life with Grandparents

It was a tradition among our people that the first-born child had to be looked after by grandparents, usually those of his mother's side. I was no exception to that tradition. At the tender age of five, my grandmother duly collected me, bag and baggage. She regarded me as the first-born of her daughter, even though I had had an elder sister, Esther, who had died in infancy.

By that time, my grandparents had been moved by the Europeans to the foot of Mount Sanzaguru near Tikwiri Mountain in the Makoni Reserve, an area assigned for African settlement under the Land Apportionment Act of 1930.

My grandparents were known as generous and gracious people. So sweet was my grandmother's temper that a million devils would not have ruffled her mien. Her face was always lit by a tender smile. And I was her favourite. Relatives tell how she would at times roast meat for me even when there was none prepared for others. We called it 'chimukuyu'—fire-dried meat. Besides the goat meat and chicken, there was lots of milk and beef, for the family herd numbered up to a hundred. I never stop wondering how heredity succeeded in keeping me at the height of 5 feet 2 inches in spite of the large quantities of meat and milk that I devoured during those growing years!

My grandfather was known as a healer, although in those days he did not possess the powers of divination formerly practised by his own father. When asked, he said that the gourd called a *gowo* which used to speak the truth had disappeared when brothers in the family quarrelled over who would possess it, and that it had never been seen again.

I can attest, however, to my grandfather's healing ability. Once when playing with a bicycle rim, I slipped and a spoke jabbed my left leg like a spear, causing a deep and ugly wound. Grandfather, when he learned of it, rushed to a nearby stream to gather certain leaves and roots. After carefully washing the wound and the leaves, he bound them upon the leg with fibres like a bandage. The roots, once pounded, dried by the fire and ground to a powder, were applied each time the bandage was removed.

6

No infection developed, although the scar remains to this day as a mute testimony to his medical skill.

Belief in witchcraft was very strong in those days. Every misfortune, of sickness or death, of failure in farming or business or even love, was believed to have a personal cause. It was hard for my parents to refute the reasoning of the elders that their first-born daughter must have died because of witchcraft.

As for my childhood, the family tells this story. Each Sunday my Aunt Edith would take me to church, when small, often strapped on her back. One Sunday, while people closed their eyes in prayer, a woman sitting beside us tried to give me food. With the innocence of a child I reached out to receive it, only to have my Aunt Edith shake it from my hand. Holding the morsel of food in her hand, she challenged that woman outside the church to give that same piece of stiff porridge to her own child. She refused. Now the woman was suspected in the village of giving poisoned food to others. When she refused to feed her own child with it, Aunt Edith could reach only one conclusion — that God had led her to keep her eyes open during that prayer so as to save my life.

As a child, I also lived in a world in which dreams and reality seemed intertwined. One night I dreamed that my father would bring me cooked green maize (corn). 'What a silly dream!' my aunt and grandmother replied as I related it the next morning. They were working to cultivate their maize field at the time and the plants were only knee high. At about nine o'clock, however, they were startled to see my father striding towards them. There, tied to the handle of the axe upon his shoulder, were freshly cooked ears of green maize! A child's funny dream had come true.

In those childhood years even the chores of herding cattle and goats seemed like fun and play to us. Fishing was also one of my preoccupations. First I had to learn the art of putting the right size of bait on the hook, before graduating from catching frogs to catching fish. These were some of the pleasant memories of those pre-school years, in which we left to our elders the burden of scratching a living from often very unyielding soil.

Chapter 2

The Village I Like Best

'East, west, home is best', the saying goes. For me 'home' is the village of Chinyadza, twelve to fourteen miles from the small rural town of Rusape in eastern Zimbabwe. The village lies cosily at the foot of Mabvuwo Mountain.

I do not remember how old I was when I returned to stay with my parents again. After his assignment as pastor-teacher, my father had decided to try his hand at farming. Finding the soils too poor at Muziti, the family home, he decided to seek a patch of fertile virgin soil. He found it at Chinyadza about ten miles away.

Visiting our village, one could see that this place was chosen carefully as a homestead. The houses and granaries were in the middle of a pocket of rich brown and black soil—in striking contrast to those infertile sandy soils characteristic of most African 'Tribal Trust' lands. These soils were the envy of every farmer in the area. Evidence of the earth's richness could be seen in the family orchard which abounded with mangoes, peaches and lemons. Huge gum trees soared into the sky, giving the village a distinctive character. Between the houses and the fields could be seen cattle kraals, pig sties, and pens for sheep and goats.

The family house was a four-bedroomed building with a separate thatched-roofed kitchen situated about fifteen yards from the main house. That modest building has become a treasured monument in my mind. It was the theatre in which the tragedies and comedies of my youth were most often enacted. There I spun out with others the fantasies of youthful innocence, and those grandiose schemes hatched by a powerful yet unripe imagination. My memories of those years are happy ones of a life of security assured by an ordered family life.

In Zimbabwe, 'family' includes more than one's own father, mother, brothers and sisters. It encompasses a far wider range of kinsfolk. For us 'home' included the huts of my grandmother just forty yards from my father's house. Just to the north lived

Mrs. Chipunza, the widow left by my grandmother's brother. To the west lived my father's sister, her husband and children. All these shared one home (*musha*) together with us. All of us were considered to be part of one family.

Our extended family system carried with it certain economic advantages. We were able to pool our resources to promote the economic well-being of all. In farming we shared the work together. Blessed by rich soils, adequate rainfall, and a co-operative spirit, we prospered.

My parents depended on me in many ways as I was their first-born son. Often I was the one chosen to carry messages to our neighbours. From an early age I accepted responsibility for herding the cattle and milking the cows. Indeed, tending livestock became a vital force in shaping my character. While doing so we children learned much about nature at first-hand. We discovered which wild fruits and plants were poisonous and which were good to eat. We observed the breeding habits of the animals we tended. We also learned much about responsibility. There was no bigger offence than to lose a beast. The punishment given was immediate and severe. But all was not work while herding. We played games, fought and then forgave each other, and learned the importance of physical courage. Thus we were prepared for both the responsibilities and conflicts of adolescence.

Near our village my father discovered some forty to fifty acres of relatively rich soil near the top of Mabvuwo Mountain. It was there that our family carried out a heroic struggle to wrest a good living from the land. First, my father made that herculean effort required to clear the land for ploughing. There were long days of felling trees, of cutting and digging and burning the stumps—all done by hand with no tools other than axe and hoe. Then the planting took place. Soon the top of the mountain was crowned with rich green fields of maize, groundnuts, *rapoko* (millet) and beans. The last was a valuable cash crop which my parents grew as much of as space would allow.

One scourge, however, remained to be overcome—baboons. Hordes of these beasts would descend upon the crops at harvest time for we had had the audacity to plant our fields at their very home. We in turn took measures to discourage their forays. Relays of up to five people, armed with sticks, bows and arrows, would be organized to keep watch over the fields day and night as the time of harvest approached. At times my father would appeal for help to the District Commissioner in Rusape, who might lend him a shotgun for use against the baboons. This was the only time that an African would be allowed to have a gun in his possession.

Baboon-duty was an exciting time for us youngsters. We thought it was fun to camp out in the fields, cooking and sleeping there. It was work, however, for it demanded our closest attention and observation. Baboons could be a danger, especially when they realized that their opponents were merely small boys who were unarmed. Sometimes they would pick up a stone which had been thrown at them and throw it right back at you.

On one occasion my father let me carry the borrowed gun to the mountain fields when he was away from home, being first careful to conceal at home all the cartridges so that I would not be tempted to try to fire it! How proud I was to carry that big gun on my shoulder, adult fashion, and to pretend that I was a big-game hunter. I had noticed that baboons were so scared of a gun that the mere sight of it sent them scampering away to safety. This gave me a tremendous feeling of power over those otherwise fierce creatures. But as my game of intimidation went on, the baboons began to call my bluff. It eventually dawned on them that I was harmless on two counts: they saw me to be a small boy and realized that the gun in my hands never seemed to make its usual bang. Needless to say that was the end of my sway over the baboons.

One evening the family assembled in the main house for evening prayers. The practice was that the children remained in their bedrooms during prayers. We felt included, however, because the house had no ceilings, the partitions were thin, and voices carried easily from room to room. On that occasion father asked my brother John Wesley Kufahakutizwi to lead in prayer. He must have been about eight years of age then. He started to pray in his childish voice: 'O God, be with father, with mother, with all my brothers and sisters, and with all those who are sick and in prisons.' Then he went on, building to a climax, 'and be with those who are chasing baboons.' He paused and repeated, 'and those chasing baboons'. He was in deadly earnest about the welfare of those persons, so much so that we young listeners were at first puzzled, then amused. When John repeated the phrase a third time, we could contain our laughter no longer and broke out in uncontrollable giggles. Fortunately, father saw the funny side of it too, or we might have all been chastized for our frivolity during prayers.

Good Neighbours

Village life entailed a web of social relationships. Especially close was our friendship with two other Christian families who lived a short distance away—the Nyatangas and the Jijitas. All three fathers had been trained at Old Umtali Mission. All three had served as pastor/teachers. All had moved into the Chinyadza area with their wives and children hoping to build a good life as farmers and committed Christians for themselves and their families.

Living apart from their traditional family homes, our three families were released from those pressures to conform with past ways that make it so difficult for many of the Shona people to be progressive. Here at Chinyadza my parents were free to build a rectangular house instead of just round huts, to dig a well for pure water instead of drawing from the same stream where people and animals bathed, and to construct the first pit latrines. They had learned to keep flies from the milk, and the benefits of a balanced diet. They desired to build a school for their children, and to put the church at the centre of their community life.

Going to church services as a child was as natural for me as eating or sleeping or going to school. At first we worshipped under a big tree at the chief's home. Later all the families helped to build a first church building of sun-dried brick with a grass thatched roof. My father was one of the three village leaders who took turns in preaching.

Even more interesting for us as children were the ten-day religious camp meetings which we attended with our parents. These, along with weddings, were the major social events of the year for us. In addition to the large gathering for singing, preaching and prayer, people used to go apart in smaller groups to confess their sins, to share their faith, and to pray for each other.

One day while in one of these groups with my mother, I was astonished to see a woman fall down as we were singing. Immediately the others sang more loudly. They struggled to keep her under control but could not contain her. I was puzzled when the woman on the ground began speaking with a foreign accent and said, 'Leave me alone; I want to go to my wife.' 'What is she saying?' I asked my mother. 'How can a woman ask to go to *her*

11

wife?' 'That is what we call a *shawe* spirit,' my mother replied. 'This woman is being possessed by a *shawe* of the Sena or Nyanja tribe from Mozambique or Malawi,' she explained. 'As we pray with her, we are doing what Jesus did—casting out demons from people who were possessed by the evil spirits,' she concluded. This was my first experience of a *shawe* spirit. It was mysterious, and yet I sensed the great faith of my mother that God is as present today to overcome evil spirits and heal as he was in the time of Jesus.

The Christian faith was a strong bond in our community which held together not only the elder Muzorewas, Nyatangas and Jijitas, but also their children. Those with whom we played were all reared on the same moral code and Christian principles as ourselves. There was no question of any of the children of these families leading each other astray.

All three families believed in applying Christian principles to everyday life. In fact, they formed something of a social club amongst themselves. All the children from the three families automatically belonged to the club. At regular intervals the families would gather at one of the homes to spend the evening singing hymns, telling stories and having a meal together. The children would add variety by singing folk songs. As for the meal, chicken usually formed the main dish. Sometimes one of the families would slaughter a goat, a sheep, or even a cow. At the end of the evening the guest families would collect money and present it to the hosts. In this way we formed an early savings club. It was our unwritten rule that such monies were to be used to purchase major household goods—bicycles, sewing machines, furniture and the like.

Christianity, therefore, for me was thoroughly indigenous in the lifestyle of our family and friends. I understood it as joyous and practical. I grew up in it and was surrounded by it. I saw it applied in countless little ways. It was never a 'Sunday-only religion'.

To School

My first recollection of school is of seeing village children passing our fields each day. I was impressed by their neat uniforms and by the books which they carried. My father, who himself had started school at a very late age, did not sense any urgency in my going. He was understanding, however. Father neither questioned my desire to go to school nor suppressed my feelings about schooling.

So it was that at the age of nine I found myself at Chinyadza School in what was called Sub-standard A at that time. The building was just one thatched room constructed of poles with mud plaster. Nevertheless, school impressed me. I saw that others could say and do things of which I had no knowledge or understanding.

I remember my first teachers with affection for their kindness to me as a new pupil. One day our dog whom we called *Kugarahunzwana* (which means 'real living is harmonious living') did not live up to its name. The dog, after following me to school, was attracted by a girl whose dress was tattered. Chasing her, it tore her dress into shreds. The girl was furious and came at me to thrash me. As far as she was concerned, I had torn her dress because the dog was mine. Fortunately Miss Katherine Kutukwa, our teacher, intervened. Taking the embarrassing burden as her own, she took the tattered dress and mended it herself.

On another day at school, while working in the garden with the other children, I suddenly felt so hungry that I could hardly walk or work. Fortunately the wife of our headmaster gave me a piece of rice meal and meat which had been left over from her previous supper meal. She took me in as if I were her own son. I should have collapsed with hunger on the arduous seven-mile hike to home across the hills but for her compassion.

While at Chinyadza I had my first personal contact with a white man. He was Rev. H. I. James, a missionary from England, who visited our school as one of the mission schools for which he was responsible. I was more shocked than thrilled to see the whiteness and unusual length of his hair. It was startling to listen for the first time to the Englishman's language. The words I could not understand, but his gestures told the whole story. He was enacting the ups and downs of his car as it went over the bumps in the road. In fact, he was threatening to close the school unless the parents were prepared to make the road smooth enough for his car to reach it easily.

At that time I was in the second and last year of studies in our one-room schoolhouse. They used to call the grades 'little rabbit' and 'big rabbit'. Our fathers hoped that new grades would be added, but there was not enough money to pay the teachers. Many pupils who finished the second grade would stay on to repeat it, for their parents had no money to send them away to boarding schools. I was fortunate to be able to go on because of my father's industry and his concern that his children have a good education.

The Europeans

Harvest time brought with it new chores and responsibilities for us all. The full white cobs of maize, the rich, loaded fingers of the millet, the plump pumpkins and the beans all had to be brought in from the fields to be prepared for storage or marketing.

It was a major expedition each year to transport our crops to the marketing depot in Rusape twelve miles away. First, the grains had to be packed into sacks and tied. Next, they were loaded on to ox-drawn carts, each with a capacity of about twenty-five bags. Each wagon was drawn by a team of as many as eighteen oxen. I was expected, as the eldest son, to lend a hand by driving one of the wagons.

The journey to Rusape took almost two days and was arduous for both man and beast. These trips took place during the month of August when the sun was already heating up the earth after our Rhodesian 'winter'. We had to rest the animals during the hottest hours of the day. But the biggest hazard of the journey was the crossing of the Rusape River. It was painful to see the oxen going down on their knees, muscles straining, pulling at their heavy loads. The river crossing had become known as '*Mudzimu ndiringe*', which means 'ancestral spirit, look with favour upon me'. Although our family did not believe in ancestor worship, we could not shake off the obsession that if we were to pass that difficult spot successfully we would need a power beyond our own.

Upon reaching Rusape we were paid two shillings and six pence (35c) for each two-hundred pound bag of maize. Today this seems like a ridiculously low price. At that time we were grateful for even a little cash, although we knew that the white buyer was making an excessively large profit at our expense.

We sensed as children that the Europeans whom we met in town and on the surrounding white farms were different from the missionaries whom our parents knew. Conversations overheard in town were punctuated constantly with swearing and harsh words. Africans who worked on nearby European farms lived in constant fear of their white masters. If a labourer came to work fifteen or thirty minutes late he felt lucky if the white farmer merely deducted from his wages. Often the white boss used one of his permanent employees to hold the tardy worker so that the European could beat him up or kick him.

Nevertheless, my parents joined with others to work for the European farmers near by from time to time in order to raise funds to build a school or church building. Then they shared the life of the average African farm worker. Work began at 6 a.m. and carried on until 5 p.m. with a brief lunch break. Often they transplanted tobacco, cultivated maize, or harvested either of those crops. The standard wage in those days ranged from fifteen shillings to one pound a month ($2.10–$2.80), with some food rations besides.

The most hated farmer of all lived just ten miles from our home. It was he who closed the path that Africans had used for a generation to reach the main Salisbury/Umtali road and rail line. When Africans continued to use the path rather than increase their journey from five to twenty miles by walking around his farm, he shot them. So it was that some of our people were murdered and dumped in shallow unmarked graves. Their relatives knew no legal redress at that time.

Hospitality
In contrast, I recall with pleasure the gracious hospitality with which visitors were welcomed in the lands and homes about us. Zimbabweans are a warmly hospitable people. They enjoy receiving and entertaining visitors. Some cynics say this virtue of hospitality contributed to the ease with which the first white settlers penetrated our country and grabbed our land. There is perhaps some truth in this, but it cannot obscure the wonderful joy which we experienced when welcoming others into our homes.

As children we looked forward to the visitors' coming as it brought a relaxation of some of the stringent family do's and don'ts. One was allowed to make a bit more noise than usual, and naughtiness did not bring immediate punishment. Visitors, especially relatives, were always some kind of advocates who explained away our indiscretions and begged forgiveness on our behalf. It was they who appeared to notice when we were clever in speech or action. We anticipated that when visitors came we would have a special meal of chicken, or even of beef if a rarely-seen or important visitor had arrived.

15

Looking back on those years, I know that it was a privilege to grow up in a small village. There I learned what it meant to be industrious. I learned also the rewards of hard work. I received the warmth and security of parental love. I grew up to appreciate the virtues of rural life, its peace and orderliness, and how we all are dependent upon one another. Perhaps one of the greatest benefits was the respect I developed for farming. Indeed, I was to take eight long years to decide whether I preferred to become a farmer or a minister of religion, whether to tend crops or God's flock. As it is, I ended up with two vocations, since farming became my favourite hobby.

Chapter 3

My Education

In the 1930s in colonial Rhodesia, the benefits of an education were still not fully evident amongst my people. The advantages of academic education were still nebulous. Many parents regarded time spent at school as time taken away from what they considered more important things. Youths were expected to supplement the family's diet through hunting. There were cattle and goats to be tended, fields to be cultivated, crops to be harvested, firewood to be collected and a hundred and one other domestic chores to be carried out. A boy who spent his time at books was often regarded as lazy or unmanly.

It was therefore an act of foresight on the part of my father to send me to the Old Umtali boarding school for further education. There was no other alternative. My parents and others at Chinyadza would have liked to build a bigger school there. They would have willingly constructed new school buildings and equipped them and would have helped to pay the teachers' salaries, as the government required in those days. The expansion of our village school, however, was refused.

I was fortunate to go to Old Umtali for that school was, and still is, one of the finest in the country. We soon came to respect missionaries because they brought such opportunities for education to us. At that time all schools for Africans were Church-run. Government grants for teachers' salaries were meagre. Missionaries solicited donations from churches overseas to pay even the wages of village teachers. Such gifts also made possible the building up of the central schools like Old Umtali and the sending of missionary teachers. Because few parents could afford to send their children to boarding school, scholarships were provided for most students. Church schools were noted for rigorous discipline and high standards. Zimbabwe owes a debt of gratitude to those missionaries and other Church leaders who pioneered African education in our country. Until recently most educated Zimbabweans received all their schooling and scholarships for advanced studies through the Church.

Now I was thirteen and it was time to leave for boarding school. My departure from home aroused in me mixed feelings. It was painful to think of leaving my family, friends and familiar surroundings. I was to be uprooted from the security which they provided and transplanted into an entirely new environment of boarders and school authorities. The stories which had reached my ears of life at a boarding school only increased my apprehensions. It was said that the school was rough, that newcomers were bullied, and nicknamed *Mafama* ('farm boys'). Those young and small, as I was, could be made miserable if they showed signs of weakness. I faced a rigorous initiation into adulthood and the wider world in which I would live.

My father accompanied me by bicycle from our village to the railway station at the town of Inyazura. Even there I was not alone, for my parents had asked a very loving and responsible cousin, Chabarwa Matthew Mataranyika, to travel with me to Old Umtali. It was exciting for us to board that train which we had seen and heard for years but had never ridden before. As the train picked up speed, it seemed as if the moon was going in the wrong direction and the light poles seemed to be receding. The steam-pulled coaches appeared to obey the command of every puffing sound.

We reached Umtali in the early morning, as we had boarded the train in the middle of the night. There we disembarked and walked the arduous ten miles over the hills to Old Umtali.

'Who is this child?' some classmates wondered as I arrived at the school, for I looked the youngest of all the students at Old Umtali. I was so small for my age that my teachers and classmates questioned whether or not I was old enough to be there. In those days the average Standard One (Grade 3) pupil was eighteen to twenty years old. There were even cases of thirty-year-old men and women studying in primary school. I was relieved, however, to find one other boy of my size in my class—Booker T. Washington Jangano, the son of one of our ministers. Some of the older boys accorded us the sympathy and protection that they would give to their own younger brothers and sisters. The class bullies, on the other hand, took advantage of our frailty and immaturity.

My first day at Old Umtali began much as I had feared. One of the big boys started firing questions at me in English:

18

'What is your name?'

'How old are you?'

'Where do you come from?'

'What Standard are you in?'

At first I was too shy even to attempt an answer. I knew that my 'bush' English would be laughed at, for I had learned very little spoken English at Chinyadza. The boy who showered those questions at me, however, was generous enough to translate each one into Shona, our mother tongue, so that I could at least understand what he was asking me.

Then the harassing began. The new students were supposed to sing songs expressing to the bigger boys who the young new-comers were, where they came from, and in an amusing manner, what they had come to school for. In addition we were required to help with such chores as cooking, sweeping and cleaning the dormitories, and doing the washing and ironing for the bigger boys.

Before long it was time to undergo an entrance examination which included oral English. It was then that I appreciated for the first time all those questions fired at me that first day, as well as the attempts made by my father in our home to converse with me in his limited English. I did amazingly well while many pupils failed to qualify to stay on.

Each week of those early studies brought with it new adventures in learning. It was fascinating to learn cursive writing. I also enjoyed reciting passages from great books, as we were taught to do in our English classes.

Most of all I enjoyed the dramatizations. I will never forget the day our Standard Three class acted out the parable of the Good Samaritan. I played the role of the person who fell into the hands of robbers. For that occasion Mr. Mazaiwana, our teacher, bor-rowed a real donkey on which I was actually carried as part of the drama. The entire Old Umtali community was invited to watch the play. One viewer remarked at the end, 'You acted so well that it seemed like the real thing!'

Just as I was beginning to catch up with the Old Umtali tempo and spirit I contracted boils. They broke out behind my knees making it painful to walk from the study hall to the dormitory. I was grateful to my cousin who cheerfully carried me on his back, though it must have surprised others to see a teenager being carried in that way.

In spite of such physical setbacks I shared in much of the mischief-making of life in a boarding school. At night we would seek ways to get into the kitchen, even welcoming a spell of duty there in order to pick up some food treats. One of our favourites was called *makoko*, the crust found at the bottom of the pot used to cook the thick maize porridge called *sadza*, which was our staple food. We enjoyed *makoko* like children do candy today. One day I took a pocketful to the study hall, desiring to munch on it there. The first bite gave such an explosive crack that a prefect on duty rushed over to see what I was up to. He charged me with disturbing the study hall peace that night.

My first attempt to join the debating sessions brought great amusement to my classmates, for I was the youngest both in age and qualification to speak on the topic under discussion. Nevertheless, I demanded a hearing. When the chairman finally called upon me I became speechless. Finally I blurted out, 'Mr. Chairman, I am happy, happy, happy!' My fellow students nearly fell off their chairs in laughter at this. For some time thereafter the girls used to call me 'Mr. Happy Happy'.

On another occasion students were relating their holiday experiences. I wished to tell how I had helped my parents to cultivate in the fields but could not remember the correct words in English to use. Instead I improvised from Shona, my mother tongue, saying that I had helped my parents to '*sakura-sakura* (cultivate)'. That's how a second nickname arose.

A third was given to me as a result of one musical performance. I was a member of a student choir which we had organized to feature African songs and dances. In one of them we acted out the farmer's life as we began to sing:

'*Tariwamba tariwamba basaredu*' (We have started, we have started our job)
'*Uyai mese muzotibatsirawo*' (Come all, and help us, please).

Then followed the response with the sound and motions of hoeing, '*Zendeu! Zendeu! Zendeu!*' as with each shout we struck the floor with our hoes. I was so completely absorbed by the song and its actions that for some time thereafter students called me 'Mr. Zendeu'.

The school curriculum in those days balanced academic with practical training. In the mornings we studied English (reading,

20

writing and spelling), Shona, arithmetic, geography, history, and general science. Much of the afternoon was devoted to such practical courses as gardening and carpentry. As a result, students who finished Standard Six (Grade 8), the highest level of African education at that time, went out not just as English speakers but also with skills for better farming, furniture-making, etc. It is ironic that several independent African nations today are discovering a 'new' approach to education which combines study and work, for that is what we received in earlier years.

My Second Birth

As a Christian I speak of two births which I had at Old Umtali Methodist Centre—that of my physical birth in 1925, and that of my spiritual rebirth when a student there.

During my school days the entire week before Easter was known as 'revival' week at Old Umtali. All academic work came to a standstill at that time. Some students welcomed this as a holiday and disliked the required attendance at religious services. Others saw it as a time for spiritual renewal.

I was one of the latter group, for I was asking myself, 'Do I believe in Christ just because my parents and teachers want me to do so? What do I believe?' At one revival meeting I found my answer. Rev. Josiah Chimbadzwa, our pastor, preached a stirring sermon and invited those who wished to meet Christ in a new way to come forward. I felt an inner compulsion to go to the altar but hesitated. Many of my classmates made fun of religion, feeling that Christianity was a religion for the aged. What would they say if they saw me kneeling at the altar? Finally I decided to go forward. I heard giggles from some beside me, but also the footsteps of other students who joined me at the altar for prayer. Then those who had responded went out together to the foot of the mountain to talk and to pray.

Although I had been brought up in a devout Christian home, I made that morning my own commitment to follow Christ as my Saviour. On that day of days Christ gave me a spiritual microscope, spectacles and earphones to see and hear for myself what Christ offers. I realized that I was a sinner, but that God loves me and forgives me.

At such moments it is often the little misdeeds that at first bring remorse. I remembered how a group of us had stripped a mango tree when asked to cut grass at the home of Sister Hansen,

21

our missionary nurse. On leaving the small group I went immediately to her and said, 'Sister, I am sorry that I took your mangoes without permission. Today I have accepted Christ and have felt His acceptance of me. I now seek your forgiveness also, Sister Ruth,' She was a sincere Christian who understood what I was feeling. Her words accepting and forgiving me gave me indescribable joy.

In the months that followed I found that I was given a new moral fibre which helped me to pass through the hazards and hurdles of adolescence. Some young men would go on hunting sprees for loose girls in order to satisfy their sexual desires. They considered those of us who refrained to be somehow 'abnormal'. I felt strengthened to resist such temptations so that later I might enter marriage with a sense of victory.

Many Zimbabweans today marvel that we as students accepted without question the moral absolutes taught us by missionary teachers, including their prohibitions against smoking, drinking, and all premarital sex. The essential commitment which we made, however, was to follow Christ and to live a life consistent with the faith we professed. Today many whom we respect as leaders of Zimbabwe are among those who can testify to a spiritual rebirth during their student days.

I believe that the Christian faith gives a unity and a centre to all of life. It is an ethic not just for the professional minister, but for every believer. It is a call to each person to seek Christ in his personal life. With it you can go anywhere in the world, to work as farmer or driver, politician or nurse, and find Christ to be your source of happiness, strength and victory.

The basic commitment to seek for wholeness in life which I made at Old Umtali that day is, I believe, consistent with our traditional Shona philosophy of life. In it we centre on the belief that life is a whole, and that it can be lived to the fullest when every thought, action and human relationship is in conformity with our spiritual values.

My Father's Odyssey

For many years my father had considered becoming an ordained minister of the Church. That choice was doubly difficult for him to make after his heroic effort to build the family farm at Chinyadza. During my third year at Old Umtali, however, my father decided to accept Dr. Murphree's invitation to study theology. This meant a radical change for the family. Cattle were sold, farmlands surrendered to others, and cash savings prepared to finance the years of study ahead. The first trauma of moving, however, was soon surpassed in intensity by a second. When Dr. Murphree went on furlough, his successor as principal did not approve of married theological students. Father, mother and family were suddenly asked to leave Old Umtali. Determined to continue in school, nevertheless, my father moved to another Methodist Centre at Mrewa, near Salisbury. He had to resign at the end of the year, however, because he could not afford to pay both for education and the raising of his family.

These were trying years for my parents. They had accepted land in Chief Mangwende's reserve which was almost desert-like in comparison with our former home. Father tried to support his eight children by working at the Mission, but soon could no longer pay their school fees from his earnings and savings. His solution was to go to South Africa to work.

At that time South Africa offered about the only opportunity for Africans of limited education to earn a moderate income. My father began to work in Cape Town as a waiter, earning sixteen pounds ($44.80) a month plus tips and food rations. At that time waiters in Salisbury earned only about three pounds a month. However, many Zimbabweans who went to South Africa to work never came back, leaving broken marriages and children without fathers. We in our family were blessed with a father who remained loyal to his family and continued to send money from South Africa in order to assist us.

Amid the political changes of 1948 in which Afrikaners gained power in South Africa, my father determined to return home. Having heard no reply to his application to purchase a farm in Rhodesia, he decided to go back to his home area in Makoni District. Still the odyssey continued. After one year's residence at Sharara, the white government decided that the Makoni district was overcrowded and forced my parents to return to the poor soils of Mangwende Reserve.

Such disappointments would have broken the spirit of most persons. Determined to educate their children, my parents resolved to make the best of a very poor situation. First, they selected a small garden plot, about one-half acre in size, to cultivate. There they concentrated all their effort on raising carrots as a cash crop. The hours of fertilizing, planting and watering by hand, reaped surprising results year after year. In fact, my brothers, sisters and I all had school fees paid during those years through father's sale of carrots in Salisbury.

It was not until 1957 that my father was successful in securing permission to purchase a farm at Zviyambe, one of the few areas reserved for private farms owned by Africans.

My debt to my father is beyond measure. Through his example I learned that if your conscience is clear you can take a stand on an issue without fear, even against those in political power.

During the 1940s the 'Native Commissioner' at Mrewa, the district administrator, introduced a regulation that levied against each family head tax arrears for all relatives who had absconded or were absent. He summoned my father to pay the back taxes for one of his sons, John Wesley.

'Do I owe the government any taxes,' my father calmly and courageously asked the Commissioner. 'No,' he replied, 'your payments are up to date.'

'I have paid *my* tax,' my father then declared. 'My son is an adult. He is working and is earning money. He owes you some money. It is your business, not mine, to make him pay the tax. As for me, I am going to my home because I do not owe anything to your government. I am a free man. If my son were to steal something from somebody, would you arrest me in his place?' he concluded.

There ensued an embarrassing silence. Finally, the Commissioner said in broken Shona: '*Nyagiende; ichafundisa wazhinji zhakashata.*' ('It (you) must go away for it (you) are going to teach many people bad things.') My father informs me that after this confrontation the unfair practice was suspended.

The real significance of this incident was the courage it took for my father to take that stand. In those years it was unthinkable for an African to oppose a ruthless white administrator. In his area the Native Commissioner was virtually a law unto himself. He was the supreme authority—the government, the law, the magistrate. People trembled when he approached, and feared to challenge his commands. But not my father.

I remember also an incident of my father's courage which took place twenty years later. The only political party for Africans, the Zimbabwe African People's Union (ZAPU), had been banned. White policemen were collecting the illegal party cards from every African in Inyazura. As my father handed in his card, he said, 'You have taken away my party card and the cards from so many people, but does that take away the party cards lodged in our hearts? How are you to impound those?' The policeman was dumbfounded and at a loss for words, for my father expected an answer to his challenge. Finally, the white man called his colleague and told him what the 'old man' had said. The other policeman was obviously worried but conceded, 'There is truth in what he says.'

Who can pay adequate thanks to their parents for their love, their self-sacrifice and their example? I cannot do so to mine. They instilled their burning desire for education in us their children and sacrificed so much for us that four sons and two daughters went on to university studies. They have taught by example a vital Christian faith and we have caught it. Their integrity and courage in standing for the truth have been my model not only when a student, but also later when chosen to lead in both Church and politics.

Called to the Ministry

I remained at Old Umtali in 1941 until I finished Standard Four, but then persuaded my father to enrol me in another United Methodist school near them at Nyadiri. There I could join my boyhood friends from Chinyadza of the Jijita family. I am sure that my father's unhappy removal from Old Umtali must have influenced also my decision to leave that school.

The following year was my most miserable one in school, as I was more in the hospital than in class due to recurrent bouts of malaria. Whenever I was well enough I used to have private prayers with my best friend, Elliot Jijita, in the thick bush near the school. Like our fathers before us, we wrestled with the question, 'Does God want me to become a farmer, or a minister?'

During those days I began to have a dream which would come back to me again and again during the following eight years. In it I saw first, as if on a movie screen, lots of property such as a wealthy person would own. Next, it seemed as if I were part of a large church congregation. There a man dressed in a long white robe would give me a hoe handle and command me to lead the congregation in singing. 'Was God in this dream calling me to become a minister?' I asked myself repeatedly.

Fortunately I was surrounded by those who loved the Church and wanted to help us to love it too. Miss Edith Parks was one

25

missionary teacher who had a great influence upon my life at that time. She taught mathematics, a subject in which I was weak. Often she tutored me in her office or at home. I felt as free to talk with her, to drink cocoa with her, to share my problems and to pray with her as I did with my own parents. This strengthened me for the difficult year that was to follow.

When Nyadiri Centre failed to open a Standard Six class for the 1943 year, I found myself returning to Old Umtali for schooling. To the surprise of my family and friends, I failed the exams at the end of that year. Friends tried to blame my misfortune on others, and especially the missionary principal, but I would hear none of it. I realized that I had not overcome my weakness in arithmetic nor really concentrated on my studies as I should have done. To fail at that level was a crushing blow. It was like a steel door cutting off the road to academic advancement. I was the only member of our large family who ever failed a grade in school.

At any rate, I did not take failure as the end of the world for me, but rather as the beginning of a new adventure.

Chapter 4

Off into the World

In those days the holder of a Standard Five (Grade 7) certificate was allowed to teach in the lower primary schools. Thus it was that I found my way to teach as an untrained teacher at Chitimbe School in the Mrewa District, from January, 1944 to December, 1945. There I earned my first salary of one pound, ten shillings ($4.20) per month. I was assigned to teach Standard One (Grade 3).

My start in teaching was like a plunge into ice-cold water. I would have given up in frustration during those first weeks but for the sensitive guidance of Rev. Samuel Munjoma, the headmaster and church minister at Chitimbe.

One day I was so annoyed that I decided to quit teaching. Without speaking to anyone, I packed my bags and started walking away. I was determined to walk fourteen miles to catch a bus to go home. Somehow Rev. Munjoma heard what was happening. Before I had walked a half-mile I heard him call me. I expected a tongue-lashing. Instead, he encouraged me to talk out my frustrations. When I had finished he responded, 'Abel, you are such a short-tempered boy. Come back. I assure you that what has annoyed you will be cleared up.'

One night the Munjoma's house caught fire and everything they had except a little puppy was destroyed. We teachers went to console them and to pray with them. When the time came to choose hymns to sing, Mrs. Munjoma asked for the popular hymn in Shona, 'There Shall be Showers of Blessing'. 'Why did you choose that hymn?' I asked, surprised by her choice. 'Because I am thankful that no lives were lost in the burning of our house,' she replied. In times like this I learned much of what it means to be a mature Christian.

In those days some people said that teaching by untrained teachers was like poisoning the children! I was, therefore, pleasantly surprised to learn that Rev. A. T. O'Farrell, our school manager, had reported favourably upon my teaching. The good examination results of my pupils at the end of the year also supported this judgment.

Outside the classroom I enjoyed teaching African music and physical training. My two groups excelled in competitions in the Uzumba area. In those days goats, sheep, pigs and chickens were the prizes for the best choirs. Sometimes my choir got both first and second prizes. In physical training I worked together with Mr. Darius Jijita, my co-teacher. It was a great day for our apt pupils when they beat the formidable Nyadiri Mission Centre physical training group.

During the next two school years I taught at the Zunga (now Rukariro) School in the same district. At that time, in addition to school responsibilities, I began to preach as a 'local preacher' in our church.

Running Away from God

Towards the end of 1947, I became convinced that I would not do anything big with my life with a meagre teacher's salary of $4.20 per month. I felt some obligation to help my family to buy clothes and pay the school fees for my younger brothers and sisters. Ten shillings a month ($1.40) wasn't much, but was one-third of my earnings. Sometimes I would save and send more, but this took some time.

To change occupations, however, was painful. I had grown to love teaching. But for me, like thousands of young people at that time, the bright lights of the city appeared to offer a better future.

When we closed school I went to Nyadiri to tell Rev. O'Farrell about my resignation from teaching. He was expectedly disappointed and took me to task over the reasons why I had decided to leave teaching. I was not supposed to leave 'God's work' to go to the city. However, I made it adamantly clear to him that I was determined to leave teaching. He revealed that I had been one of his best teachers in the district. But no words would dissuade me from my determination to leave. With great reluctance, Mr. O'Farrell finally signed me off on my Registration Certificate (*Chitupa*).

As I left the room, I felt as if I was carrying a bag of cement on my shoulders. I suddenly felt a great sense of nakedness, and avoided meeting anyone as I walked out of Mr. O'Farrell's house. I was leaving my work and the place I had adored so much for no other apparent reason than for love of more money and adventure.

I was struck by a mixed feeling of regret and guilt for having taken an impulsive decision against the Church. I finally walked into the thick bush behind the boys' boarding department to pray. It was getting dark and I was all by myself. I vividly remember that short prayer:

'God, if I have made a wrong decision by leaving teaching, and preaching, please bring me back somehow. Amen.'

When I rose up my anxiety was completely lifted. The next morning I was on my way to the capital of Salisbury, eighty-six miles away.

I was struck on this my first trip to the city by the number of people there. The towns of Rusape and Umtali that I had known as a boy were small by comparison.

Immediately I sensed a different relationship between whites and Africans than I had known before. My missionary teacher, Edith Parks, had often said when I was working at her house, 'Abel, let's sit down and have a cup of cocoa.' Here in Salisbury I heard whites speak of their African servants as 'my boy' and Africans of their employers as 'my white man' (*murungu wangu*) in a strict master-servant relationship.

Fortunately like most African newcomers to town, I did not enter Salisbury as a lonely stranger. Relatives, young men from my village, and former school friends, all welcomed me to stay with them and eat with them, even when I had not a cent in my pocket. That is our Shona way of hospitality.

On the first night in Salisbury, I had a dream. It was a vision of a hut full of ministers of religion, all clothed in clerical garb. They surrounded my shabbily dressed figure. I was the only dirty fellow in that room. Was God saying to me that I should join the company of the ministers of the Church? I doubted it the next morning as I set off for the city centre to look for a job.

At that time I had no clear idea of what work I might do. I only expected that it would pay more than teaching in school. I thought that I could work as an office clerk. Although I could not type, I had learned to read and write English quite well. Perhaps I could work as a waiter—a job that many who had not gone to school were doing. I wanted to learn to drive. Perhaps I could work as a driver.

Already my friends had told me how to look for work. It meant walking from door to door, house to house, office to office. Never mind those 'No work here' (*Hapana Basa*) signs. Just ask. Never mind those shouts 'Get away from here! There is no job.' Just ask. And don't let the rudeness of those European bosses discourage you.

So I started out. As I entered the doorway of the first shop, to ask for work, the owner advanced towards me and said, 'On your way! Come on, out! If I were you I would go to work at the Mission.'

His words shook me in a big way. Here was a complete stranger telling me to go back to work for the Church. If he had first asked to see my registration book listing my previous employment I would not have been surprised, but he had not done so. I reflected on what this meant. Was God sending me a message through this stranger?

A Lay Evangelist

The answer came three months later. After three months of fruitless searching, just as I was despairing of finding work in Salisbury, I met Darius Jijita, my former fellow teacher. Darius had remained in the employment of the Church. 'Rev. O'Farrell has sent me to look for you, Abel,' he said. 'He wants to appoint you as lay evangelist to the Nyadiri East Circuit in the Mtoko District.' For me, these words seemed to be God's answer to that prayer which I had said before leaving Nyadiri. As I packed my belongings I felt strongly that I was going to enjoy what I was about to do.

Nyamakope, Gurure, Chindenga, Dunda and Gumbutsa— these were the small congregations placed under my care. The last was little more than a preaching point under a tree. My work was to visit house to house, to preach and lead in worship, and to guide the fellowship groups for women, men and youth. Fortunately, Rev. Jonah Chitombo, the minister in charge of the wider circuit, was a flexible and kindly pastor. He would visit to baptize, administer holy communion, confirm and receive church members, and lead the church meetings. I gained a lot from his wisdom and rich experience.

Soon I became a familiar figure in the district—the small preacher trudging along the dusty road with his blankets and Bible on his back. Wherever I went doors opened to welcome me, and a daughter ran to catch a chicken to put in the pot. Wherever

I went the people fed me—a gesture fully appreciated by this itinerant bachelor! But I was relieved when after three months the church bought me a bicycle to speed me on my way.

Those were happy days for me. I felt very close to God. The people responded and the church grew. This confirmed my strong belief that God had called me to become a minister of the Church of Jesus Christ.

As I reflect upon my experience in the circuit a few incidents remain fresh and indelible in my mind. For example, during an evening service at Gwenambira about three miles away from Nyadiri, a twelve-year-old girl started screaming amid the singing and praying. The church people who were present at the time explained to me that the girl was 'possessed' by an evil spirit (*shawe*). I recalled a similar experience years before when I had accompanied my mother to a church meeting as a child. However, what actually puzzled me was that the strong men and women who were present failed to contain that little girl. By a mere stretch of her hand she sent down most of the men and women who tried to quiet her. Then I witnessed the power of prayer. The sound of fervent prayers for her deliverance drowned out her screams, and she was healed.

After this experience, I asked myself, 'To whom does God give this power to heal?' Some time later, while attending a revival meeting at Katsukunya near Mtoko, I dreamt that a sick woman was brought before me. A voice commanded me, 'Put your hands on her head; she will live.' As soon as I did so and after I had prayed, the woman rose up and walked. The dream was so real that when I woke up in the morning it was difficult to dismiss it as a mere dream.

The following morning I joined others in witnessing house to house. I surely expected to see a sick person in one of the many homes I visited that day, but the revival meeting came to a close without seeing one. Then I went back to Nyakabau where I was stationed.

Two weeks later some colleagues accompanied me for an evening prayer meeting at a home about a mile from our church. Upon arrival we moved on to another home to pray for a friend who was seriously sick. As soon as we entered the house I was struck by the fact that the scene reminded me of the Katsukunya dream which I had almost forgotten. There was an inner voice of assurance which seemed to say within me,

31

'Abel, this is the person you saw in that dream; put your hands on her and she will live.'

I did not share that message of spiritual conscience with my colleagues, or with anyone else in the house, but I laid my hands on the woman's head as I prayed for her. It was the first time that I laid hands on a sick person. After the prayer, the woman actually rose up and in an emotional voice charged with praise and thanksgiving, she said, 'Last night I dreamt a man was praying for me. Now as I think of it, this man who has just prayed for me has the image of the one I saw in my dream.'

There was singing and praying in praise of God for the miraculous healing of the woman. The woman's dream was startling as she described it, and if I had retold my dream also, I would probably have been branded as a faith healer.

When He Calls I will Follow

It was while working in the Nyadiri East Circuit that I finally decided to become a minister. The Christian leaders there recommended me for theological studies. It was not unanimous, however. One leader commented that I was 'somewhat short-tempered'. The majority supported my application enthusiastically. The approval to enter into God's service marked the end of my eight years of indecision and struggle against God's will. I felt an inner satisfaction that I was going to train for what I believed God wanted me to be.

My days of teaching, however, were not yet ended. While waiting for the new school year, I moved to the Nyadiri Methodist Centre and was asked to teach a Third Grade class. Other teachers labelled that class the 'condemned idiots' as they were the slowest and most backward class in the whole school. For me, however, each was a child of God with potential to grow as a person. Once again careful tutoring brought results. Many did quite well in their final examinations to the surprise of their parents and other teachers at that school.

In the School of Theology

'Can such young men serve as ministers?' That was the common reaction of the pious faithful at Old Umtali Mission as eight of us began our theological studies. It had been almost a tradition in our Church to choose new ministers from among experienced

32

schoolteachers forty years of age and older. We as a class were much younger than those who had preceded us in theological school.

The new content of our preaching did little to alleviate their fears. Previously the evangelistic message of our Church in both hymns and sermons stressed the heavenly rewards to be given to the faithful who must endure suffering here on earth. I recalled that our favourite hymn in my childhood home had been 'Take the name of Jesus in all your poverty'. The early missionaries had given a literal interpretation to those Bible verses that implied that the poor, and not the rich, would inherit the kingdom of heaven. African evangelists and pastors went out from training to preach the same message. It was found in the words of another hymn which we sang, 'I don't want much money'.

My classmates and I disliked that emphasis. We labelled it the 'pie in the sky by and by' gospel. We found more appealing another side of the Church's ministry—that of giving to those who follow Christ not only a faith but also the skills of agriculture, carpentry, teaching, etc., so that they might live a fuller life here and now. The crops which our parents sold to buy clothes and bicycles and to pay our school fees—were these not also blessings from God? Did God want some to seize the good land of our country leaving the masses to scratch the dry and sandy soil and starve? We wanted to proclaim a whole gospel for the whole man that would speak to what was going on in the day-to-day life of our people.

To prepare us, the Rev. Josiah Chimbadzwa took us into the woods of Chiremba Mountain behind the school to preach and criticize each other's sermons. It was there I received from him the nickname *Chikurumuzinga,* which literally means 'what is big is the power of a gun'. It implied that I, although small in stature, was explosive in my delivery of sermons.

Today it is the living example of my teachers more than their formal teaching that remains impressed on my memory. Dr. M. J. Murphree, our principal, was a conservative but exceptionally well-experienced man. His wife Lois gave us a love for music and Christian education which was later to become my field of graduate study. Dr. Arthur Mansure brought from Boston University not only new insights in New Testament interpretation but also an example of humility that remained with us all.

One day news came that Darius Jijita, my close friend and brother of my classmate, was seriously ill. The usual practice was for the Principal to give a student permission to return home by his own means. Imagine our surprise and pleasure when Dr. Mansure himself offered to drive us there in his own car, to sleep in our modest home, and to pray with us there for healing. Such involvement by a white person in the problems of an African family was not common in Rhodesia in those days.

Struggle into Love

During my second year at the Theological School I met Maggie Rutendo Chigodora who was working at the Murphree's home. Maggie was one of four daughters of a devout Christian widow. Before I made my first approach to her, like any well-cultured African young man of the time, I inquired of the elders about Maggie's character. My uncle, who then worked as chief labour officer at the Mission, replied, 'Yes, she is a very good and hard-working girl.' So I resolved to court Maggie. This, according to tradition, had to be done slowly and precisely according to custom.

The Shona traditions of courtship and marriage at that time meant for young people a long struggle into love. A boy must first write a letter to the girl he would court proposing his love for her. This is done before any real friendship develops. A good girl will say 'no' to the first proposal, even if she is longing for the boy deep down in her heart. She may give the excuse of their age difference or another reason. The boy will then show his sincerity and seriousness of purpose by answering each excuse. Next the girl might think of other reasons why she should not permit his advances. The boy is supposed to show persistence and perseverance if he would win the girl he loves. Finally after several weeks or months the girl may accede and in a carefully worded letter tell the boy of her love for him. The boy then acknowledges the girl's favourable reply in another letter or through an emissary. He asks for a love token, a ring or handkerchief, to prove that she has agreed to be his girl. He in turn gives her a token to symbolize his love for her. Not until these steps have been taken does the formal courtship begin.

A boy who follows traditional custom does not have a high regard for a girl if she concedes to his proposal on the first approach. He would say, 'She may be of loose and weak character.'

34

The girl, too, must be convinced that the boy is not trying to 'play' with her.

Thus there was a lot of correspondence and consultation before I finally convinced Maggie that I meant serious business. My classmate's young son, Norman Jijita, carried letters to and from each of us. On the day that she accepted my proposal I went to see her in her room after she had finished work. There both of us knelt in prayer to thank God for leading us to that stage in our relationship. We asked Him to give us strength and moral discipline in the conduct of our new-found friendship. We prayed for our future together, and agreed to place our sexual desires under God's control from that day until after our wedding.

The marriage negotiations which followed were even more lengthy and detailed than our preliminary courtship. Following Shona custom, I could not speak directly to Maggie's parents. Instead, I chose a go-between to negotiate the marriage on my behalf. The intermediary carried to the Chigodora family home in a rural area an initial sum of money to ask for marriage. The negotiations that followed included setting the amount of *lobola* to be paid (sometimes incorrectly called 'bride-price'). In traditional society *lobola* was usually in the form of cattle, but from my time onwards it was more often a sum of money—money paid to the family which would be poorer because the services of a daughter had been lost. It was agreed in my case that £25 ($70) and two head of cattle would be the acceptable payment.

Finally on August 11, 1951, we arrived at the joyous day when Maggie and I stood at the altar to pledge our loyalty to each other. There was added community excitement as ours was the first wedding in the new church building at Old Umtali. The majority of the school's teaching staff, however, stayed away. Perhaps it was because it was merely the wedding of a widow's daughter to a poor theological student. We did not care. Frankly, I felt well-dressed in my beautiful black suit bought at an auction sale in Umtali for £1.10 ($3). The wedding reception which followed at the bride's home and that of my parents were, as usual, times of festivity for the entire community.

My first year of marriage was to be my busiest one at school. About half-way through my theological studies, the Principal informed me that I would not be given a graduation certificate because I had never passed Standard Six. Troubled that I would not get a certificate, I determined to sit for Standard Six (8th

Grade) and theological school examinations in the same year. The results were successful.

On December 11, 1952, I graduated from Hartzell Theological School. The following day our first son was born. In naming him we chose words meaningful in both the Christian community and in traditional culture. We named him Blessing because God had honoured us in the same week with a first-born son and with graduation. His Shona name, Tendekayi, means 'be honest and faithful'.

Chapter 5

A Rural Village Pastor

In 1952 the Rhodesia Conference responded to a world-wide call for Methodists to emphasize visitation evangelism by appointing two teams of evangelists. Thus it was that my first appointment after theological school was as Assistant Conference Evangelist to Dr. M. J. Murphree. ·

At that time fewer than ten per cent of the African population were committed Christians. Many more had attended mission schools, as these were the only ones available to Africans in the rural areas. Some persons had never heard of Jesus Christ. Our goal was to win persons for Christ and to train committed Christians in witnessing to their faith.

The work meant weeks of travel, leaving the family at Vengere township in Rusape, a town between Salisbury and Umtali. Our programme commenced in each new community on a Sunday with a challenge to local Christians to share their faith with others. During the next four days we taught local Christians how to win others for Christ. Then together with them we visited two-by-two those families in the community who were not active in the church. Finally on the last Sunday the people gathered at the church to give their testimonies during the main service.

Sometimes opportunities to witness arose when least expected. One day while waiting for a train at Bromley station about thirty miles from Salisbury, I greeted a young man waiting there. After some general conversation I asked him, 'Do you know Jesus Christ?'

'Does he live in Salisbury?' the young man replied in the accent of a person from the neighbouring country of Mozambique. Realizing that I was talking to one who had never heard of Jesus Christ, I gave a brief summary of His coming to earth, His life and death. When I talked about the resurrection, the young man was amazed. 'Did this Jesus actually rise up from the dead?' he asked. 'Yes, and He is right here now with us in spirit,' I replied.

I went further to enquire whether the young man wanted to 'talk' to Jesus. He welcomed the idea even though he still wore a puzzled expression on his face. As we bowed in prayer together, after a moment of deep silence, he prayed with me, saying, 'Lord Jesus, I give my life to you.' The prayer ended, to be followed by another silence. My new friend broke it as he said excitedly, 'Man, when I get to Salisbury, I will tell my brother too about this Jesus!'

As time went on, however, I found this direct approach to witnessing as taught by the missionaries to be inadequate. Too often the missionary witnessed to Africans as if they had no religion, speaking only of Christ without reference to our rich religious heritage. Such an approach I found to be both ineffective and disrespectful to our Shona culture.

One day I visited an old woman, possibly in her seventies, who lived just two miles from a strong church congregation at Chitenderano in Chiduku Reserve. During our conversation there was nothing to suggest that she had ever heard of Jesus. I started by asking her to tell me about traditional Shona ways of worship. She related how the elders used to go to a sacred *mushakata* or *muhacha* tree and there ask the spirits of the departed ancestors to hear their pleas. They would begin by addressing the spirits of those most recently departed, probably their grandparents, and then would address those who were higher in ancestral seniority. Reaching the last known ancestor, their prayer would end by asking the last named to pass on their request to *Musikavanhu*, the Creator of man.

'Who is the creator of man?' I asked her. '*Mwari* (God),' she replied using the name common both to Christians and to those who follow traditional religious beliefs and practices.

At that moment I felt the way open to lead the old lady to Christ. 'That God whom you have mentioned has a son called Jesus Christ,' I explained, giving a brief summary of the life and work of Christ and how He had died and risen from the dead. I told the old lady that Jesus was there with us in spirit and asked if she wanted to 'talk' to Him. She agreed. As I began praying she started that ritual clapping which was customary in addressing the ancestral spirits. It felt good to her. Before I left she accepted Jesus as her personal Saviour. Soon she was baptized, and eventually died peacefully as a Christian.

At other times the Church was not so open to receive new believers. One day we had an evangelistic campaign at Muziti near my parents' original home. I teamed with Mr. Matthew Mataranyika, the school headmaster and a strong Christian, to witness to a famous man called Toto. Mr. Toto was short and stout, with round fat cheeks and big eagle eyes that conveyed intelligence. He was well known as a polygamist and as a medicine man (what many Western writers have wrongly referred to as 'witch-doctors'). He had never been to church in the over seventy-five years of his life. Mr. Toto had known both of us as boys. We wondered, would it do any good to witness to him of Christ?

We decided to present the gospel story in about fifteen or twenty minutes. Already we had learned that if we did not lead a person to respond in that time our conversation would degenerate into futile argument. After telling Mr. Toto the story of Jesus and what Jesus had done to us individually, we expressed our deep desire for him to accept Jesus as his personal Saviour. As we prayed, the old man spoke after us his prayer of commitment, adding here and there words of his own. We left him in great joy.

'Can it be true that Mr. Toto has accepted Christ?' I asked my colleague. Both of us knew that he had earned a nickname of *Chirwembe* for being a 'professional' liar. The answer came in a knock on our door at 5 a.m. the next morning. Opening it, we found, to our surprise, Mr. Toto who had walked five miles to reach us. 'I could not sleep,' he told us. 'Please, I wish to be baptized here and now!'

Alas I replied, 'No, I cannot baptize you now.' As Methodists we believed that first a person must be enrolled in classes as a 'beginner' for several months before being baptized. We also insisted that a person be subjected to the rules of the Church. I could see on his face his keen disappointment. Sadly, Mr. Toto left, and went to a Roman Catholic priest who baptized him immediately.

Five years later, I heard of the death of this prominent man. His funeral drew large crowds, partly because of his former reputation as a medicine man, and partly because of his exemplary life as a new Christian. Christ had worked through the ministry of a Catholic priest to confirm Mr. Toto in the faith. Otherwise, he might have left his new faith and gone astray because of our refusal to baptize him.

It was not easy, sometimes, to get Christians to witness in the homes of those in their communities who were known to be hostile to the Church or to be backsliders. One day, Dr. Murphree and I failed to find men who would go to visit a certain man who had left the Church. To our surprise two women volunteered to go and pray with him. This forced us to change our system. Hitherto men had gone only to visit men, and women to visit women.

Upon their return the two women told this story: 'Before going, we felt we needed to spend much time in prayer together. Yes, we were afraid to visit that disgruntled man. Fortunately we met him outside his house as he was coming home. We told him of our desire to talk with him alone, not even in the presence of his wife and children. When we sat down, we asked him no questions about his past problems with the Church. Instead we simply told him that we had been sent to him by Jesus Christ through the Church. We told him that Jesus loved him, and that the joy with which Christ had filled our lives could be his also.

'We asked the man if we could pray with him, but by that time this huge and strong man was weeping profusely like a two-year-old boy. And then he started praying and remembered a Bible story in his prayer:

'God! Oh, God! Thank you for sending Martha and Mary to come to me. I am Lazarus who is now dead and stinking in the grave of my way of life! I give myself to thee now!'

The man had been reclaimed for Christ. That night he was the first to come to the evening service. He did what many people do not want to do, he sat in the front row. And when the time given to speak came, he did not fear to stand and give his testimony. That night the faith of many was strengthened and others were won also to Christ through his testimony.

Pastor in My Home Village

My appointment as Assistant Conference Evangelist ended in a most dramatic way. In the midst of an evangelistic campaign at Gurure near Mtoko, a local church I had served before, a letter arrived from the bishop instructing me to drop everything and go immediately as pastor to the Chiduku North Circuit in Makoni District.

Naturally my first reaction was one of deep consternation. It was hard to accept the abrupt manner of taking up a new appointment. When I shared the news with my parents, however, they asked, 'How can the son of Mary and Joseph be accepted in the place of his childhood?' They recalled how Jesus had been rejected when he sought to preach in his home village and were asking whether their own son's ministry could be taken seriously in the villages where his parents and grandparents lived and where he had grown up as a child. So it was that we began our new ministry with some fear and trepidation. Such a fear, however, was groundless. Instead of hostility, my family and I were welcomed with joy and love.

The people to whom I was called to minister were scattered over a wide area. The farthest church was forty-five miles away from Muziti where we lived. In fact, the sixteen churches under my charge represented the largest circuit of our Church in the country.

I realized immediately that careful and systematic visiting from church to church would be required if I were to serve effectively as a pastor to so many. And all I possessed for transport was a bicycle. I remembered with some bitterness the day when I asked Dr. Murphree to sell me one of his three cars, only to have him refuse, saying that I could not afford to maintain it. Probably that assessment was correct, but I would have preferred to make it myself!

For years I had seen my father heap his bicycle with bags of produce to market them in town. The slightest shift of weight would then send the bicycle crashing to the ground. Could I travel like that with blankets, clothes, and books? I determined to try.

Each Thursday afternoon I would set out by bicycle to one of my congregations, planning to hold a prayer service with them in the evening. During the following day I visited my people. Often that meant joining them in hoeing or carrying water to their gardens. Usually we ended the day's work with prayers at a church building or someone's home. Sunday was the busiest day of all. By careful planning and fast cycling I could often preach at one church at 11 a.m., reach another at 2.30 p.m. and conclude the day with a third congregation at 7.30 p.m. After that I really needed Monday as a day of rest, before tackling office work, study, and correspondence at home on Tuesdays, Wednesdays and Thursdays.

This was my plan. But like any African pastor, I observed it more as a guide than as a rule. When someone died in the community I was expected to visit the home and stay to mourn with the family much of the ensuing night. I never knew what counselling with a family might result from accepting their hospitality for dinner and a night's rest (rarely did I prepare food for myself).

I was made uneasy if someone spoke of 'Pastor Muzorewa's church'. Pastor I was, but could I claim the church as mine? Certainly not! I knew that soon I would be transferred to another circuit. It was the local leaders, the local preachers and Bible class leaders, the officers of groups for men, women and youth, who form the backbone of the Church. To train them for their leadership was one of my major goals.

My wife and I truly fell in love with these people. But it was hard at first. When we began our ministry the circuit was far in arrears financially. How could I tell the family that for a whole month there would be no salary? In fact, I went without salary for two and three months at a time, although the total was only eleven pounds ($30.80) a month. As months went by, however, the church grew. Revival meetings strengthened and deepened the faith of older Christians and new members were won for Christ. So it was that by the time I left the circuit there were enough contributions to meet all the church's expenses.

I could fill a book with the experiences of those first years as a village pastor. One day God spared my life when I almost drowned in the Inyazura River. It had rained heavily. The river was overflowing its banks, and there was no bridge by which to cross to reach the Rukweza Church. Nevertheless, I attempted the crossing, carrying my bicycle over my head. Just as I was about to reach the opposite bank, I slipped. Instantly I threw the bicycle to the bank before me, and grasped for some nearby reeds. Fortunately they held firm so that I was saved from being carried away in the swift-rushing stream. A church family soon opened their home to me, although I was embarrassed to enter with soaked clothes, blankets and books.

The rains (or absence of them) had a way of uniting all farmers in our district, both black and white, in common concerns. One day a local white farmer, Mr. Taylor, came to the church to ask us to pray for rain. His crops, like ours, were dying for lack of water. He had always had respect for the church and had encouraged us to begin preaching services for workers at his farm. As I was not well, my wife Maggie and some members from Muziti agreed to go to pray there. That evening I heard from my bed first thunder and then the sound of raindrops. Soon Maggie and the other women came running through what was by then a downpour. Our prayers for rain had been answered.

Relationships between Africans and Europeans in our area, however, were not often that harmonious. Many of our people, faced with grinding poverty and the pinpricks of insults and abuses, burned with a smouldering, though oft-hidden, hostility towards whites. Even committed Christians shared such feelings.

One day I entered a European-owned shop in the nearby town of Rusape. The African clerk asked me whether I still had chickens, as he knew that poultry-raising was my hobby. 'Yes,' I replied, 'I have a lot of them.' Suddenly he drew closer and in a whisper continued, 'Look! Just look around over there . . . do any of those women's overcoats appeal to you? If you want one of them, I will see that I get it out and give it to you somewhere outside if you can give me six pullets in exchange.'

I was surprised, for I knew this man was a staunch member of an African independent church called the Apostolics which believed that no Church received the power of the Holy Spirit as much as they did. 'Now,' I replied, 'I do not understand. This is not your store. How can you buy my chickens with someone else's overcoat?' Then I challenged him: 'You have always proclaimed as Apostolics that you are the only people who have the Holy Spirit of God. What is the Holy Spirit saying to you now?' 'Nothing,' he replied, a bit perplexed.

'Do you want me to tell you what the Holy Spirit is saying to me now?' I asked the man. 'Yes, if you want to tell me,' he replied in a startled voice.

'The Holy Spirit is telling me that you are tempting me to steal another man's property—that overcoat—for it belongs to the owner of this store,' I said. He then shrugged his shoulders and replied, 'Well, Reverend, it is not sin to steal from a white man.'

I then told him that for me it is always a sin to steal, whether from those black or white. At the same time I realized that he was a victim of that racism which was endemic in our country.

The man probably was being paid less than ten dollars, whereas the store owner was making a profit of thousands of dollars each month.

A New Crusader

In 1956 we welcomed Dr. Ralph E. Dodge as our new bishop. His area comprised Angola, Mozambique, South Africa and Rhodesia—all countries under white racist rule during his twelve-year episcopacy. We of the Church looked forward to his coming as our first bishop to reside in Rhodesia.

From the start we knew he wanted to change things. As he spoke to the pastors, he said, 'I would like to visit all of you, my brothers, in your circuits and get to know the people and the Church well. But I am going to be radical. I will not carry any food when I come to visit you. I will come and stay with you in your homes, wherever you are. I know that is the African custom, and we will observe it.'

Such action was a radical break from the past, for missionaries had always stayed in special 'missionary guest houses' and carried with them their own bedding, food, and a cook to prepare it. Inviting the bishop to visit first our Chiduku North Circuit meant that we pioneered together with him. Fortunately my wife Maggie was an excellent cook, and soon we found volunteer cooks at each of the churches where we visited.

Bishop Dodge's radicalism continued to be manifested in his sermons, teaching, conversations and above all in his example. In former years missionaries and African Church workers ate in separate dining-rooms during Church conferences, only joining together for worship and discussions. Saying nothing, Bishop and Mrs. Dodge merely went to eat with the African ministers and laymen. One day the Annual Conference delegates were going to the dedication of a new church. Missionaries jumped into their cars while Africans boarded a hired bus. Many were embarrassed as the bishop boarded the bus with his African pastors. But the old patterns of segregation within the United Methodist Church were breaking down, even as the white settlers were building stronger ones in the society at large.

A Fledgling Nationalist

During my years as a village pastor (1955–8) our country was experiencing an awakening of African nationalism. The honeymoon of racial partnership was over. In 1953 we had welcomed the formation of the Central African Federation joining Southern and Northern Rhodesia with Nyasaland as one nation. We as Africans had great hopes as the Hon. Garfield Todd, a New Zealand missionary of the Church of Christ, became the Southern Rhodesian Prime Minister. The new government's slogan was 'racial partnership'. Already, however, the Federal Prime Minister, Lord Malvern, had been quoted as saying to white voters that this was to be likened to the partnership between a horse and its rider.

While young leaders in Salisbury and Bulawayo formed the City Youth League to focus African opposition to white rule, we in the Rusape area began to think also about politics. The staff at nearby St. Faith's Mission organized in 1957 a series of meetings on political issues—one prelude to the formation of the African National Congress (ANC).

My first encounter with this new spirit occurred in 1957 as I attended an ANC meeting at St. Faith's Mission. Mr. Winston Field, who in 1962 was to become the first leader of the Rhodesia Front Party, was one of the speakers. He was then a member of the all-white Dominion Party.

I do not remember all that Mr. Field said that night. Burned indelibly in my memory, however, was his statement, 'I do not believe that an African will go to heaven.' I could scarcely believe my ears as he said that an African is a sub-human being, and that God would not accept the African as his child. 'Is he projecting a South Africa Dutch Reformed theology to support his racial arrogance?' I wondered. I grieved that any white person in our country would think like that, but was too hurt and humiliated to respond.

Fortunately, the Anglican Bishop of Mashonaland, who was present, the late Cecil Alderson, rose to challenge Mr. Field's statement. 'Christians do not believe as you do,' the bishop replied. I breathed a deep sigh of relief. Here was another white Christian leader like my own bishop who was fearless in opposing the white racists who ruled our land. But I wondered how soon we as African Christians would rise up to join them in that struggle for justice.

Chapter 6

Love and Prejudice

In 1962 the Reverend Ndabaningi Sithole, National Chairman of the Zimbabwe African People's Union (ZAPU), visited Old Umtali Methodist Centre. Students crowded around him eagerly. They waited breathlessly to hear his words, for they admired him as a committed Christian who was active in politics. But his words that day left them hurt and bewildered as he said:

'Your place in the struggle for liberation is here, at school. Do not leave school. Do not engage in political demonstrations and protests. If you do you will be expelled. We shall need you tomorrow as the well-educated leaders of Zimbabwe. Leave to your elders the active political struggle now!'

I did not hear Mr. Sithole's striking words. They described my life, however, during the five eventful years from 1958 to 1963. Those were the years of the ANC, of NDP, and of ZAPU* when our elder nationalist politicians openly challenged white rule. Although political parties were banned and leaders thrown into political detention camps, our people grew in their commitment to the struggle for majority rule. Among them were students like myself who had chosen to continue our education so we would be prepared to assume leadership in a free country.

In colonial Rhodesia formal education was a luxury enjoyed by only a few Africans. No university within the country would accept them. To study overseas seemed to many of us the wildest daydream. I was, however, determined that this stark fact should not thwart my ambition for higher education.

Like many others, the only road forward for me in school was to study by correspondence while I was employed. I started my secondary school education in that way. My immediate target was to pass the Junior Certificate examinations. I began while travelling around the country as an evangelist and continued

* African National Congress, National Democratic Party and Zimbabwe African People's Unions.

when reassigned as pastor in the Chiduku Circuit. I was able to use textbooks which I had brought with me from Old Umtali.

Finding time and energy for correspondence studies was a constant problem. My work as a pastor involved extensive travel, and I had frequent meetings to attend. My only opportunity for study was after others had retired for the night. The local shopkeepers knew me as a frequent customer for candles, as they were my only source of light during those late-night sessions.

Looking back I marvel that I succeeded in passing the Junior Certificate examinations after eleven months of private study, for it takes two years for a regular full-time student to prepare for the same examinations. The fact that I passed all the subjects at one sitting spurred me on to register immediately for the Senior Secondary course. I continued my studies night after night, and was on the point of sitting for the General Certificate of Education examinations when a surprise came—the offer of a scholarship to study in the United States of America.

The opportunity came unexpectedly while I was attending the 1958 Annual Conference of our Church. As usual, there was tenseness in the air, for each minister may be notified of a transfer to new work at that time. I was breathless when Bishop Ralph Dodge said to me: 'One of our former missionaries, Dr. Charles E. Fuller, has raised money to send an African student to America for higher education. Would you like to go?' My first thought was: 'Of course I want to go!' My second thought was, 'Can I leave my wife and children?' Quickly I went to break the news to Maggie. She did not hesitate, however, to face separation for my sake. She urged: 'Take up the offer. I will remain with the three little boys. I think we can go to "Zvikomborero" (my father's farm) and stay there until you return.'

I will always be grateful to Maggie for her wisdom and for her willingness to face a year of separation. Otherwise, with my limited education, I would have been less effective as God's servant. I hurried back to report to Bishop Dodge our decision, and soon thereafter heard the announcement to the church leaders: 'A. T. Muzorewa—Left without appointment to attend school.'

I, and many others, will never forget that it was Bishop Ralph Dodge who had the vision and determination to crash through the barrier to higher education for Zimbabweans. He secured funds so that more than one hundred of us could go to Europe or America for study. It was he who encouraged those selected to train not only for teaching, journalism, law and medicine, but also for the Christian ministry. I owe a great debt also to Dr. Charles Fuller for raising money for my scholarship.

A Farewell with Wet Eyes

The time came for me to tell the people on our circuit that I was going overseas. It was not an easy task, for both Maggie and I had fallen in love with the people of the churches where we served.

The day of our farewell, in July 1958, was one filled with tears. Speaker after speaker recounted what together we had accomplished in a few brief years. The spirit was that of a revival meeting. We were especially touched when Mr. Mugauri, one of our most devout Christian leaders, stood up and declared: 'Rev. Muzorewa has led many of us to receive the Holy Spirit.' In the five years of separation from our homeland which were to follow, we were sustained by the memory of this intimate Christian fellowship, and our desire to prepare ourselves to serve more effectively such people.

One detail remained—to ensure that my family would be provided for during my long absence. Here again the Church helped by appointing Maggie matron of the girls' boarding department at the Nyamuzuwe Secondary School. There she and our three boys found a home.

I must admit that the thought of my first ride in an aeroplane chilled me. That morning, August 17, 1958, our newspaper reported an air crash in which ninety people had died. Little wonder that I was apprehensive.

To my surprise, when I was about to board the plane, one of our best friends, Mrs. Barnie Higgs, handed me an envelope on which she had written: 'Read only. after getting on the plane.' As soon as I fastened my seat belt I opened it and read: 'Abel, you are in the air, but you are in the perfect hands of God, your loving Father.' She must have sensed my apprehension.

After landing in America, I went directly to Columbia, Missouri, where I enrolled as a 'special student' in the Missouri School of Religion. My courses included Old Testament, Church history, theology and homiletics. Most of my classmates were university graduates working on their Bachelor of Divinity degrees.

That year I had my first meaningful encounter with ministers of various denominations. This ecumenical relationship had a significant influence upon my life. Here, also, for the first time, I had an inter-faith experience. Old Testament was taught by Professor Caiphus, a gifted and inspiring teacher who as a Jew could interpret the scriptures out of a profound knowledge of his own culture.

Close friendship with faculty and students, most of whom were whites, could not shield me from the reality of racial bigotry as then practised by many in Missouri. It was as if the white community had not yet heard that the Supreme Court had ordered desegregation of schools, or that blacks led by Dr. Martin Luther King had already won desegregation of buses in the Deep South.

My first exposure came in St. Louis when our professor of Old Testament invited our class to join him for lunch. Most of my classmates, all of whom were white, went ahead of me in the cafeteria line and ordered their food. When I reached the counter the cashier announced: 'You can't eat here.' The whole class reacted to the bigotry, dropped their trays on the table, and walked away with me.

Other blacks soon told me of similar insults which they had experienced in hotels, schools, and even churches. So for the six months I served as interim pastor of the St. Luke Methodist Church, a black congregation in Columbia, Missouri, I led our people in prayer that the wounds of racial prejudice might be healed.

In those years Dr. Martin Luther King gave inspired leadership in the civil rights movement. It was plain that he was trying to change an unjust, segregated system, but he always spoke without hate, in a steady, convincing way. That was something which I never would forget.

On to University

Towards the end of the first year my grades were sent to Rhodesia. Eagerly I awaited word from the Church leaders concerning my future. I was overjoyed to learn of their decision that I should stay in the USA for university studies, and that finances would be made available so my wife and children could come to America to be with me.

Assured that the family would join me soon, I began my new studies at the Central Methodist College in Fayette, Missouri. I pursued a double major in religion and philosophy. Courses in psychology and sociology proved to be helpful as well, giving insights which in later years would enable me to be a better judge of human behaviour.

When my family arrived in November, 1959, it became a struggle to make ends meet financially. Fortunately the college granted us a married student's apartment, with space for a small garden where we grew vegetables and sweet corn to supplement the family budget, as we had learned to do in Africa. During the winter our classmates used to go rabbit hunting for sport. We were happy to get the rabbits which they sold to us for 25 cents each. Other friends helped us to buy our first car for the grand sum of $75. It was sixteen years old, and not always reliable, but neither was its learner-driver.

Much as I wanted to spare my wife and sons the raw edge of racial discrimination, I could not. Unintentionally we joined the civil rights movement on our first Sunday together as a family, for twenty members walked out when we entered a white congregation to worship. Fortunately the minister was prepared for this crisis in his church, and the majority of worshippers either tolerated us or accepted our presence among them.

We soon learned that among Missouri towns Fayette rated low in racial justice. One day my sons, four and seven years old, innocently entered a drugstore to buy ice cream cones, only to be thrown out! We learned as a family that, like all blacks, we were barred from parks and theatres and most public places in Fayette.

Meanwhile I had chosen to write my first research paper on *Apartheid* in South Africa. My reading reminded me that the ugliness and ruthlessness of that society was not unlike what was being experienced by my own brothers and sisters in Rhodesia.

Life on the college campus, however, was far better than that outside it. Upon the graduation of a black woman student during my first year, our family became the only remaining blacks in that campus community of around 4,000—counting students, teachers, and their families. Dr. Charles Caldwell, pastor of the college community church, invited me to be one of his student associates. The white students responded amicably to my pastoral work among them. Some would say, quite frankly, 'I wish I could take you to my home for a weekend, Abel, but I am afraid my parents will not accept you on racial grounds.' Rather than being hurt by such remarks, I felt touched by their open honesty. Among this new generation were some who were determined to wipe out the ruthless racism in America and to create a more Christian society.

Southern Hospitality

In the spring of 1962, when once again our family faced the crossroads, Bishop Dodge invited me to return to Rhodesia to work as his administrative assistant, but he left open the possibility of further studies. I chose the latter course and enrolled for a Master's degree at Scarritt College for Christian Workers in Nashville, Tennessee.

From my first hours in Nashville I knew that there I would be exposed to the full brunt of the racial strife in America. Arriving too late to eat in the college dining-hall, Rev. Mark Eloride and I looked for a nearby restaurant. The waitress quickly said to my friend, 'You know our custom in the South; I cannot serve this gentleman.' Mr. Eloride, whom I affectionately called a 'transformed Georgian', argued: 'This man is not from Tennessee. He is a pastor from our church in Africa thousands of miles away.' 'Well, I give a lot of money to missions, but I am not going to serve him,' insisted the waitress. While my friend, in vain, carried the argument to the owner, I stood by and thought, 'Yes, this is what has been called "the Deep South".'

Our experience in churches was a strange mixture of love and prejudice. Upon our arrival in Nashville friends invited us to worship at the nearby Belmont Methodist Church. Their friendship was warm and genuine, but it was not shared by many at Belmont. A crisis developed when we applied to become church members. The Committee on Membership and Evangelism supported our application, but the pastor refused to receive us. He feared repercussions from the third of the congregation who opposed having a black family as members. We were keenly disappointed, and decided not to present our son for Christian baptism lest we provoke a second conflict.

Such rebuffs, however, made many members more concerned to share their Christian hospitality and love. Often we visited their homes during weekends. When Maggie gave birth to our fourth son, Scarritter, women of a Sunday school class took turns sending food to our home during the first ten days. Those who came to care for our children while Maggie was at school were like substitute aunts and grandmothers to them. We felt we were among friends at church and school. We were living on an island of love in the midst of an ocean of indifference and hatred.

The year of study at Scarritt passed all too quickly. I chose to concentrate on Christian Education and the Ministry to Youth, knowing that this was a great need in my own country. Courses in anthropology gave me a chance to reflect upon my own country and its values, which had been so unappreciated by missionaries and other Europeans.

Soon I learned that my training at Scarritt would be put to immediate use back home. I had written to Bishop Dodge that I was prepared to serve in any capacity, wherever there was need, either in rural or urban areas. I was appointed pastor and station chairman at Old Umtali Centre, a challenging responsibility for one so young.

Chapter 7

Back to the Valley of Dry Bones

Excited and apprehensive, and with mixed emotions, the Muzorewa family returned to Rhodesia in June, 1963. It was exciting for the children to spot their grandparents waving from the airport balcony. Our mouths watered for the welcome feast ahead. Each of our four sons would receive special gifts with baby Chido, born in America, the focus of attention.

With apprehension, however, we faced the initiation rituals at the airport and the discrimination of racist Rhodesia. Immediately upon arrival white immigration officials searched me and my luggage, then took me away for interrogation. 'Why did you go to America? What did you do there?' they asked. This time the questioning soon ended, but in the days to follow I was told that the secret police watched my movements, noted those I spoke to and monitored my meetings.

I felt our people showed in 1963 an intense interest in politics that I had not experienced in earlier years. In the confidence of our own home relatives and friends eagerly briefed us on the latest developments. Indeed, our politicians had succeeded in developing a high political consciousness amongst our people. At that time I sensed also a powerful spirit of unity. Little did we know that this would be shattered in the near future.

Reports in the white press, however, spoke of political uncertainty. The Federation of Rhodesia and Nyasaland was on the rocks. Ten years earlier it had been heralded as a marriage of black and white for racial partnership, but it was an ill-fated marriage in which the latter partner reaped all the benefits. Our brothers and sisters in neighbouring Zambia and Malawi had fought successfully against Federation which for them meant domination by the white settlers of Southern Rhodesia. Already the Rhodesia Front party—led by those settlers—was arguing in London: 'Give Rhodesia full independence at the same time that you give it to Zambia and Malawi.' 'What would independence offer to the black majority?' I wondered.

As we drove to our village I looked and listened for the changes which ten years of so-called 'racial partnership' had brought. The farms of the Europeans looked as prosperous as ever. The improved main roads helped them to transport their goods to market. The whitewashed villas of the farmers were barely visible through the trees. Beyond, almost out of sight, I glimpsed the mud and pole shelters of their African labourers. The contrast spoke eloquently of who owned Rhodesia.

I recalled the incident when a European motorist spat upon the face of a Mr. Sauramba as he walked along this very road to Umtali. Other whites observed the incident but spoke no word of rebuke.

Friends briefed me on the latest twists of the so-called 'Law and Order Maintenance Act', and how it was used to silence African opposition. This ordinance was like a giant net within which you could swim until the authorities chose to catch you. Under the latest amendments, statements likely 'to have the effect of inducing any person or group to resist, either actively or passively, any law or lawful administrative measure' were judged to be 'subversive', and the offender was subject to up to five years' imprisonment. Appended to the ordinance was a mandatory death sentence for anyone who threw a petrol bomb.

'What about abuses against Africans by whites?' I asked. 'Do European farmers continue to seize the wives and daughters of their farm workers for sexual gratification? Are farm workers beaten and refused their pay at the whim of the white boss?'

'Yes,' the village elders replied. 'These practices continue.'

As a family we found that our experiences in America had sharpened our sensitivity to racial discrimination. We were shocked and hurt by the hypocrisy of many so-called 'liberals'.

I had looked forward to my new appointment as pastor at Old Umtali Methodist Centre, succeeding Rev. Larry Eisenberg, a missionary. Already the Church, under Bishop Dodge's leadership, had adopted a system of 'interchangeable houses' for missionaries and nationals in such appointments. Their failure to provide similar arrangements for furniture, however, was to provoke a major incident.

To our surprise Maggie, our four children and I moved into a practically empty house. The 'missionary' furniture had been removed. Fortunately we had some blankets which we spread on the wooden floor to sleep on. But we did not sleep well. To us the barren house symbolized the stupid straightforward segregation that still infected the church community. In order to buy furniture I would have to go deep into debt, for I was to be given the same salary as any other pastor in the Conference—£25 (US$50) per month. Impulsively, I lashed out at those who were responsible for this injustice, and this led to a strained relationship with certain missionaries. Soon kind friends helped us to get furniture and emotions subsided; but in the eyes of many I was branded as a radical. The controversy did lead to policy changes, however, which greatly improved relationships between African and missionary staff.

It seemed at the time as if we had returned to 'a valley of dry bones'. That expression comes from the prophecy of Ezekiel in the Old Testament. His people were scattered in exile, crushed politically, and spiritually despondent. Ezekiel had a vision of a valley filled with dry bones, and he heard the voice of the Lord, saying 'Can these bones live?' In the vision the dead came back to life as they heard the word of the Lord.

Like Ezekiel I felt that my people were like dry bones—oppressed and depressed under the rule of a small white minority. They were without a united spirit as a nation, or as a Christian community. Like Ezekiel, I felt I had been called to preach the word of the Lord to such a people.

The Whole Gospel for the Whole Man

I began my ministry at Old Umtali preaching on the text which Jesus used in his first sermon:

> 'The Spirit of the Lord is upon me, because He has anointed me to preach good news to the poor. He has sent me to proclaim release to the captives and recovering of sight to the blind, to set at liberty those who are oppressed, to proclaim the acceptable year of the Lord.'
>
> (Luke 4: 18–19)

I was sick and tired of hearing missionaries and African pastors preaching for the conversion of souls and promising a heavenly reward to those who would repent and be saved. Our people needed to hear a total gospel—that God created a man, or a woman, as a total person, having a body, a mind and a spirit; and that our Heavenly Father would save that total person. I believed, and preached, that to love as God loves means to be in total service to the total man. That includes politics. Participation in politics is not a 'secular' activity. It is part of the Christian's duty if he is to serve as Christ served.

Had this message come too late to be accepted by our students? I wondered. Already African nationalists had promoted an anti-Church feeling which had swept across the country, and even into the thinking of our students. Politicians accused the churchmen of preaching a one-sided gospel of 'pie in the sky by and by.' They charged that the Church offered a spiritual tranquillizer which put oppressed people into a coma, and condoned the aims and activities of the imperialists who were oppressing and exploiting black Africans. Some called Christianity 'the white man's opiate for the black people'.

Stories were circulated justifying such accusations. One was told of a white minister and principal at a Dutch Reformed school, who received a report that his students were troubled by an outbreak of bedbugs in the dormitories. When the students incessantly complained the principal shamelessly replied: 'We did not come to Rhodesia to save your bodies but your souls!'

Often missionaries were taken aback by the sharp attacks of their critics, feeling that their good works in health, education, and social welfare deserved praise, not condemnation. 'Where would the African people be today if the Church had not built schools and clinics for them?' they replied. They had a point, but our new generation of young students were extremely sensitive to any expressions of paternalism. They knew as well that the Churches were now dependent on government funding to pay teachers' and nurses' salaries and to build and equip many buildings at the Church centres. Could the Church, when so tied to the white government's purse-strings, stand prophetically with the people in their liberation struggle?

Student excitement ran high the day I invited Rev. Ndabaningi Sithole to the campus. He was the first prominent African nationalist to speak to our high school and teacher training students. He encouraged them all to work for a free Zimbabwe. 'Your place now is in the classroom,' he advised, 'so that you can prepare for future leadership in a free Zimbabwe.' Then he told the story of 'The Little Engine that Could' which pulled an immense load over the steep mountain. He said, 'Our struggle for freedom is like that. On the upward grade progress is painfully slow, but like the little engine we must persist, saying: "I think I can". Finally we shall reach the summit. Only then can we come down into a free Zimbabwe with shouts of joy, saying: "I knew I could, I knew I could, I knew I could".'

Sithole's presence on our campus spoke eloquently of our commitment to the liberation struggle. Other Churches, however, had not yet reached this level of involvement. In August, 1963, I met a multi-racial delegation of our Church attending the Southern Rhodesia Christian Conference, which assembled at Morgenster Mission, a Dutch Reformed Church centre. Missionaries were taken as guests to the homes of white missionaries, while we Africans were sent to the compound for 'native' pastors and teachers. I felt deeply hurt. My missionary colleagues shared my annoyance, but we did not make an issue of it.

Driving home we shared our feelings and stopped for refreshments at a small hotel at Beitbridge. The day was very hot. No sooner had we ordered refreshments than the waiter said to the missionaries: 'You can drink here, but your friends will have to drink outside.' 'We are together,' we replied. 'Serve us in here, or not at all.' Our loud protest brought the white owner on the run. 'Get their licence number!' she shouted to the waiter, as if to have the last word. And she did; for the next day the police tracked down the car in which we rode, even though it was 250 miles away at a mission farm. Police interrogated the owner concerning this racial incident.

Unity Broken
The trip to Morgenster Mission showed me that I was not alone in my sensitivity to racial discrimination in our country. Even at the citadel of Afrikaner religion, people were talking national politics. What we lacked was a clear sense of direction, as the events of that month were to demonstrate.

On August 8 the incipient split among our leaders burst into full public view. ZANU (the Zimbabwe African National Union) under Rev. Ndabaningi Sithole's leadership gained support both within and outside the country, some coming from those who were disappointed that Joshua Nkomo had gained little if anything in his struggle to further majority rule.

57

Many people were confused by these developments. They admitted that they did not know where to put their loyalties. Before long discussions turned to arguments and then to quarrelling, even among members of the same family. Then the violence began. News reached us quickly of violence in Salisbury's African townships, where people started manufacturing petrol bombs to attack homes and stores of those of the opposing party. Our whole struggle for liberation from white minority rule turned inward and led to fighting amongst ourselves for power.

It was disturbing to hear that ZAPU (the Zimbabwe African Political Union) leaders exhorted the masses to oppose ZANU as the party of the educated élite. Schoolteachers, nurses, doctors and even ministers like myself were to be viewed as 'the enemy'. This was the basis for violence against schoolteachers in some rural areas, as well as in the cities.

It was equally disturbing to hear the conservative reaction of many Church leaders who used this crisis as their opportunity to preach again that a 'true' Christian should not be involved in politics, nor be active in the national struggle. As a result there were some violent confrontations between churchmen and politicians. Politicians scheduled their rallies at the same time as church services to force people to be loyal to one side or the other. Some church buildings and schools were burnt down. At our Nyadiri Centre volunteers, fearing arson, guarded the hospital day and night for two weeks.

The Church Awakens
In the towns, however, a new movement for unity and political involvement by African Christians was under way. The African Ministers' Fraternal in Salisbury tried its strength, and on March 13, 1964, organized a Day of Prayer for Peace and Unity. Crowds of 8,000 and 18,000 responded in Salisbury's African townships—the largest religious gatherings in the country's history. People demonstrated their hunger for unity, despite the continuing political dissensions among their leaders.

There were many of us who longed for an inter-Church body that could speak for us on national issues. The Southern Rhodesia Christian Conference met only once every two years and then was afraid to attack the very government which supported mission schools and hospitals. African ministers' fraternals in Salisbury and Bulawayo expressed the views of many of us as they urged the formation of a Christian council which would speak prophetically on social issues as they arose, and would affiliate with the World Council of Churches. The result was the formation of the Christian Council of Rhodesia. It was launched in April 1964, the same month in which Ian Smith became Prime Minister.

The Council gave us new hope. It voiced the concerns of the African people at the very time when our parties were banned and our leaders silenced in political detention. Gradually, the youth of Rhodesia started again to have faith and hope in the Christian Church.

Mere statements, however, did not convince the doubters of the Church's stand. They wanted concrete actions, and had not long to wait. In July 1964 the government deported Bishop Ralph Dodge and Rev. Robert Hughes of our Church. Bishop Dodge was not only head of The United Methodist Church, but also the first President of the Christian Council of Rhodesia. He had preached a total gospel for the total man, and he had led the Church in a denunciation of the proposed unilateral declaration of independence. He had severely criticized the government's practice of detaining persons without trial.

My first contact with white officials of the government in Salisbury came over these issues. With other church leaders I joined in a fruitless attempt to persuade government officials to cancel the orders to deport Bishop Dodge and Rev. Hughes. Our lawyer advised us to write a formal letter of protest to the government, but he let us know that he held out no hope that anyone would listen to our pleas.

One avenue of protest remained—public demonstrations. White police had quashed protests by political activists, but they were startled to find churchwomen in their blue and red uniforms, men with blue sashes of their Fisherman's organization, and black-suited clergy with clerical collars demonstrating in the major towns. They all wore black armbands, signifying that they were in mourning, and they carried placards protesting against the deportation of Bishop Dodge. Fifty-six clergy of various denominations carried the protests to Ian Smith's office in Salisbury. The words fell on deaf ears, but the demonstrations initiated many church leaders into a new style of political involvement.

Bishop Dodge then was given two weeks to say farewell to

his people. His words to us at Old Umtali reminded me of Jesus' final words to his disciples, as he encouraged us to continue with the fight for justice and peace. In reply the people said to the beloved bishop: 'Deportation has only taken your flesh, but not your spirit. You have speeded up the educational, medical and African leadership in church work. We wish you a speedy return to take up the unfinished task.'

At the airport farewell I met my old friend Darius Jijita who had, like so many others, drifted away from the Church as he became active in politics. He was there not because he loved the Church, but because he admired what Bishop Dodge stood for. Upon seeing the bishop again and the support of the people for him, Jijita resolved to return to the Church and today he is a staunch leader.

Little did the white regime realize what was happening in those days. Although they expelled anyone who spoke out courageously for justice, by that action they stimulated hundreds of African churchmen to take up the torch in the struggle to end discrimination.

The Churches and UDI

UDI (Unilateral Declaration of Independence) was the next issue on which the Churches took a prophetic stand. The banning of African political parties and of the *African Daily News,* in 1964, left a political void which churchmen sought to fill. Some of them called the impending rebellion against Britain 'immoral and unchristian'. Others enjoined Christians to obey the existing authorities under every circumstance. To foster that argument, Ian Smith, in announcing his action on November 11, 1965, declared that he had struck a blow in order to 'preserve Christian civilization'.

I was in Kitwe, Zambia, on that fateful day, attending a youth leaders' course. There was no celebration, but sadness in the hearts of African students. 'Would there be any hope for our freedom as blacks in Zimbabwe?' we wondered. How disgusted and shattered we were when we heard the announcement made by Britain's Prime Minister Wilson: '. . . under no circumstances will the British Government use force in Rhodesia'. Naturally these words encouraged the white minority to seize power. It was dismaying to hear that the few heroic protests by our people in Salisbury and Bulawayo were easily crushed.

Press censorship denied to our people news of the prophetic rejection of UDI by many church leaders. The Christian Council on November 26 declared:

'In humble submission to Almighty God and to the judgment of our Lord, we affirm our present loyalty to Her Majesty the Queen within the Constitution which is at present the Constitution accepted by the lawful Parliament of Rhodesia in 1961. . . . We judge the proclamation of a new Constitution of Rhodesia by a group of Ministers, without the assent of the Parliament of the Crown, to be an unlawful act, and any further enactments of Parliament to be unlawful unless confirmed by the lawful Governor . . . We look forward earnestly to and pledge ourselves to work for the rapid restoration of constitutional government in our land.'

I did not expect that many white Christians would heed this injunction. They were too much a part of the ruling élite for that. In fact, the Christian Council was suspect in the eyes of many whites from its inception. But to African Christians it gave a sanction for that opposition to white rule that would flower again.

Travelling for Youth

I felt proud upon returning to Rhodesia in December 1965 to begin work as Youth Secretary of the Christian Council, and as the Travelling Secretary for the Student Christian Movement. This was a joint appointment. Earlier that year I had moved into full-time youth work at the request of Bishop Dodge. At first I served as the Conference Youth Director for the United Methodist Church. It seemed an excellent way to utilize the education received at Scarritt College in that field. No sooner had I begun that work than the invitation came to work with youth of various churches. Bishop Dodge kindly encouraged me to accept it, and to attend a course in Zambia for youth secretaries of various Christian organizations and countries. This training would prove valuable in my new appointment.

My new responsibilities involved travel to each high school in which there were students who were interested in the Student Christian Movement. Often as I stopped for petrol the station attendant would ask, 'Who do you drive for?' Since few Africans owned cars he assumed I was the driver for some white man. Such marks of colonial mentality were common throughout Rhodesia.

The students whom I visited, however, were in rebellion against white domination. Some older teachers and ministers found their questions threatening. To me they were refreshing in their openness and honesty. They were signs that a new age was coming.

However, in their desire for freedom and equality some of the students wanted to throw out 'the white man's religion'. 'Why not stick to our own traditional ancestral worship?' many asked. 'Why worship Jesus? Wasn't he a white man and not an African?'

In response I preached on the topic, 'Why worship Jesus, a European God?' Today my reply would be called 'Liberation Theology'. I explained that Jesus was not from Europe, but from the Middle East. His people were themselves in bondage, and Jesus announced that his mission was 'to proclaim release to the captives (and) set at liberty those who are oppressed'.

One day I sat with a young man who said: 'We should destroy the Bible and find some Africans who can write our own Bible.' He thought that the Bible had been written by people like the Prime Minister of Rhodesia, Ian Smith. The fact that so many whites in Rhodesia claimed to be Christians (although few attended churches) and that the vast majority, including some missionaries, supported white minority rule, made my witness to African students extremely difficult. I found that most of the students saw the Church as part of the system of oppression—a system that would deny to the majority the opportunity to finish high school, and would permit only a select few to go on to university, or to find skilled employment.

Preaching a total gospel had its impact, strengthened by the witness of a few of their fellow-students. Some of the members of the SCM boldly declared: 'We believe in a Saviour who suffers on behalf of the oppressed and who walks with us in our struggle for liberation.'

The SCM programme was based on the conviction that persons are not just spiritual, but also social, cultural, physical, political and economic in their concerns and interests. It affirmed that a Christian should relate his or her Christian faith to all these concerns. Many students found the SCM to be the one group on the campus where they could discuss social and political questions along with issues of religious faith.

Some Protestant leaders were suspicious. They preferred to have the Church abstain from every form of political involvement. They discouraged the discussion of political issues in church schools. We found it impossible to organize branches of the SCM in schools of the Dutch Reformed, Salvation Army and Free Methodist Churches.

Work in government schools became increasingly difficult. Those in authority suspected that my influence would make the students restless. Soon officials in the Ministry for African Education began to write letters to headmasters recommending that I be denied permission to speak to their students. In fact, the Student Christian Movement came close to being declared illegal on several occasions, being branded by some white settlers as 'communist', 'atheist' or 'political'.

I chose, therefore, never to discuss openly certain controversial topics. In private, however, students bombarded me with questions and our conversations often went on after 'lights out'. They were eager to learn of my visits to the political detainees at Gonakudzingwa and Hwa Hwa. Some were surprised that I had visited political leaders both of ZAPU and of ZANU.

There came times when fear of informers muted our discussions. It was said that wherever ten Africans gathered you could assume that one was in the employ of the Smith regime as an informer, with instructions to report to the police anything political that was said.

Ways remained, nevertheless, by which we could share information and express common aspirations. In April, 1966, for example, I sensed a new excitement and hope amongst many students. News had filtered through of the 'Battle of Sinoia'* which launched the new armed phase of the liberation struggle. Almost everyone, however, was afraid to talk about it openly.

* A combined military operation by guerillas of ZAPU and the ANC of South Africa, marking the beginning of the armed struggle.

Chapter 8

In the Footsteps of Bishop Dodge

In July 1968 visitors to our home brought a startling request: 'Abel, we want you to stand for election as bishop.'

United Methodist bishops in Africa, unlike their American counterparts, have to go through the rigour of quadrennial elections. Since preparation for indigenous African leadership was one of Bishop Dodge's priorities, and he had served as bishop-in-exile for four years, people were speculating about his possible African successor. The United Methodist Churches in central and southern Africa would send delegates to the Africa Central Conference meeting in Botswana in August 1968 to make the selection.

Many persons assumed that Rev. Jonah Kawadza would be the automatic choice, since he had acted as Bishop Dodge's Administrative Assistant for four years. Tall and handsome, a good preacher, with an amiable personality, he won favour with many, including most of the still-powerful missionary community. Rev. Kawadza appeared an obvious choice. In contrast, I was considered a more controversial figure, having been outspoken on many issues. Some even feared that many missionaries of our Church would leave the country if I were elected.

Urging me to stand for election, a friend argued: 'Abel, if people think you have what they are looking for in a bishop, and you refuse them, you will be failing both Christ and the Church.'

Several weeks later I found myself sitting alone on the bus carrying the Rhodesian Church delegates to the Central Conference. No one wished to side with me openly lest they be found later to have backed the losing candidate. I understood then the loneliness that political candidates must feel at times, even amidst crowds of anonymous well-wishers.

I did not care for the type of electioneering which too often characterized such elections, even in the Church, nor did I wish to promise anything to my supporters. A layman came and said to me. 'We think we are going to elect you . . . What new things are *you* going to do for the Church?' I quickly replied, 'I am not in a political campaign. As you know I have not asked one person to vote for me, nor have I paid or promised anything in order to be elected. I am not promising any individual or the Church anything new whatsoever. If what I am saying makes you change your minds, you had better do so now before the balloting takes place.'

Balloting started the morning of August 28. As expected, Bishop Dodge was re-elected bishop on the first ballot. Also as planned, the bishop immediately announced his retirement. Balloting continued for his successor until after the sixth ballot the presiding bishop announced: 'Number voting—seventy. Number needed for election fifty-three. Rev. Abel Muzorewa received fifty-six votes and is elected bishop.'

People jumped from their seats and dashed forward to congratulate me, embracing me with shouts of jubilation. It was overwhelming. But I was aware through it all of the absence of my colleague who had slipped away as the voting turned in my favour. Breaking away from well-wishers I sought to express to Rev. Kawadza words of friendship and respect. I said, 'I will need your help. Let us work together.'

An Awesome Task

As the Conference drew to a close I felt the heavy responsibility before me as leader of our United Methodist Church and the first African head of a major denomination in Rhodesia. It was appropriate that Bishop Dodge, my predecessor and mentor, should give the charge to me at the consecration service. He challenged me to follow five principles of leadership. These have continued to be an inspiration to me even to this day:

'First, maintain your personal integrity; honesty in dealing with other people, honesty in dealing with yourself, honesty in dealing with the Father . . . Second, maintain your concern for people; do not forget those of different classes, those who walk far from where you normally walk. Don't forget the despised . . . Third, maintain an open mind; learn from others as well as teaching them; listen as well as speak; admit your mistakes . . . Fourth, maintain vision and foresight; he who would lead people must be ahead of them; he must look into the future. You must begin now to build the foundation in Africa upon which our

Church of the year 2000 can stand . . . Finally, maintain contact with the true vine; your ministry will fail if you are out of harmony with God's plan and purpose for you and for His Church; keep sensitive, deeply sensitive to the whisper of God's voice. As God has spoken through the prophets in past generations, so prophets must continue to speak to His people today. Listen to the Holy Spirit, and as you listen you will be taught, and as you are taught you will go forth in faith to help to establish God's Church—a *new* Church in a *new* Africa and a *new* world.'

The Daily Life of an African Bishop

I have dwelt on the charge which was given to me because it helped me to keep in perspective the multitude of demands I faced each day as bishop.

My day usually began at 6 a.m., and sometimes earlier. It became increasingly common at that hour to find a queue waiting outside our house—people wanting to 'catch the bishop before he leaves for work'. Some came to borrow money for families of political detainees. Others told of water or electricity about to be cut off because they were unemployed. I felt like a welfare officer without a budget! Friends said, 'You are soft-hearted.' I know my family often was deprived because I found it hard to turn anyone away. There were many pleas which I could not resist, so again and again I dug deep into my own pockets. Often it was hard to get away and turn my attention to other pressing responsibilities.

My preference was to reach the office by 7 a.m. so as to launch into my correspondence before the office opened at eight o'clock. I tried to keep the early morning free from visitors so that I could do creative thinking and writing. At 10 a.m. there was a break to have prayers and tea with the staff. From 10.30 a.m. to 4.30 p.m. days in the office were filled with all manner of appointments, with only a brief time for lunch, usually consisting of bananas, apples and tea.

Rarely did I return in the evening to a house free from visitors, or eat an evening meal alone with my family. Maggie followed our Shona customs of hospitality. Sometimes she fed visitors as they arrived; cooked five or six meals a day; and the tea kettle remained hot on the stove, so she could pour those unending cups of tea which the British had introduced into our way of life.

One day, like many, I arrived home to find a stranger among us. Assuming that he had come to see my wife, I greeted him and soon we sat at table together. He listened amiably as we conversed with missionary friends visiting us. Late that night he accepted a ride to town with our visitors. 'Who was that?' I asked Maggie upon his departure, only to have her reply, 'I don't know; I assumed that he was someone who had come to see you.' A newcomer needing a hot meal? A government informer? We shall never know.

More difficult to answer than the request for a meal were the incessant pleas for financial help, mostly from simple folks who believed that a bishop has an endless supply of money. At the times we have been unable to respond, some have rudely insisted: 'Give us some of that money you have. What do you do with all your money?' It was as if our home was looked upon as 'Standard Bank—Highfields Township Branch'!

In the face of these requests and needs, the salary of a United Methodist bishop in Africa seemed woefully inadequate. The salaries as set by the African Central Conference are below those of some African doctors and school inspectors in Rhodesia, and far below those of American bishops and of many pastors. Many persons in need came to me for assistance, rather than going to government officials, or even to a wealthy African businessman. Friends claim that I am generous to a fault yet that seems to me a lesser failing than to turn a deaf ear to those in genuine need.

Fortunately I neither faced these requests alone, nor found the work of administering the Church solely on my shoulders. Rev. Kare Eriksson, my Administrative Assistant, was noted for his fatherly sensitivity to others' needs. The onset of his physical blindness seemed only to increase his mental alertness and sympathetic understanding. Pat Fulmer, as Administrative Secretary, gave continuity and competence to that important work, carrying an especially heavy load of appointments during my absences. Isaac Musamba and John Shryock maintained unquestioned integrity as our church treasurers. Our receptionist, Susan Chitombo, now Mrs. November M'tshiya, gave that friendly welcome which put the visitors at ease.

This competent staff sought to free me as much as possible from office routines so that I could fulfil the varied responsibilities of a bishop. On Fridays I hoped for a day of quiet study and writing away from both office and home. Each weekend I tried to visit one or more of our 333 congregations. District conferences, church revival meetings—led by women, men, or youth—and dedications of church buildings were given a place of priority. Each Monday I hoped for a day when I could exchange my clerical garb for that of a farmer and work with my hands in our garden plots.

Major Concerns

It soon became plain to me that our theology needed to be clarified and our concerns needed a broader base. I felt at ease in following in the footsteps of Bishop Ralph Dodge. He, too, had stressed that the Christian faith must be proclaimed as a total gospel for the total person.

I wanted our people to be liberated from over eighty years of colonialism and the implication that Africans are by nature inferior. The Church had to work hard to exorcise the demons of that inferiority complex. I wanted people to be liberated from the teaching that it was all right to suffer now on earth because believers can look forward to a better life in heaven. I wanted them to be liberated from the doctrine that God has more sympathy for the poor than for the rich. I wanted them to realize that getting a good life was not the exclusive right and privilege of white people. I had to preach against the false belief that politics is a dirty game which Christians should avoid.

The whole gospel for the whole person I believed—and still believe—has a dynamic that will lead many to Christ as their liberator, their Saviour and Lord. To the Annual Conference I threw out a challenge to win 50,000 new persons for Christ and his Church. But I knew that the resolution adopted to that effect would be empty words without a systematic programme of reaching out to others. To that end I agreed to speak at evangelistic meetings in a number of our churches. The Smith regime had banned political rallies, but fortunately not religious services. In one of the fast-growing city congregations, St. Mark's United Methodist Church in Highfields, Salisbury, a hundred persons, mostly young men and women, stood up in response to a call for commitment of their lives to Christ.

Even at such a high moment, I was troubled because we had developed few church leaders who were able to respond creatively to the needs of young and old, educated and uneducated, amongst our people. Bishop Dodge's crash programme of higher education, from which I had benefited, trained mainly school-teachers and administrators. It seemed as if there was a subtle feeling among our people that higher education, salaries, good houses, etc. were for the laity rather than the clergy. Ministers as 'servants of the Lord' were not to worry about 'earthly possessions'.

One day a young pastor, Josiah Kurewa, came to my office to talk about his desire for higher education. 'I heard your challenge to ministers to study by correspondence if they have not had the opportunity to go to high school,' he said. He continued: 'I've passed one subject already. Can you consider me for further studies overseas?' Before me as he spoke was a letter from Dr. D. D. Holt, President of Scarritt College, offering one of our ministers a scholarship for study there. Remembering my own fortuitous start, I responded: 'Yes, Josiah, there may be a way for you to study overseas.' He became the first of more than seven of our church ministers to receive university training in the next few years.

Another challenge was to build a self-supporting church. Some pastors doubted that their people could provide their salaries, in the face of reduced contributions for church work by our sister churches overseas. Fortunately lay leaders, among them those who had studied overseas, were determined to lead the way to a self-reliant church. Matthew Mataranyleka, a skilled teacher, accepted an appointment to work full-time conducting workshops on stewardship and fund-raising. He was to travel to all of our circuits. As a result of his efforts, and those of others, the local churches were able to pay almost eighty-five per cent of their pastors' salaries by 1976, despite the ·tragedies of war, poverty, and social disturbance.

Women deserve much of the praise in leading the way to self-reliance in our church. The women's report at each Annual Conference brings great excitement among the delegates. Not only is it lively in dramatic presentation, but it includes remarkable achievements in projects to help the needy, to educate girls left without school places, and in building dormitories and church buildings.

Of the many church dedications I have conducted as bishop, that at Nyakunu, near Umtali, stands out most vividly. Here was a new congregation, just fifteen miles from town. Although most men worked in town, the women were determined to build a church in their own community. They began by gathering stones for the foundation, carrying them on their heads across the hills to the new church site. Chagrined, the few men who remained at Nyakunu hitched their oxen to wagons and hauled the larger rocks. Next the women started moulding bricks, and once again their initiative spurred the men to join in that back-breaking work. Then the women raised money by selling vegetables in town and before long there was enough to hire a builder for the little church. When I came to dedicate that building I knew that the church was there to stay—a people's church.

In spite of all that women have done for their local churches, they now face a new challenge. They must assume their full share of leadership in the general Church and in society as well. They must be liberated from that archaic African tradition that allows the relatives of the husband upon his death to take the deceased's property as their own, leaving the widow destitute.

Is it possible for the Church to become a model of the kind of community we desire the nation to become? I believe so. But the Church has much to do to achieve this goal. It requires setting an example of human freedom which will allow all its members to speak freely irrespective of their colour, sex or age. Such freedom would be unusual in a country accustomed as we are to authoritarian rule in which five per cent of the population pretends to speak for the other ninety-five per cent and controls their destiny. It requires destroying every practice of tribalism, racialism and regionalism. Pastors and teachers must be appointed to the places they are most needed, and this should promote genuine Christian brotherhood and fellowship.

The Colour Chasm
We found that every attempt to reach across the colour bar in Christian fellowship was difficult. Our denomination has an almost entirely African membership, except for a few missionaries and one small congregation in Rusape. Although this fact left us free to develop vigorously our own African leadership, it handicapped us in dealing realistically with the barriers to racial understanding. 'Let us welcome white families living near our churches,' a senior pastor urged year after year at our Annual Conference. No one opposed his recommendation, but the social barriers to integration prevented any concrete action. It became

increasingly clear that some of the ideals of the Church could not be attained until there was widespread social change.

I felt a growing urge to speak to the nation concerning the racism which was our country's undoing. In 1969 Ian Smith and his Rhodesian Front party appeared to emerge victorious over Britain in the post-UDI manœuvres. In June the white electorate approved the 'republican' constitution. The last symbols of Britain's *de jure* rule over Southern Rhodesia collapsed as the Governor, Sir Humphrey Gibbs, resigned and the British residual mission withdrew from Salisbury. On March 2, 1970, Ian Smith declared Rhodesia a republic and called for new elections to sweep away the last vestiges of white opposition. Smith's followers felt victorious over every opponent, internal and external, black and white.

In that month I was invited to the USA to attend a special session of the General Conference of our Church and invited to Central Methodist College—my alma mater—to receive an honorary doctorate. Before my departure from Rhodesia I addressed the following message to the nation. It was my first effort to reach a national audience, both black and white:

'Since I am leaving Rhodesia for a length of time, I feel I should voice my distress at the present situation in this country.

'First, I want to address myself to the electorate. Since only two per cent of our total population can vote in the coming election, they bear a heavy responsibility to the voteless masses.

'We need free men—men free from fear. The freedom I talk about is needed by all of us—Black, White, Coloured, and Asian alike. Even the Rhodesian Front is not free, for it fears the loss of white privilege. It needs our liberation.

'During this election the voters shall hear many appeals to protect the narrow interests of one racial group. Let's vote instead for people who are free from the intoxication of racialism. Let us vote for a party we believe will offer equal opportunities for advancement to all in education, employment, social and political life.

'I am sorry to think that at the very time when scientists and theologians are coming to a common understanding of the basic common nature of Man, the rulers of Rhodesia are still believers in the false doctrine of racial superiority and inferiority.

'The human race is one. Why then do people spend money, energy, and time on schemes of compulsory separation? Racialists

71

talk about forced integration. I do not believe there is such a thing. Voluntary integration is one mature way whereby Rhodesians of all races could really get to know one another.

'I hate to think that our children in Rhodesia fifty years from now will still be victims of racial hatred and distrust when people in other countries have achieved racial harmony.

'I believe that we should emphasize our unity rather than our differences. Africans are equally guilty of not seeking this unity in the coming elections.

'Another point I want to touch upon are midnight raids in the townships. Many whites in our towns do not realize that Africans in the townships go to bed every night in fear of police raids. The whites do not understand what life is like for people unable to speak openly their opinions and frustrations for fear of police informers. Some Africans are held for questioning without any charges being brought against them. Others are held for so long that they lose their jobs.

'This is terrorism—rule by a system of coercive intimidation.

'It is this government terrorism which causes our young men, both black and white, to be fighting one another in the Zambezi Valley.

'Why should children of the same country fight against each other? Will this promote racial harmony and peace?

'Some hide the real cause of the warfare by saying it is a fight against Communism. If Communist influence spreads among the African people in Rhodesia, it will be the Smith regime which is to blame. It is the denial of opportunities for advancement on merit to persons of all races which has caused African young people to look elsewhere for help.'

In historical perspective such words seem mild indeed— temperate when compared with the hard-hitting attacks of our African politicians against racist domination. They were only a rational plea for reform compared with the violent liberation struggle which is now under way. But for a freshman bishop, they marked my entry on to a national, rather than denominational, stage. For the first time I addressed concerns which were political rather than religious in nature. In doing so I joined in a new wave of Church opposition to racism in Rhodesia, and I was to face the consequences in the months ahead.

Chapter 9

The Church in the Liberation Struggle

Upon my arrival in New York City, in March 1970, I met with Zimbabweans living there and was shocked to find how many were bitter in their criticism of the Church. One Zimbabwean after another prefaced his or her comments with 'When I was still a church person,' or 'When I used to go to church,' or 'Before I left the church,' and so on. The church appeared to be a thing of the past to these young men and women. I was concerned that they identified the established church with the minority racist regime which had oppressed our people for so long.

I replied: 'I appreciate your frankness in making these comments about the church to me, a clergyman and practising Christian. But your rejection of the church hurts me. It would be helpful if you could share why you left the church and why you condemn it in this manner.'

One was quick to reply: 'I attended a mission boarding school where one day we were forced by a missionary to eat the meat of a beast which had died of an illness—meat which was stinking and unfit for food.' He went on, 'I said to myself, if this is what men of God acting on Christian principles can do, then I will have nothing to do with Christianity.'

Another said: 'At the mission school I attended one of the missionary fathers used to fool around with us girls, touching our bodies and wanting to seduce us. From that experience I became disillusioned with the Church and Christianity.'

Citing his denomination, another gave this rationale: 'Christian missionaries practised racial discrimination to the same extent as the white settlers. White ministers baptised black babies, but black ministers never baptised white babies. The white missionary had privileges over his black counterpart. The black priest travelled up and down on a bicycle, while the missionary drove by in his car. The white missionary was paid a much higher salary than the black priest. I became disgusted and lost faith in Christianity.'

I had no defence for the Church in these particular examples which had been cited. I have no defence for many other instances of social injustices by ordained priests and missionaries of the Church. Facing my fellow Zimbabweans, however, I felt impelled not only to agree with them in condemning injustice when it is found within the Church, but also to affirm the outstanding contributions of the Church to the uplifting of our own people.

I replied: 'Yes, I share your disgust at these injustices done by some churchmen. I, too, could cite innumerable instances of racial discrimination practised by white missionaries. Furthermore, I am outraged by the frequent condemnation of African culture as evil and devilish, and the identification of western civilization with the 'Christian' way of life. Our songs, dances and even drums were banned as "pagan". Our traditional healers were derisively dubbed "witch-doctors" and called "forces of evil". Why were we given names like George, Margaret and Basil as "Christian" names at our baptism, while our African names with their beautiful and deep meanings were to be used almost secretly and apologetically?

'But that is only one side of the missionaries' impact on us and our people,' I went on. 'Here we sit condemning the Church, yet without the church schools which each of us have attended we would not be here today. And have we forgotten those teachers who made great personal sacrifices so that we could have an education and a better way of life?

'I, too, remember missionaries who seemed little different from white settlers in their racist attitudes. However, I have also known those who struggled against the settlers' immorality, cruelty, drunkenness, injustice, arrogance and racism. I remember my own former teacher, Miss Edith Parks, who when meeting her former students on the streets of Salisbury did not hesitate to greet them with warm affection according to African custom. One day a white bystander rebuked her, saying, "What are you doing shaking hands with Africans, shaming our race?" But such remarks did not deter Miss Parks from inviting us to her home, or to sit in the front of her car beside her or from doing any of those things which some regarded as "shaming" to the white sense of superiority.'

I continued: 'You and I often accept education in mission

schools as our right, and we criticize the Church for not providing more and better schools for us. We often forget that white settlers opposed every advance in African education proposed by the Church. White settlers never forgave the missionaries for "making natives clever", or "spoiling the natives", to use their terms.

'I shall never forget a drama I witnessed as a boy at the annual conference session of our United Methodist Church. The late Bishop Newell Booth and other church leaders had fought for years for permission to open a high school. We had excellent facilities—teachers, money and classrooms, but every request to the Government had been "tabled for further consideration". But this year Bishop Booth invited the Government's senior school inspectors to come to our annual conference. There, in front of the church delegates, the dauntless bishop requested an explanation of why the church had not been given permission to open a high school. The white officials gave evasive excuses, but no straight answer. Shortly after this public confrontation, however, permission was granted to open Hartzwell High School at Old Umtali.'

Our conversation continued long into the night. My young Zimbabwean friends accepted much of my argument, yet persisted: 'Yes, but that's not enough. Where does the Church stand today? Is it siding with the oppressor, or with we who are oppressed?'

I understood then that we of the Church could no longer rely upon the good will built up through our past efforts in education, medical or agricultural work, as if it were a deep well that would not run dry. The Church in all this work was so tied to a government which young people now called 'the enemy' that we too stood in danger of being condemned. But how could a disengagement from the State take place so long as ninety per cent of African pupils attended 'mission' schools run by the churches, but financed and supervised by the State? How could the Church move into more active opposition to the policies of white settler rule? How could it identify more clearly with the Zimbabwean liberation struggle?

I returned to Rhodesia determined to seek answers to these questions, only to find that the Church in Rhodesia was about to enter into vigorous confrontation with the State. Between 1969 and 1971 I became involved along with leaders of other denominations, in seven issues which brought us into conflict with Ian Smith's racist government. These were the 1969 Constitution, the Land Tenure Act, the schools issue, a five per cent cut in government grants to schools, my own ban from entering Tribal Trust Lands, reactions to the World Council of Churches' grants to liberation movements, the struggle of the Tangwena people, and the banning of the Cold Comfort Farm Society and its leaders.

1969 Republic Constitution

My baptism in political involvement as a church leader took place in 1969 as Protestant and Catholic church leaders united to reject the new constitutional proposals of the Smith regime.

The churches became involved in this issue in this way. Since the rebellion against Britain by the Smith regime in November 1965, various attempts had been made to devise a new constitution acceptable to the contending parties. The British Government enunciated five principles which they would require, including progress towards majority rule and an end to discrimination. Twice Harold Wilson met Ian Smith to negotiate in talks named the 'Tiger' and 'Fearless' after the warships where they took place. Each time Smith failed to get the backing of his party for the British proposals.

Meanwhile Ian Smith decided to sample opinion on Rhodesia's constitutional future within the country, and invited various groups including the churches to submit evidence to the Whaley Commission which he appointed for that purpose. At that time the Catholic bishops gave suggestions that any new constitution should 'promote the common good, guarantee the dignity and the freedom of every individual, build up a true social order, bring about the unity of the nation, and establish concord with other nations.'*

As Protestants we did not have the tradition of pastoral letters like those addressed periodically by Catholic bishops to their people. In South Africa, however, the major Protestant churches during 1968 adopted 'A Message to the People of South Africa' which performed the same function. In it church leaders set out the biblical and theological bases for the Christian's rejection of *apartheid*. In Rhodesia the invitation to discuss proposals for a

---

* 'A Call to Christians: Pastoral Message of the Catholic Bishops of Rhodesia, 5th June 1969.'

new constitution stimulated the churches to make a parallel statement.

The Christian Council of Rhodesia staff, led by their General Secretary, Rev. Herbert Chikomo, drafted the statement entitled 'A Message and Appeal from Church Leaders to the Christian People of Rhodesia'. Having so recently been a CCR staff member, I was enthusiastic about their initiative. Fortunately the Catholic bishops agreed to sign the CCR statement although they were preparing their own pastoral letter as well. Joint publication of the statements on June 5, 1969, hit the newspaper headlines which read: 'BISHOPS SLAM PROPOSALS; Church warns: This will breed hatred'. As predicted the papers received a flood of letters from whites protesting church involvement in politics.

Next the Christian Council prepared a flyer called 'An Appeal to Christians'. It was their aim to distribute it to every European church congregation, since whites alone would have a say on the coming constitutional referendum. Most Protestant clergy failed to present the flyer. Many Roman Catholic priests obeyed and read the bishops' pastoral letter from their pulpits. 'An Appeal to Christians' summed up our position as follows:

'If, as a Christian, you believe:
1. that every individual person has his own dignity because God made him in his own image, and because Jesus Christ lived, died and rose for him;
2. that, through Christ, God has broken down the walls of division between God and man, and under his rule all human differences of race, tribe, culture or nation cease to matter;
3. that this is God's world, that it is He who shapes history, and that it is only in obedience to His ways that we shall find our security;

can you say 'Yes' to proposals for a constitution which would:
(a) be introduced in a country, the vast majority of whose people will be given no opportunity to express their opinion by democratic means;
(b) divide African and European by replacing a common voters' roll with separate rolls, and by its distribution of land;
(c) use the payment of income tax as the assessment of a people's right to representation in Parliament;

(d) take away from the individual and from the judiciary basic rights and safeguards, and place absolute power in the hands of the government of the day?'

Church leaders, of course, were not the only opponents of the new constitution. The University of Rhodesia was another rallying point for opposition. Often it loomed as an island of multi-racialism above the fogs of segregation that pervaded Rhodesian society. Periodic deportations of 'political' faculty members and the expulsion of students who took part in demonstrations would quiet the regime's opponents at the University for a while, only to have courageous new voices heard and new leaders emerge.

1969 was no exception. When student friends from SCM days urged me to support a Week of Protest at the University, I consented. Knowing how volatile student emotions are on political issues, I wondered if that week I would be branded as 'a bishop who backs violence'. As it turned out, the debates on the constitutional proposals reached a high level of presentation and discussion. Dr. Ahrn Palley, the Independent MP representing the African constituency of Highfields, said that the constitutional changes would lead to *apartheid*. Mr. Guy Clutton-Brock, the well-known former member of the banned African National Congress, agreed and said that Christians should know that their Lord would oppose such racism. I applauded his statement: 'Jesus Christ was an extremist—He was one hundred and fifty per cent for love.' It was Mr. Sam Whaley, chairman of the Whaley Commission which prepared the constitutional proposals, however, who raised emotions to fever pitch. African students shouted him down when he said that the economic and political power in Rhodesia should remain in white hands for the foreseeable future. Following the debates, three hundred students with placards demonstrated in the centre of the city, but fortunately returned to the campus without incident.

Despite these protests, eighty per cent of the voters approved of the new constitution and voted for Rhodesia to become a republic. Those who cast votes, however, formed less than five per cent of the total adult population. I saw the proposals as a real implementation of *apartheid* such as is found in South Africa. I viewed them as political assassination, such as was done to the native Americans by European colonists, who limited both the ownership of land and the political representation of the historic inhabitants of that country.

The failure of the churches to sway white opinion did not surprise me. Churches which had been quiescent in the face of tyranny for so long could not expect one moral appeal to sway the actions of the privileged élite. But the success of church leaders—Protestant and Catholic, black and white—to speak with one united voice was certainly a major step forward.

The Land Tenure Act

Following its victory in the constitutional referendum, the Smith regime hastened to pass a Land Tenure Act which would entrench land *apartheid* in Rhodesia for all time. Under its provisions the land of Rhodesia was divided into two parts. One half, 45 million acres, was reserved for all time for that five per cent of the population which is white. The other 45 million acres was assigned to the ninety-five per cent of the people who are black. Furthermore, the government was to possess wide powers 'to eliminate racial friction arising out of the ownership, occupation and use of the land'. This could include regulations to prohibit persons of one race from entering, attending meetings, or living in areas designated for the other race.

This time the regime did not call for public discussion of the issues involved. Churches were not invited to express their views concerning the bill. Instead it was rushed through Parliament in October 1969 with only five days for debate, and published in December.

Catholics were the first to be shocked by its implications for the life and work of the Church, and they set aside a senior priest, Fr. R. Randolph, SJ, to lead the Church in study and action related to the new Act.

I was concerned that United Methodists immediately begin discussion of these issues. At our annual conference in January 1970 the delegates agreed on this declaration:

'We . . . view with great alarm the passing through Parliament of the Land Tenure Act. The philosophy behind this Act and the possible grave results issuing from the enforcement of it, will, in our opinion, not avoid racial friction but on the contrary will seriously intensify it.'

The declaration went on to state the Christian basis for these judgments: 'The Church is one. We cannot tolerate any divisions

79

into African and European congregations . . . We stand for equal rights for all racial, cultural, and religious groups.' We called for united action by the churches under the leadership of the Christian Council.

When the Christian Council met for its annual meeting at Umtali in March, I sensed a new unity and a determination to resist the Smith regime on this issue. It was appropriate that our resolution was moved by Anglican Bishop Kenneth Skelton of Matabeleland and seconded by former Prime Minister Garfield Todd—two outstanding champions of racial justice. It included the judgment that the Land Tenure Act 'based on racial separate development . . . is incompatible with Christian commitment to non-racial free development but also permits interference with the free worship and witness of the Church'. The Council called for a meeting of heads of churches to take united and positive action.

Catholics were the first to propose civil disobedience as the appropriate Christian response to this racist legislation. In their pastoral letter entitled 'A Crisis of Conscience', the Catholic bishops on March 21, 1970, said that the fundamental freedom of the Church to perform a mission of service and reconciliation to all sections of the community was being endangered. They quoted St. Peter's famous battle cry, 'We must obey God rather than men' (Acts 5:29), and they refused to accept any limitation on freedom of movement, or freedom of worship.

I was in America attending the Council of Bishops of our church when the Protestant and Catholic church leaders of Rhodesia held their first meeting. Eagerly I received reports from our United Methodist representatives. Upon my return I was chosen as one of seven church representatives to lodge a strong protest to the Prime Minister.

This confrontation with Ian Smith took place on June 4 in his office. At that meeting I came face to face with the racist white leader for the first time. The seating arrangements intrigued me. Though the churches' delegation was multi-racial, all the white people sat on one side of the table while we blacks (Rev. Andrew Ndhlela, General Superintendent of the Methodist Church—UK, Rev. Christopher Chikasha, Moderator of the African Reformed Church Synod, and I) sat on the other. The feeling for kith and kin and racial division had penetrated so deeply into our society that it had virtually become second nature.

The meeting was a head-on clash. We from the churches' side stated what we felt the bad effects of the Land Tenure Act would be. 'The churches,' we said, 'are determined to oppose the Act on Christian principle, and place the onus on Government to make possible the continuation of our work.' Mr. Smith presented the Government's view that different racial groups have to be kept separate in the interest of peace and harmony. 'Look at the United States where they are trying to enforce integration,' he said. 'They are having a lot of trouble there because they are trying to integrate different races.' In reply I gave my opinion that the race problem in America was gradually being solved, whereas his Government's policies were fomenting the racial strife in Rhodesia. A subsequent press release described our meeting as 'cordial and constructive', which was like calling a boxing event a 'friendly match'.

Next, we as church leaders had to report back to our respective denominations and secure their mandate for further action on this and other pressing issues. To that end, I called for a special session of the United Methodist Conference to be held at Old Umtali on June 12-13.

It was a new experience at that time for our people to be addressed by a Catholic bishop and a priest. Bishop Donal Lamont of Umtali gave the keynote address on the 'World Reaction to the Problem of the Church in Rhodesia'. I knew that it was the bishop's drafting of the pastoral letters and his prodding of his colleagues to make public statements against the Smith regime that had awakened many persons overseas to the Rhodesian problem. Then Fr. Randolph spelled out what the new Land Tenure Act meant for the Church. I can remember how everyone was really depressed as he said:

'The Land Tenure Act has restricted the Church in the following ways:

The Church is no longer at liberty to move freely among people of all races to carry out her mission.

People of different races may no longer freely associate for the worship of God in churches outside their own prescribed racial areas.

The Church has no longer the right to admit to her schools whomsoever she wills.

The Church is forbidden to admit to her own hospitals people of a race different from that of the prescribed area.

The Church can no longer—without a permit from a Minister of State—admit ministers and other church workers of different races to live in the same communities.

The Church can no longer use freely its own land or property.'

Then the Conference fully supported and endorsed the ecumenical statement concerning the Land Tenure Issue—that it 'cannot be reconciled with the Christian Faith', that we refuse to register as voluntary associations under the Act, that we will continue to live and work among persons of all races without asking the Government's permission to do so, and that we call upon Government to make possible the continuation of this work.

During this conference it struck me that my very presence at our Old Umtali Centre could be prohibited under the Act. Old Umtali is in the area designated 'European' and I as an African would be required to get a permit to be there. My statement that day excited many as I said 'Let it go on record that I will fight as a Christian and by Christian methods of non-violence. I will sit in the same chair as I have been sitting in the church before . . . and I will not move from it. I will not move from it! They will have to carry me away instead.'

Such vehemence had its effect. By August Ian Smith introduced amendments to the Act to exempt the churches from registration, or from the necessity of applying for permits to enable them to continue their work on mission lands. Nevertheless, the Act remained in force, while our missionaries continued to violate its provisions regularly as they travelled without permission into African areas to carry on their work.

The Schools Issue
At the same UMC special conference a very hot debate took place. The regime had backed the churches into a corner on an issue concerning the schools. It gave us these choices: either we would begin to collect taxes for the Government to cover five per cent of the African teachers' salaries, or we could give up the administration of schools.

You will recall that the churches had pioneered in African education. Even in 1970 virtually all schools for Africans outside of the towns were run by the churches as 'mission schools'. For some time there had been signs that the Smith regime planned to phase out this tradition of partnership with the churches in African education, in which the Government set the curricula and paid grants for teachers' salaries to the denominations. The regime wanted to enhance the authority of traditional chiefs and headmen who were paid government salaries and were therefore considered more loyal than other community leaders. Their authority would be enhanced if they could run the rural schools for Africans.

The increasing criticism of the regime and its policies by church leaders also made the Government uneasy in the old partnership. To put the churches at a disadvantage the regime cut grants for teachers' salaries in those primary schools which were managed by missions, but not in those run by the Government.

The debate was vigorous at our conference on the issue of whether we should collect the five per cent from the parents or give away our schools. Delegates from rural areas wanted to keep the schools and the opportunities for Christian influence provided through them, but they felt that parents were unable to pay the five per cent. Most delegates came from the Tribal Trust Lands where each family had only four-six dry acres of sandy soil to plough and six head of cattle. They felt strongly the injustice of shifting the burden of increasing educational costs upon those least able to pay.

The debate degenerated as some delegates from rural areas called upon the Church to give up *all* schools, even those on mission lands. Others opposed vehemently that view. At that point I let my views be known by way of this analogy. I asked the conference: 'If a madman came to your house and over-powered you and killed two of your children and left two, would you say to him, "Now that you have killed the two I want you to kill the rest of my kids?" '. Because the emotions and frustrations were so high some people called out, 'We don't care!'

The final resolution incorporated our mixed feelings, for the conference decided both to retain its 200 primary schools *and* refuse to collect the five per cent tax. 'Now is the time to stand firm against the payment of the five per cent (or its equivalent) by parents, church, local school committees or councils,' it declared. 'If, as a result of such opposition, schools are closed, it is the Government which is to blame.'

In the weeks that followed we took the issue to our people. At district meetings they spoke as with one voice resolving to close the schools rather than pay the five per cent. When the regime refused to back down, however, we and most other denominations decided to give up the management of rural primary schools from January 1, 1971. Only the Anglicans and Salvation Army reneged and kept their schools.

In the months that followed, our despondency over this impasse melted away. We had feared that both teachers and pupils would lose interest in the church if the schools passed out of our control. Those teachers who had grudgingly led youth activities at church as 'school duties' took this chance to fall away, but we were happily surprised to find hundreds of teachers continuing to be loyal to the church and active in giving leadership. But this was now on a voluntary basis, like the service of other members.

Bannings

A flurry of speaking invitations greeted me following our special annual conference. Many pastors said: 'We need to hear your views, Bishop, on the land tenure and schools issue. Please preach to them as you did in January about the dry bones.'

In that sermon I had compared Rhodesia to Israel at the time of her political bondage and exile in the days of the prophet Ezekiel. I said that Africans are considered fourth-class citizens in the land of their birth, and are victims of massive unemployment, segregation in education, and police harassment and torture. 'Can Rhodesia be resurrected and transformed into a new country?' I asked the people. 'Yes, if the people trust in God and lift up men and women who courageously speak out against injustice,' I said.

One afternoon in August my secretary entered my Salisbury office looking downcast. It was not normal to see her in that state of mind.

'There are two men out there in the reception room who say they want to see you.'

'Do they have an appointment?', I asked.

'No. They said they are from the Ministry of Internal Affairs.'

'Let them in,' I said. 'Let's see what they want.'

They were ushered in. Both were tall, nice-looking white fellows. But their message was not good. One of them pulled out a document issued by Mr. Hostes Nicolle, the Minister of Internal Affairs. His name was notorious among our people as one ruthless and cruel to Africans. The paper was a notice that

Nicolle was going to ban me from entering any of the Tribal Trust Lands where three-fourths of the African population live.

I responded that I had done nothing in the sight of the law to deserve that. I was going about doing what I believed was my Heavenly Father's business. I declared, therefore, that I would not be intimidated by anything and said, 'I think I would rather obey God than man.'

I had been given the right to appeal against the banning notice, but knew that this was only a formal ritual. The President, Clifford Dupont, did nothing about our appeal. All our pressure achieved was an explanation that one cause for the ban was my sermon about the dry bones!

When the regime issued the banning order in September I was away in Maranke TTL attending our churchwomen's convention. Upon my return to Salisbury telephone calls of sympathy and solidarity poured in from across the nation. The whole country was surprised and angered by it. 'Congratulations!' many said. At first that response puzzled me. Later I understood its meaning. If I was considered a threat by the regime, then I must be honoured as a leading Zimbabwean nationalist. In a matter of hours the district superintendents who formed our church cabinet came together in our Salisbury headquarters. Several of them were more experienced than I in facing such blows from the Smith regime, as they had supported Bishop Dodge and several missionaries at their time of deportation in 1964. None appeared cowed by such repression. Instead I read on their faces great determination to struggle on. That very day three hundred of our churchwomen, returning from their convention, demonstrated with placards in Umtali.

The following Saturday, Salisbury shoppers, politicians and police were startled to find persons at every major intersection of the downtown area who were protesting against my banning. Without any notice they had descended on Salisbury by night so as to be in their places by 6 a.m. There were women in the sky-blue dress, with red sleeves and belt and white turban— the uniform of United Methodist Women. Men wore the blue sashes across their chests which were the insignia of 'Fishermen' (Vabvuwi)—a churchmen's organization. Missionaries from America and Sweden demonstrated side by side with their African colleagues.

That morning a demonstrator overheard this radio report to

headquarters by a policeman: 'They are everywhere. There are at least two people standing with placards at every corner of the street. I guess we were caught unawares.'

The demonstration came like a clap of thunder among people cowed so often into fear and apathy by the white police. Nothing in the history of the country could be compared with it. Two old grandmothers stood outside Ian Smith's office holding a placard saying, 'Woe to Christian oppressors!' Mbuya (grandmother) Lydia Mandizera said when interviewed, 'I do not care what they do to me!' The demonstration's immediate effect was that it made people more aware of oppression, and more willing to fight against it. It gave them self-respect, self-confidence, and a sense of accomplishment.

In the days that followed we learned of additional demonstrations in the smaller rural towns of Rusape and Mrewa. It was rougher there. Thirty demonstrators were themselves detained overnight by police in Headlands. In Rusape a middle-aged European dashed out of his car and spat in the face of a man holding a placard.

During the following months I concentrated my work in visiting our church centres and urban congregations. Fortunately there were one or more churches in each district which were in areas designated for Europeans, so our leaders could gather there to meet with me. I still had my passport and planned to make visits to neighbouring countries as well.

In May of the following year I was invited to speak to an association of churches in Beira, in neighbouring Mozambique. I travelled with Mr. Matthew Mataranyika, our Conference Director of Stewardship, who wished to learn more about the successful ways of church-giving in the Mozambique churches.

Passing without incident through Rhodesian immigration formalities, we moved on by train to the Mozambique Immigration Office at Nyamapanda, ten miles inside that country. The immigration officer came to our compartment, looked at my passport and returned it to me. He went away, but returned a few minutes later. This time he took my passport to the Immigration Office. When he came back again he ordered Mr. Mataranyika and me out of the train.

'You are not wanted in Mozambique and must go back immediately,' he said in the sinister whisper so characteristic of the racists' security officers.

'How do we go back?', I asked.

'Get your luggage and follow me,' was the cryptic order.

'Why do these people always want to be so mysterious,' I remarked to my colleague.

We were lead to a goods train facing in the direction of Rhodesia and unceremoniously bundled into one of the empty cars. Since it was night we were unaware that we were actually in a wagon for livestock. Sitting in the unlit wagon we could not read each other's faces. I knew my brother must have been very apprehensive at this turn of events. As for myself, I reflected on this clear evidence of collusion between the secret police of the Portuguese and those of the Smith regime.

Aid to Liberation Movements

During 1970 I was encouraged by the strong and nearly unanimous support expressed by church people, both black and white, for my right to freely preach the Gospel. It disappointed me, however, that so few whites understood why we as Africans supported the liberation movements and applauded the overseas churches for whatever assistance they had given to them.

In 1970 the World Council of Churches became the focus of white wrath. 'It is not the function of a Christian world body to advocate force and terrorism,' argued the Anglican Dean of Bulawayo Cathedral, Rev. Allan Shaw.

Meanwhile there was conspicuous silence in the churches concerning the force used by the Smith regime to hold African leaders in political detention without trial and hang those who had thrown bottles of gasoline against buildings.

In September 1970 the World Council of Churches announced that its battle to combat racism would include grants totalling $143,000 to various liberation groups in Southern Africa, and some funds went to the banned ZAPU and ZANU. Immediately white clergy and laity filled the newspapers with denunciations of this action. Mr. Garfield Todd, however, swam against this tide as he commented: 'No Christian wishes to see force used, but a growing number of members of world churches hold that the violence being done to the spirit of the black man in South Africa and Rhodesia is intolerable and that it must be resisted. It is the white leaders who spring to attack the WCC, not the black leaders. While there may be a great deal of unanimity amongst our white Christians in condemning the WCC, there will

87

be wide appreciation among the great African membership of the Church for this gesture of concern. The aid is being given for social welfare programmes, not for armaments.' This last point was seldom recognized by the WCC's critics.

Garfield Todd assessed correctly the cleavage among churchmen on this issue. We as African churchmen decided to carry our views to the Christian Council in hopes that it might be our forum of opinion. On November 11, 1970, while white settlers in Rhodesia celebrated their so-called 'independence', the Council met in Salisbury and voted 30 to 4 to support the World Council of Churches' 'gesture of concern and compassion for the oppressed people of Rhodesia'. The next day newspapers, however, featured a headline which stated that Bishop Paul Burrough of the Anglican Church had opposed the resolution and said it raised 'the spectre of religious schism'. Actually, there had been no serious racial split at the Council meeting, as fourteen whites and sixteen blacks voted together. Nevertheless, white churchmen possessed certain sanctions that could be exercised. The Salvation Army withdrew its membership from the Council, and the Presbyterians threatened to do the same. When Bishop Burrough proposed to his diocesan Standing Committee that Anglicans withdraw, Mr. Percy M'kudu, an outstanding Anglican layman and leader of the African opposition in Parliament replied: 'Bishop, *you* can withdraw from the Christian Council if you wish to, but *we,* the African members of the church, will not.' The bishop quickly withdrew his trial balloon.

The Rev. Canaan Banana of the Methodist Church (UK), later to become the Vice-President of the African National Council, was a casualty of the conflict at that time. His church synod tried to assuage white members' feelings by a resolution which said: 'The Methodist Church in Rhodesia believes that Christians ought not to support violence in any form.' Rev. Banana resigned from the ministry of his church in protest against this distortion of the intent of the WCC's action.

Fortunately these controversies did not deter the churches from continuing their humanitarian aid within Zimbabwe to persons involved in the liberation struggle. We as United Methodists, for example, set up a special fund to relieve some of the sufferings of persons in political restriction and detention. The major effort, however, was carried out by *Christian Care.*

This is the social welfare arm of the churches—both Protestant and Catholic. Quietly working behind the scenes, *Christian Care* provided monthly allowances for the families of detainees and restrictees, paid the school fees of their children, gave clothing, money for correspondence studies for the men being held, and travel money for their families to visit them.

Cold Comfort Farm

One *Christian Care* project, however, was destroyed at this time by the Smith regime—the Cold Comfort Farm Society. Five years earlier the World Council had provided funds for the purchase of Lord Acton's farm on the outskirts of Salisbury for a multi-racial experiment in co-operative farming. Didymus Mutasa and the Clutton-Brocks (Guy and Molly), its leaders, had worked together since the 1950s to establish models of racial co-operation, but their every effort was seen as a judgment on white racism. The fact that these leaders had not only helped in the founding of the first African National Congress, but had given encouragement and succour to Zimbabwean nationalists, did not endear them to the authorities.

The regime acted to crush Cold Comfort Farm in December 1970. First they threw Didymus Mutasa into political detention. Next they deprived the Clutton-Brocks of their Rhodesian citizenship as a prelude to their deportation. On January 15 Government troops seized the farm while the Parliament banned the Cold Comfort Farm Society. By April the farm was sold at auction for nearly twice its purchase price, with the regime pocketing the proceeds despite protests by *Christian Care* and the World Council of Churches.

'Where are the voices of those churchmen who had so vehemently opposed violence?', I wondered. 'Is this not violence too?' But the church leaders were conspicuously silent.

The Tangwena People

Related to the Cold Comfort Society's ban was the regime's oppression of the Tangwena people, which reached its height in 1971. For several years Cold Comfort members had supported the struggle of Chief Tangwena and his people to retain their historic lands on Rhodesia's eastern border. They had helped to provide schooling for the children when, in August 1968, police destroyed homes, confiscated cattle, and removed the people

89

from their lands. It was then that Chief Tangwena chose with his followers to defy the regime by returning to their homes.

The history of Zimbabwe's liberation struggle must include Chief Tangwena, one of its gallant freedom fighters. His struggle against oppression made him as well-educated as if he had been to school, and as brave as if he had received military training.

I admired Chief Tangwena and drew upon church resources to help fight his legal battles. Many times we talked together in my office about the courageous resistance of his people. Once he said to me, 'Tenzi Bishop (Lord Bishop), I have told Smith that I am not going to move. If they want to kill me and move my body where they want it, that will be up to them.' No wonder many people were saying, 'If only we could have just five chiefs like Tangwena we would go a very long way towards defeating Ian Smith.'

In this chapter I have sought to outline the Church's involvement in the liberation struggle for Zimbabwe during three critical years—1969 to 1971.

Students of comparative African politics may be surprised at the extent and depth of the Church's participation in politics in Rhodesia, in contrast with what happened in other countries. Because their political parties had been banned and rallies had been outlawed, African congregations tried to fill the void. 'Freedom', 'justice', 'liberation'—these biblical terms were given new interpretations as a result of our struggle for survival. Gradually preachers began to speak from their pulpits of the new nation 'Zimbabwe' and of the aspirations of its people.

It is not surprising that political leaders emerged from among those trained by the churches. Not only did the Church provide the schooling for future Zimbabwean nationalists, but also it gave significant opportunities for leadership. For example, the United Methodist Church is proud of its team of black primary school headmasters, principals of high schools, hospital matrons, superintendents of mission schools, doctors, theological lecturers, church lay leaders and treasurers. The councils of the Church have been under their direction for more than a decade. The Church conducts elections by secret ballot as fairly and smoothly as any independent state. It provides a practical training ground for self-government.

The clergy have been called up to fill a national void in political leadership due to the detention of so many others. The Salisbury

African Ministers' Fraternal included many who later were tapped for political leadership. Among them is Rev. Henry Kachidza, General Secretary of the Bible Society in Rhodesia. He had been outstanding in his work for unity among nationalists of competing groups, during 1970 and 1971.

I do not subscribe to the romantic and unhistoric view that the liberation struggle is won by armed clashes between the forces of liberation and the colonial army. Important as they are, such acts of war form only sporadic episodes in the total process of liberation. Neither do I call for whole congregations to march en masse, guns in hand, against the Smith regime in order to be considered part of the liberation effort.

Liberation embraces the whole process of opposition to all forms of the colonial oppression. This opposition is at various times moral, spiritual, mental, economic, political and physical, as appropriate. The Church's contributions are manifold, including its attack on the very rationale and philosophy of racism. In the future it must continue in the struggle for liberation even after the overthrow of the Smith regime. At that moment the struggle for liberation will not end but will enter a new and perhaps more difficult phase.

Chapter 10

In Search of Freedom for Zimbabwe

In September 1971 the air was full of persistent rumours that the British Government was anxious to patch up its quarrel with the rebel Rhodesian Government, the quarrel arising out of Mr. Smith's UDI of 1965. The Conservative Party had pledged to make 'one last try' at negotiations. To that end Lord Goodman paid a secret visit to Salisbury in April 1971, and a more public one in June. This paved the way for the British Foreign and Commonwealth Secretary, Sir Alec Douglas-Home, to come to Salisbury in November.

Sir Alec made a big show of consulting all shades of Rhodesian opinion. I joined the group of churchmen from the Christian Council who were invited to meet him in the old British House, the official residence of the British representative before 1965.

At our interview Sir Alec appeared to be talking in riddles. 'We must avert drifting into apartheid,' he kept repeating. To us this seemed a negative approach. The black people of Zimbabwe were not fighting to avert something. We were struggling for majority rule. The quarrel between the Rhodesian leaders and the British was of little interest to us, being virtually irrelevant to our main objective. I left the meeting feeling that the interview had been a waste of time.

We were but one of several delegations invited to make representations to the British Foreign Secretary. African Members of Parliament, businessmen, the chiefs and the trade unionists were there too. Also included were white professionals, opposition party leaders, etc. Sir Alec specifically asked to see some ex-detainees, so Ruth Chinamano brought together a combined ZAPU/ZANU group composed of Edson Sithole, Michael Mawema and Cephas Msipa, who succeeded in preparing a joint declaration to Sir Alec.

The coming of the British, and the continuous movement of people to and from the British residence, created an atmosphere of excitement among our people. There were many curious bystanders. Perhaps they thought the black aspirations were now to be met, and that the British were prepared to deal with their responsibilities in Zimbabwe.

Proposals for a Settlement

Finally Ian Smith announced at the end of November 1971 the 'Proposals for a Settlement', commonly called the Smith-Home Proposals after their two principal architects. They consisted of amendments to the illegal 1969 Constitution. By a complicated formula of income and property qualifications Africans were to be able to register to vote in increasing numbers. They declared that by this means Africans would ultimately gain majority rule. Division of seats by race was to continue, however, with African representation theoretically able to reach sixty in a Parliament of 110 members. The British were to offer £50 million for development, to be matched by the Rhodesian regime and to be controlled by them. Although a bill of rights was included, it did not apply to any existing legislation, including the notorious Law and Order Maintenance Act and Land Tenure Act. The State of Emergency which overrides a bill of rights would remain. A British royal commission was to be appointed by the Queen to test the acceptability of the Proposals to 'the people of Rhodesia as a whole'.

I was eager to sense the reactions of my colleagues and friends to the Proposals. A few were cautious, preferring to await the full text before giving judgment. Expectations, however, soon turned to disillusionment. Those of us who had made recommendations to Sir Alec looked in vain for evidence of their inclusion in the Proposals. Our opinions had been completely ignored in what had been essentially a public relations exercise.

We felt used and abused. The nasty smell of a sell-out deal became evident. The opinion spread among Africans that the Proposals were merely Britain's way out of their quandary without abandoning their kith and kin. In clandestine meetings the Zimbabwean leaders met to analyse this latest piece of Rhodesian-British intrigue. Soon a strategy for rejection began to emerge.

I found some persons saying, 'What hope is there of defeating the Proposals if both the British Government and the Smith regime have already agreed upon them?' One opportunity remained, however, since there was to be the Commission on Rhodesian Opinion to test public opinion. Ian Smith agreed to this because he believed that the Commission could go to rural areas and gain the support of the chiefs and headmen who, as persons on government salaries, would vote for acceptance. I was disappointed, as were other Zimbabweans, that the idea of a referendum had been thrown out. We were suspicious, also, concerning the composition of the Commission. Nevertheless, our only hope as Zimbabwean leaders lay in organizing a massive 'No' response.

The Formation of the ANC

Our people were now faced with a crisis. They were convinced that the proposals before the country were a betrayal of their aspirations. They wanted to fight this betrayal and frustrate it, yet there was no organized political activity amongst us. There was no political party to act as a vehicle of our struggle and the old nationalist leaders were largely in prisons and detention camps.

It was then that the four former members of the ZANU and ZAPU executives who had presented a joint declaration to Sir Alec (including Josiah Chinamano) decided to form a new unity movement to fight the Settlement Proposals. They named it the African National Council (ANC), using the same initials as our first nationalist movement, the African National Congress. Their problem was to find a 'neutral' leader of national stature who was neither former ZANU nor ZAPU.

I was surprised when the full committee arrived at my home to ask me to head the new movement. Already they knew of my agreement with the main outline for it. The new organization would aim, they said, to unite all our people, establish a new orientation to the struggle, and bring about majority rule. The immediate objective, however, would be to fight and defeat the Smith-Home Proposals. 'How do our nationalist leaders feel about this?' I asked. Both the representatives of ZANU and ZAPU assured me that they were in touch with their leaders in detention, and that Rev. Ndabaningi Sithole and Mr. Joshua Nkomo would give their support to the new movement.

I requested time to consider the matter seriously. I wanted to be absolutely convinced that the old rivalry between ZAPU and ZANU would not be resuscitated. I did not want to be associated with a new outbreak of inter-factional fighting and thuggery between rival nationalists such as that which had given the Smith regime an excuse to ban both ZAPU and ZANU. I also wished to confer with leaders of my Church and with my family concerning the invitation. Above all the matter deserved my prayerful consideration. At the end of three weeks of prayer and meditation I accepted the call and challenge to lead the ANC.

Time was of the essence. First, we chose a ten-person Executive Committee, balanced carefully between ex-members of ZANU and ZAPU. As Vice-Chairman we chose Rev. Canaan Banana who, like myself, had not formerly been involved in nationalist politics.

News spread like wildfire on December 16 that a press conference was soon to be held at Mutanga Brothers' Restaurant in Highfields. There was great excitement as I stood to read the press release: 'The Anglo-Rhodesian proposals for a settlement have been critically studied, analysed and found to be a vicious and subtle device for the recognition of the UDI by the British Government.' I went on: 'The proposals as contained in the White Paper do not reflect a single suggestion made by African leaders. Their views were completely ignored.' Concerning the Proposals I concluded: 'We are convinced beyond a doubt that acceptance of these proposals by Africans would be a betrayal of the Africans, dead, living and yet to be born. We cannot be vendors of our own heritage and rights. Therefore, the African's responsible answer should be an *emphatic* "*No.*" '

Next I announced the formation of the African National Council to be a body 'that represents the voice and will of the silent African majority throughout the country. Its aims and objectives will be:

1. To call our people to realize the essential power of unity at this critical moment. And to move on as one people to achieve our ultimate goal of freedom.

2. To explain, advise and expose the dangerous implications that would result if we accepted the Anglo-Rhodesian constitutional settlement proposals.

3. To raise funds for the promotion of the organization. It is a temporary body to execute the Task before us.'

I ended the press statement with a call for youth to be active, obedient and disciplined. I urged them to work for the common good of all, and in doing so to join hands with the adults and our allies—the coloureds, Indians, white liberals, and with Christians to reject the Proposals. It was a promising start.

The Churches Say 'No'

Fortunately our fledgling organization was not alone in its fight against the proposals. Many church leaders, in the absence of the professional politicians, stepped in and fully identified themselves with the aspirations of the Zimbabwean people at this crucial time. The Christian Council of Rhodesia led in this effort. First, the Council published a pamphlet entitled 'A Guide to the Proposals for a Settlement'. This contained the main proposals in the major languages of the country—English, Shona and Ndebele. In actual fact it was an ingenious document which systematically refuted the arguments put forward for the Proposals saying 'the Proposals promise . . . BUT.' By Christmas Eve volunteers distributed the first of 120,000 copies to workers travelling by bus or train to their rural homes for Christmas. No wonder one African detective of the CID (secret police) said in frustration: 'How is it that this pamphlet is spreading so fast that it seems to be everywhere we go?'

Attention next focused on a special meeting of the Christian Council, held on December 30, to consider the Proposals. It was the first national body in which intelligent discussion of the issues took place between black and white members. Although Canon Sydenham and Rev. Elliott Kendall of the British Council of Churches attended 'merely as observers', their request that the Council assist in the distribution of the British version of the Proposals indicated their hope that the Council would accept them. The outcome, however, was a strong 29 to 9 vote against the Proposals—the first national multi-racial organization in the country to take this stand.

Organizing the ANC

Once I had assumed leadership of the ANC I found myself with an extremely packed daily schedule. I had to juggle my new responsibilities as National Chairman of the ANC with my continuing duties as head of the United Methodist Church in Rhodesia.

Much of my time was spent in consultation with members of our ANC Executive Committee. Michael Mawema as National Organizing Secretary worked full-time from the start. Rev. C.

Banana (Vice-Chairman) and C. E. Ngcebetsha (Secretary-General) met with us frequently. Edson Sithole, from his law office, served as legal advisor as well as the ANC Publicity Secretary.

There was no time to get down to the detailed organization of the ANC. The Pearce Commission was due to arrive after Christmas to begin its opinion-testing exercise. We had to get moving and get moving fast. The task seemed enormous with neither funds, nor office, nor vehicles, nor professional staff.

Despite these handicaps, ANC branches sprang up like mushrooms throughout the country wherever Africans wanted to protest against the Proposals in the name of the ANC. Sometimes an old branch of either ZANU or ZAPU formed a nucleus. Without detailed by-laws, or a constitution, or opportunity to formally register these new groups, we of the Executive simply enjoined them to 'promote the work of the organization in their regions, districts or areas'.

In later months a more rational structure emerged, although the ANC remained essentially a grass-roots organization. The 'unit' or 'cell' comprised persons of the same rural village, or members of eleven households in an urban township. Several units formed a local branch. Branches then were grouped in districts according to the density of the population. Then district ANCs selected representatives to form a provincial Executive. Leaders at each level were to be chosen by the respective membership, including leaders of the wings for men, women and youth. At the national level our goal was to hold a national congress annually as a thoroughly representative body which would choose the officers for the ANC and its National Executive.

Normal Political Activity

The *Proposals for a Settlement* included this statement: 'In the period before and during the test of acceptability normal political activities will be permitted to the satisfaction of the Commission, provided they are conducted in a peaceful and democratic manner.' The Commission, however, faced immediate problems, as did the ANC, because the definition of 'normal political activity' is radically different in Rhodesia than in Britain.

Difficulties mounted in the towns. First we had to get permission to hold a meeting or rally in an urban township, and often there was a delay in getting any government response. Permission, when it was granted, included the proviso that the meeting must be held in a hall, that the owner of that hall (usually the Government itself) must agree, and that the hall must be insured. It was that last hurdle which proved insurmountable. All insurance companies were European-owned and none would take the risk to insure the ANC, even though all meetings held to date had been peaceful. As a result, we succeeded in holding only ten urban rallies.

Our chances of holding rural meetings, however, were even more dismal. We made application after application for ANC meetings to more than 200 district commissioners, only to be refused every time. Later Hostes Nicoll, Secretary for Internal Affairs, revealed that it was he who had instructed his district commissioners to refuse our applications because ANC meetings are not 'normal political activity' in Tribal Trust Lands.

Lacking meetings to address, we of the ANC National Executive concentrated on providing materials to local branches (posters, stickers, and the initial press statement published as a pamphlet); and we had frequent consultations with local ANC leaders.

Beginning the Test of Opinion

The Pearce Commission started the actual testing of opinion on January 12, 1972. About 4,000 people attended the first rural meeting held with Chief Mutasa's people at Manyika Bridge north of Umtali.

I remember waiting with my colleagues for the outcome of that meeting. We were both expectant and apprehensive. It was the very first probe by the Commission which would test the effectiveness of our 'No' campaign.

'This is almost like waiting for the first result of a General Election,' I said. 'The outcome at Manyika Bridge will set the trend for the future.'

'There is no doubt that the Mutasa people will say "No",' one replied.

'We can't be too certain,' another colleague cautioned. 'I have heard that Chief Mutasa himself will agree to the Proposals. As usual the district commissioner has been intimidating people into agreeing with the Proposals. Some have been bribed.'

'In a way,' I observed, 'it is the ANC which is being tested. We have staked our reputation and our very existence on this issue. If the people accept the Settlement Proposals we will have failed. We will have become sell-outs.'

Just then the phone rang. It was our official ANC observer reporting, 'The verdict was a resounding "Kwete!" (No).' We were overjoyed. I turned and hugged the nearest person and danced a sort of jig with him.

When eyewitnesses brought their report we realized that our anxiety had been campaign jitters and nothing more. The Mutasa people had never wavered in their verdict.

We were amused to learn what had happened. After the Pearce commissioner explained the Settlement Proposals to the crowd he sat to wait for their answer. Just at that moment someone at the back of the audience let loose a dog with posters on either side of its back. One said 'Kwete' and the other 'No'. The people simply shouted: 'There is your answer. Go and tell your people what we think!'

Several persons spoke against the Proposals. Then came the moment for Chief Mutasa to state publicly his position. The chief said: 'My people do not want these Proposals. I am chief of the people. I do what my people want. I therefore say "Kwete" —No!'

At that word the 4,000 people rose up and started jumping, shouting, dancing, throwing their hats in the air, and cutting the earth with their axes. Women shrilled a joyful noise in the true African tradition.

The commissioners were shocked, bewildered, and a bit frightened by this explosion of emotions. 'Why are the people doing this?' one asked. 'They are happy because the Chief has rejected the Proposals,' the interpreter replied.

We were fortunate that *The Rhodesian Herald*, the national white-owned newspaper, gave an accurate coverage of this first meeting, for it helped to set the pace and direction which the test of opinion by the Pearce Commission was subsequently to take. After the Mutasa test we began to look forward with greater confidence to receiving the verdict of other tests of opinion.

Other Tests

Gradually reports emerged concerning the various ways through which the people expressed their rejection of the Smith-Home Settlement Proposals.

In Chief Ngorima's area about 4,000 people gathered to give

evidence. When the hour arrived the commissioner invited the chief to go into a tent to register his 'No' or 'Yes'. He stayed inside for a long time with the Pearce commissioner. When the commissioner emerged a man in the crowd stood up and shouted. The commissioner asked his interpreter what the man wanted. Overhearing the question the man answered directly, 'I want to say something.'

'Let him speak,' the commissioner replied.

Evidently the man was a prearranged spokesman for he said: 'We know what our chief thinks about these things. We believe he has told the commissioner, "Yes, I support these Proposals," but we his people say "Kwete" (No)!' As soon as he said this the whole crowd applauded and shouted their approval, while some danced in jubilation. This so impressed the chief that he stood up and said to the commissioner: 'I am chief of the people. If my people reject these proposals as has been indicated, I also say "Kwete" (No)!' Upon hearing those words the crowd burst forth with a second round of applause.

On other days, however, the news reaching us, as ANC leaders, was disappointing. One evening Rev. Henry Kachidza, our new General Treasurer, appeared crestfallen as he arrived at my home. After our formal Shona greetings he said, 'I have come to tell you some unpleasant news. Today the councillors, headmen and sub-chiefs of Mrewa District have been to a feast where they were given meat and beer by the district commissioner of that area. It is quite apparent that he provided the food and drink to bribe them so that when the Pearce Commission gets to the district the people will reply, "We accept the Smith-Home Settlement Proposals". ' He continued: 'It is reported our people seemed to enjoy themselves so thoroughly that it is doubtful they will be able to seriously consider the ANC position and reject the Proposals.'

I was silent for some moments, thinking what to say to my dispirited friend. 'Your report is not encouraging,' I finally replied, 'but let us trust, wait, and see.' Knowing how the Mrewa people feared that district commissioner because of his ruthlessness, I too was concerned as to the possible outcome.

On the day to test opinion people flocked to Mrewa Township from all corners of the district. In front of the Agricultural Show Hall sat Chief Mangwende. Many people called him a stooge of the regime, since he was appointed chief following

100

the government ousting of his popular predecessor—Chief Munhuwepayi 'Chiwoko' Mangwende.

Once again a Pearce commissioner followed the procedure of speaking first to explain the Proposals to the assembled crowd. Once again he turned to the people to ask them for their opinion and response. Suddenly there were placards waving in the air, which the crowd of thousands had until that moment kept carefully hidden under coats, skirts, dresses, in cars, or under nearby bushes. All of them said 'KWETE' (NO).

It was reported: 'The local district commissioner was glued to his seat in shock. Obviously he was very angry and yet knew no way to express it. He managed to suggest that the councillors, headmen and sub-chiefs stay and have another round of talks with the Pearce commissioner. The people then shouted, 'No! We have come, and we have expressed ourselves together. What else needs to be said and done?'

That was the end! The bribe had not worked.

In Zviyambe, the African Purchase Area where my father lives and farms, the Pearce commissioner tried to change tactics to avoid what he thought was mob psychology infecting the people. This time only a few councillors were called in to give their opinions. On their arrival, however, they responded: 'This issue is not for leaders only to decide. We want all the people present.'

In the nearby Tribal Trust Land the local district commissioner tried again to sway the votes by offering them a big feast, but again the people would not be bribed. Later the district commissioner was heard to say: 'I slaughtered beasts for them, but still they rejected the Proposals.' Hearing this one brave African got to his feet and responded: 'You people did not bring one single cow from Europe. All these cattle you have at the expense of our cheap labour.'

We were also interested in the early reports coming from the outlying towns. In Umtali the commissioners organized a meeting at which women, both black and white, were to give evidence. At first the African women from Sakubva Township feared to go until Mrs. Arthur Kanonuhwa, the United Methodist pastor's wife, offered to lead the way. She cut an impressive figure upon entering the hall as she was eight months pregnant.

A white woman, the first of four designated speakers, turned to the Zimbabwean women present and said: 'You Africans

101

must be thankful. We came into this country when you did not have schools, roads, bridges or hospitals. Why, you were just dressed in skins then! After we have developed this country to be what it has become today, now you want us to leave it!'

A hushed silence fell on the hall. Each African woman looked furtively to her neighbour, wondering who would have the courage to answer such provocative remarks. Finally one woman jumped to her feet and replied: 'Yes, you whites came to this country when we did not have all the things you have enumerated, but if you are making that a justification for denying us our human and political rights then I want to propose that you take all the schools, all the hospitals, all the roads, all the bridges and everything else you built in Rhodesia and go, but *leave us our soil!* Yes, you have given us all that you have named—plus oppression.' That was more than the white woman could take, and she hastily left the hall.

Repression and Violence

I have already mentioned how difficult it was to have our ANC meetings accepted as 'normal political activity' during the weeks of the Pearce Commission's visits. But the regime did not stop there. On January 18 Mr. Garfield Todd and his daughter Judith (now Mrs Acton) were arrested and placed in political detention. They had been fearless in expressing their opposition to the Proposals, both in their home district of Shabani and in Gwelo. They were among the most respected of liberal whites in our country at that time. Our revulsion increased when, three days later, our ANC Treasurer, Mr. Josiah Chinamano, and his wife Ruth were also placed in political detention.

'Was Smith trying to cripple us by immobilizing our Treasurer?' I wondered. 'If so, why detain his wife as well, leaving their children uncared for?' Yet I knew in my heart that there is no logic in the oppressive acts of an enemy desperate to stay in power. Reluctantly, we asked Rev. H. Kachidza, our Deputy Treasurer, to take over the post of Treasurer. There was a strong feeling among the ANC Executive that to replace a detained person only exposed his successor to the same fate.

The arrests of the Todds followed incidents in Gwelo after the people had feared that the Pearce commissioners would talk only to the chiefs. When the vast crowd attempted to march to where the commissioners were, the police opened fire with tear gas and bullets, killing one person and wounding many others.

A similar crisis developed soon afterwards in Umtali with tragic results. The people had been told that they could meet the Pearce commissioners at two o'clock in the Sakubva Beit Hall. Long before that hour the hall was packed to overflowing, with thousands more outside. At the appointed hour the police announced: 'The commissioners are not coming. You must leave and go to your respective places.' The people refused to believe it, and suspected that the commissioners would meet only the chiefs and their councillors once the crowd had dispersed. So they remained glued to their seats. Tensions mounted when the police tried to move the people with dogs and tear gas, until a peaceful group became an angry crowd. Police opened fire with machine guns, Africans responded by throwing stones (the only weapons at hand) at the police and at any buildings which symbolized to them white rule. The death toll mounted. With tears in her eyes a member of our church recounted to me how she saw a child shot to death as he stood in front of his parents. The official police report listed eight dead, but other bodies were later discovered by our people, for many had run away, mortally wounded, to die later in the wooded areas around the town.

As similar incidents erupted in Gwelo, Shabani and Salisbury we of the ANC Executive felt deeply upset. Our people were supposed to express their grievances to the Commission, and they were—in most cases—peacefully making their demands for justice and human dignity. Yet again and again they were being met with bullets, injury and death. Speaking in Salisbury I condemned the 'anger' of these days and expressed regret over the violence that had occurred. The ANC, I stated, did not have any connection with this violence and was completely against it. But the outbreaks, I warned, were only a sign of more anger and frustration beneath the surface.

The ANC Gives Evidence

Despite this wave of violence, we of the ANC Executive felt that the campaign for a 'No' vote was moving well. The people were responding to our call for a massive, overwhelming rejection of the Proposals. Posters and car stickers broadcast the message. When public meetings could not be held, house meetings took their place. Now it was time for the ANC to give its formal response to the Commission.

Our work began on January 28, the day set for our testimony, with a flurry of activity to complete the preparation of the ANC statement. In those days we had to rely on the duplicating services of the United Methodist headquarters, as the ANC possessed no equipment. Volunteers with ink-stained hands pressed the copies upon us as we hastened to nearby Ranche House College for the meeting. Upon arrival we found a large crowd waiting for us. Their loud cheers as we entered the conference room were welcome moral and political support.

Calmly I presented the ANC statement to Lord Pearce and his commissioners. Our words were uncompromising. *'The ANC unhestitantly rejects these proposals,'* I began. 'The basic demand of the ANC is that no settlement of the Rhodesian problem can be achieved without the active participation of the African people, through the leaders of their choice, in the actual process of negotiation. Any settlement must be approved by them.' These words formed the heart of our argument, although I went on to read detailed evidence for rejecting various items in the Settlement Proposals. We rejected all that had been arrived at without consultation with the people of Rhodesia. Furthermore, I said that the ANC cannot in any circumstances 'accept a settlement whose result, directly or indirectly, is the legalization of UDI and the Republican Constitution.'

In the discussion which ensued I reassured the commissioners that the ANC was pledged to seek a non-violent response to the Proposals, but predicted that 'the alternative to a peaceful settlement is bloodshed'. To adopt these Proposals would 'legalize a constitution which we believe is a seedbed of bloody revolution.'

Leaving the hall my colleagues and I were satisfied that we had presented the people's message—Zimbabwe's case—in the most effective way possible.

Pros and Cons

One day Mr. Ronnie Sadomba, a Centre Party Member of Parliament, visited me. His party had been formed as a 'multi-racial party', and tried honestly to bridge the growing chasm between blacks and whites in Rhodesia. Mr. Sadomba came to share with me his own heart-searching concerns. I was glad to discover that there was a lot of heart-searching in politics, too.

He said: 'Our party has decided as a party that these Settlement Proposals should be accepted. But I have discovered that the Africans whom I represent are definitely rejecting them. My conscience can no longer allow me to go on like this. Therefore, I want to join the ANC and be an independent MP.'

I was deeply impressed by the moral stamina which Ronnie Sadomba displayed. 'Of course,' I said to him, 'the decision is yours, but you will be more than welcome in the ANC.' About two weeks later he joined us.

This was the first of several contacts with the Centre Party. About the same time their President, Mr. Pat Bashford, came with some of his colleagues to see me. It struck me as strange that a party which was avowedly 'multi-racial' should send an all-white delegation.

Mr. Bashford went straight to the subject of their visit: 'Bishop, your people may have started their campaign as a protest, but if you don't stop it your organization will go on the rocks.' He continued: 'We have inside information that Smith plans to lock up the ANC leaders except for the bishop, for he may fear public opinion if he did that.'

Mr. Bashford spoke eloquently, and I noticed that the five members of the ANC Executive who were present listened with great seriousness. He carried on for about thirty minutes, with a tone and manner not unlike what we had experienced years before as schoolboys when the headmaster lectured to us.

We listened attentively—so much so that he must have concluded that he had won us over by his arguments. Certainly he was not aware of how deep was our dedication to fight for our rights. When our turn came to reply, our words cut through his arguments like a surgeon's knife. We spoke confidently. We showed that we respected his right to hold his views, although we differed with him. Neither side changed the opinions of the other that day, yet I felt that there had been some growth in understanding, for Pat Bashford said as he departed, 'I wish my African MPs were of the same calibre as the men I found here today.'

Just when it seemed clear that everywhere the Pearce commissioners went people were rejecting the Proposals, a rash of new groups, ostensibly led by Africans, sprang up to say 'Yes' to the Proposals. Companies in Salisbury began to circulate form letters to make it easy for their employees to write 'Yes' letters to the Commission. One chief in Matabeleland announced that 17,000 people under his jurisdiction had all said 'Yes'. A new party called the Congress National Union, which claimed an African membership of 50,000, said that it supported the Proposals. Fortunately, the Commission saw through this trickery and exposed the fraud.

Peace Mission

By February 1972 it was becoming clear that victory was possible. The Pearce commissioners had been 'all' around the country. There were many indications that the Proposals would be massively rejected. What we feared, however, was further collusion between the British Government and the minority Smith regime. We needed to make doubly sure that this would not happen, and to do so meant someone should influence British public opinion and talk with government officials there. Therefore, the ANC National Executive decided that I should accept an invitation to the United Kingdom, one extended by the Rhodesia Emergency Campaign Committee there.

It was a very cold February morning that I arrived at Heathrow Airport, near London. Among a sea of strangers I spotted a group of Zimbabweans who had braved the bitter weather to welcome me. Among them was Mr. Eshmael Mlambo who was to serve as the first ANC representative to the United Kingdom.

This was the time to press every button available to convince the British Government and people that the Smith-Home Settlement Proposals were a dead-end street, and that a constitutional conference with African leaders offered a new road forward.

I found church groups open to receive my initiatives, so I met with officials of the British Council of Churches and with those of the Methodist Church. Archbishop Ramsey of Canterbury, whose earlier statements on violence in the Zimbabwe liberation struggle had raised the hackles of white Christians in Rhodesia, invited me to talk with him. I shared news of recent political developments and how in Rhodesia the Christian Council worked with the ANC to demand majority rule. He responded by supporting the objective of achieving majority rule as soon as possible, but expressed fears of increased violence and an intensification of armed conflict if negotiations failed. I felt encouraged as I left his office, yet surprised that one as old as he could sound so militant.

During my two-week stay I lived in the home of an Anglican priest whom I had never met before. The warm hospitality and Christian friendship which he and his family gave to me touched me deeply.

I came to Britain, however, not as a bishop but as Chairman of the African National Council. As such I gladly accepted an invitation to speak at the House of Commons. In my address to the British MPs I repeated the central theme of my initial press conference in London—that the time had come to settle the Rhodesian problem constitutionally, or the country would deteriorate into bloodshed. 'If the British Government continues to ignore the Africans of Rhodesia in their constitutional ventures,' I went on, 'then the responsibility for a future holocaust in Southern Rhodesia will lie heavily upon them.'

When I finished speaking, at the time for questions, a lady MP stood up and made a comment (not a question) and said: 'You, a Christian and a bishop of the church, are threatening the whites with bloodshed.'

After she sat down I responded directly to her and said: 'I was not praying for bloodshed to come to Zimbabwe. I was not saying I was going to cause bloodshed, nor did I say that the blood to be shed will be of whites only, but I was saying that *there would be bloodshed,* and that meant the blood of all the people.' I made it clear that this was a responsible observation of real concern, and not a threat. 'You may call it a prophecy of doom,' I continued, 'but it was a prophecy that calls for immediate attention and action in order to save a nation in the making.'

Many Conservatives found my words a bitter pill to swallow. They had not yet reconciled themselves to the imminent defeat of the Smith-Home Proposals. Opposition party spokesmen, however, were more accessible, so it was arranged that I talk with both Mr. Jeremy Thorpe, then the leader of the Liberal Party, and with Sir Harold Wilson, leader of the Labour Party.

During my meeting with Sir Harold I could not help but recall that it was Mr. Wilson who was Prime Minister of Great Britain at the time of Smith's UDI. I knew that it was Wilson who had assured Smith at that time that the British Government would not employ force to quell any rebellion, and thus in one sense had precipitated UDI. 'Could Sir Harold Wilson have averted the bloodshed which became widespread in Zimbabwe?' I wondered again. To recall these events was for me like reopening an old wound.

On this occasion Sir Harold told me, 'We shall be making a formal statement in the House about your presence in this country, Bishop.' How charming, and how disarming! On reflection afterwards, however, I felt that Mr. Wilson, like many British politicians, favoured a settlement in Rhodesia which would be acceptable and amenable to the whites there. We remained for them 'the Rhodesian problem' which they eagerly wanted to get rid of as one would a hot potato in the hand.

Meeting followed meeting in quick succession during those busy days. Some were informal gatherings like those with members of the House of Lords, and with leaders of the Anti-Apartheid Movement. Others, such as the engagements at the Universities of Birmingham and Cambridge, were major addresses with time for questions.

My most antagonistic audience, however, turned out to be a rally of my own people. I expected Zimbabweans to be my most sympathetic audience as I briefed them on recent events back home. To my surprise the first questioner asked, 'Why are you a "globe-trotter"?' Immediately another student chimed in, 'Why are you spending the people's money and seeking pleasure in luxury hotels?' In response I launched into a spirited defence of my mission and my life-style on it and concluded, saying, 'Besides, if I wanted pleasure I would go to New York, since London looks like a pre-historic ruin and has such depressing weather.'

That brought laughter, and the tension subsided. At that moment a most eloquent Zimbabwean lady stood up and launched into a spirited defence on my behalf. She extolled my virtues and the virtues of the ANC which had been fighting so courageously against the Smith-Home Proposals. 'Can you tell us one little thing you have done for the liberation of Zimbabwe other than sitting here and criticizing Bishop Muzorewa?' she concluded. Needless to say I found her contribution most pleasing and welcome.

The storm had abated. I felt it appropriate to end by saying, 'I forgive you all'. Somehow the artificiality had been removed, and we were Zimbabweans in good humour again.

Later I reflected on this incident and realized that my accusers were afflicted with the 'exiles' disease'—the disease of dis-orientation, division and general confusion which results when politically-minded persons are separated for too long from their people. To this day Zimbabweans in London are divided into a host of factions which do not see eye to eye with each other. Blinded by the exiles' London fog, they were not aware of the new Zimbabwean political unity achieved by the ANC. They still thought of ZAPU, ZANU, and FROLIZI. As for their stereotype of politicians, it had been built up, alas, on the demerits of our Zimbabwean leaders in the 1960s, many of whom had been globe-trotters and pleasure-seekers who squandered the people's money recklessly. Seeing me they had assumed that I came out of the same mould as my older brothers in the Zimbabwean nationalist movements.

Trafalgar Square

The climax of my all-too-brief British tour had now arrived—the Trafalgar Square rally. It had been organized by the Rhodesia Emergency Campaign Committee in support of our 'ANC Says No!' campaign, and the Zimbabwean struggle for independence.

Before the rally a colourful procession wound its way through the streets, with banners lifted high. As I followed the progress of the demonstration—unobserved in the back seat of a slow-moving car—I pondered one of the contradictions of our liberation struggle. At home I battle against white people largely of British extraction who are die-hard racists—sworn enemies of the black Zimbabweans, and advocates of the superiority of the Caucasian race and of western civilization. Here in the centre of London I found myself surrounded by white people who were loudly condemning the racism of the Smith regime.

We arrived at the Square and immediately observed another phenomenon. As soon as my feet touched the ground I was instantly surrounded by a number of tough-looking men who formed a protective position throughout the rally. This was the first time I became really aware that my life was a gamble—that political leadership carried with it grave security risks. This was the first time I felt an uneasiness, a kind of fear for my personal safety. And this fear accompanied me on to the platform. Having experienced it so acutely, I resolved that day to subjugate such fear by a single-minded pursuit of the liberation of Zimbabwe and her people.

On the stage I confronted another enemy—the English weather. It was bitterly cold. Fortunately someone in the crowd noticed me shivering and came forward to offer me his gloves. I was eternally grateful. Still my lips felt frozen so that I wondered if I would be able to speak. Some in the audience must have winced at my slowness of speech.

It was comforting, amid the sea of strange faces, to sit beside someone whom I knew and respected—Rev. Colin Morris. We had first met during his participation in the struggle for black rights in neighbouring Zambia. Now he served as President of the Methodist Church in Great Britain and as our chairman at the rally. After a few opening remarks he introduced the dignitaries present, including bishops of the Church of England and Roman Catholic priests. Then he presented me.

I sensed the enthusiasm of the crowd for our cause. Soon they were singing the refrain with me, 'ZIMBABWE SHALL BE FREE!'—fifteen thousand voices blended in one mighty chorus.

In the address I chose to stress that whatever the verdict of the Pearce Commission the Settlement Proposals 'cannot and will not be accepted by my people'. To emphasize our total rejection of them I continued: 'The Settlement Proposals that have been arrived at without the participation of the Africans are a constitutional fraud, a prescription for increased racial bitterness, the making of an inevitable bloodbath, and an insult to the dignity of every African in Rhodesia.'

Then I answered the accusations that agitators had intimidated the masses to reject the Proposals. 'On the contrary,' I said, 'it is we who face constant intimidation by white racists.' I pointed out that my very presence alone on the platform was a symbol of that intimidation, for I alone of the ANC Executive had a passport to travel outside Rhodesia (although I was not free to travel in the land of my birth). I spoke of the various forms of intimidation of my people—by the district commissioner who 'is free to take away a man's land or cattle at his own discretion', by the cabinet minister 'who without explanation or reason can take away a man's or woman's freedom for any length of time, from one hour to fifteen years', etc. I said: 'We reject a policy and a regime that can justify the murder of thirty-one unarmed human beings on the streets of Gwelo, Salisbury and Umtali, and the arrest of the Todds and Chinamanos, and over 250 people whose only crime is to stand up for their dignity, and to ask the world simply to treat them as human beings.' I concluded: 'We reject the intimidation of a government of thugs. Above all, my brothers and sisters, WE REJECT INJUSTICE AND DEMAND OUR FREEDOM.'

The crowd roared their sympathy and their encouragement, with a forest of placards raised to support our cause. Not everyone, however, was sympathetic. One lonely and pathetic group of racists waved a banner which read, 'Stand with the whites in Rhodesia'. They were quickly dragged from the rally and retreated, I understand, to the nearby security of Rhodesia House. The rally ended, nevertheless, in an orderly manner.

My work, however, was not yet over. As soon as I finished speaking, friends accompanied me to nearby No. 10 Downing Street, the Prime Minister's official residence. There I delivered a petition rejecting the Smith-Home Proposals and demanding majority rule in Zimbabwe.

To the United Nations

With my mission to the United Kingdom complete, I turned to another body which has an influence on events in Rhodesia—the Security Council of the United Nations. The Council had kindly invited me to address them when Somalia, Sudan and Guinea sponsored a resolution for renewed debate on the Rhodesia issue. Mr. Eshmael Mlambo, ANC representative in the UK, accompanied me for this representation.

Before reaching the Council chamber, however, I faced reporters at a press conference. My introduction was a new experience for many of them. When the journalists had set up their equipment and were ready to write and record, I informed them that in Zimbabwe I normally started my press conferences with a prayer. Fortunately there was a respectful hush as I prayed with them before making my statement.

I began my address to the Security Council of the United Nations by saying: 'The African National Council is a spontaneous grass-roots reaction . . . not a political party. It represents the overwhelming number of persons in Rhodesia who have rejected the Proposals as being unacceptable to them.' Next I outlined in detail the reasons for this rejection. I emphasized to the UN, which is concerned about granting independence to colonial countries: 'The Proposals, contrary to some arguments, do not de-colonize Rhodesia, rather, they re-colonize the country and to ensure the success of this dangerous and dishonourable venture the British Government seems prepared to subsidize it.' Summing up this argument I said: 'Our rejection of these proposals is therefore unanimous.'

Next I dealt with Sir Alec Douglas-Home's statement that this is the last chance and that there would not be another offer, or constitutional conference, if the answer is 'No.' I declared: 'The African people are already preparing themselves for a long confrontation with the racist regime, and therefore call upon the international community not to recognize the independence imposed by the British Government.' My statement showed our real fear at that time that Britain would override the findings of the Pearce Commission—so desperate were they to get rid of the Rhodesia problem, and again to open up channels of trade and investments in our country.

Finally I discussed economic sanctions. 'The Africans accept sanctions as a price of their freedom,' I said. I called for their intensification, for a full blockade of the ports of Beira and Lourenço Marques in Mozambique, and asked that the United States be brought before the International Court of Justice for its blatant violation of sanctions by its continued purchase of chrome from Rhodesia.

During our Security Council discussion, as well as in subsequent meetings with UN delegates, I obtained some very clear impressions. It was evident that the socialist countries had greater interest in our problems of liberation, and were more positive in their approach. By contrast, delegates from western countries seemed unwilling to be committed, and dragged their feet on every proposal aimed to bring down the Smith regime. Their responses were cold, and they became alarmed when I proposed mandatory sanctions, as if protection of their business interests in Southern Africa was their major consideration. When I pointed out that the alternative was a bloody revolution, they simply refused to believe me. Then I remembered that the first time the United States used its veto at the Security Council it was to block a resolution which might have peacefully brought down the Smith regime.

After expressing thanks to those who had opened the way for my UN visit, I proceeded to Washington DC to meet congressmen and officials at the State Department's Africa desk. This was my time to put before American leaders certain proposals which we believed could bring down the Smith regime without bloodshed, and ensure a smooth transfer of power from the minority to the majority. First, I asked the USA to stop all trade dealings with Rhodesia, including the importation of chrome ore. Next, I asked that the USA join in pressing for mandatory sanctions by the United Nations against Rhodesia. Another request was that the Rhodesia Information Office in Washington be shut down as it was a moral and material boon to the Smith regime. Finally, I pleaded with the US leaders to discourage the flow of American tourists to Rhodesia, as their presence supplied foreign exchange and was of propaganda value to the white government.

This was a discouraging visit. My pleas fell on deaf ears. It was brutally obvious that there was to be at that time no hope of support from the US Government for the Zimbabwean liberation struggle.

Return to Zimbabwe

After that cold reception, I was eager to return home—back to Zimbabwe and the real struggle. My mission to promote peace through the United Kingdom and America was over.

At that stage it was becoming clear to me that the battle for our freedom might have to be fought solely by us Zimbabweans. The West seemed too preoccupied with the protection of its investments in Southern Africa to want to upset Mr. Smith and his government. The West was showing little faith in us as custodians of future peace, of democracy, of stability, and of balanced economic progress.

I was feeling depressed as our plane winged its way south. I did not know that Zimbabweans were preparing a surprise welcome for me at the Salisbury airport—one which would exceed those organized in previous years for heads of state. Never before had I experienced such a thunderous and jubilant crowd as the more than 8,000 people waiting to say 'welcome home'. Dr. Edson Sithole actually kissed me with joy and excitement, while other comrades threw me up on their shoulders and carried me from the terminal to the waiting crowd.

These are the people whom I love, who are faithfully waiting, nobly proud of their heritage, and confident of their ultimate success.

The New ANC

One of the realities to which I returned was that only one battle in the struggle against white minority rule had been won. We had hoped for a solid victory in the Test of Acceptability of the Smith-Home Proposals, and the results showed overwhelming approval of our stand. What then was to be the future of the African National Council which had been formed simply 'to explain and advise people to reject the Anglo-Rhodesian Constitutional Settlement Proposals'?

During my absence the ANC Executive received delegations from various districts petitioning for the continuance of the ANC. My overseas experience convinced me, also, how imperative it was that our people remain united and determined to continue to work through the ANC, inasmuch as our political parties were still banned and their leaders held in political detention. A permanent political organization, the ANC Executive agreed, was essential.

Therefore, on March 10, the day that Lord Pearce and his fellow commissioners left Rhodesia, the ANC was reborn. To a large crowd assembled in Highfields Township, I read the new 'Manifesto Under the Banner of Unity' (see Appendix B).

The ANC, we declared in the *Manifesto,* is the heir 'to the People's Struggle which has ceaselessly been waged since the imposition of alien rule in 1890'. We declared the African National Council 'to be the one sole voice and instrument of the African masses of Zimbabwe, and all people of goodwill in their just and normal struggle for national emancipation from the yoke of a racist and oppressive minority rule'. Carefully we welcomed 'those members of other races dedicated to the establishment of human brotherhood'. We affirmed our beliefs including those in 'the power of the unity of the African masses', 'non-racialism', protection of the rights of minorities, and in a 'non-violent, peaceful, orderly, but permanent and continuing struggle'. Our summons was: 'Be UNITED until UNITY is strength and strength becomes POWER.'

The new ANC needed an expanded leadership to carry out its tasks. Although the officers remained the same (with Rev. H. H. Kachidza having taken the place of the detained Josiah Chinamano as Treasurer), we determined to enlarge the Executive to fifty-five in number, to add a Central Committee of twenty-three members, and a General Assembly of 160 persons. We also set up new

114

national committees for education, internal affairs, and commerce and industry.

The Nation Awaits the Verdict

As the whole nation waited in limbo for the Pearce Commission's verdict, my continuing responsibilities as bishop called me back to America. In April I addressed the Council of Bishops at St. Simon's Island, Georgia, and the General Conference of the Church in Atlanta. The Conference, with delegates from fifty-five countries, afforded another opportunity to impress upon many leaders our determination to unite as Zimbabweans to secure our freedom and basic human rights.

'You are limited to ten minutes—no more,' the presiding bishop told me. After a long night of drafting, I packed my message into nine minutes.

First I contrasted the Rhodesian Government's claim that it is 'preserving civilized standards' with the realities of life for Africans in our oppressed society. I told how the Government spends an average of $30 a year for the education of an African child while spending $300 a year for that of a white child, and how under the so-called Law and Order Maintenance Act any person who 'behaves in a manner which is likely to make some other person apprehensive as to what might happen . . . ' can be imprisoned for up to ten years.

I spoke of the prophetic voice of the Christian Church in Rhodesia as the voice of the voiceless, and of new unity found through the African National Council.

'Time is running out,' I declared. 'Rhodesia is on a collision course with disaster.' I appealed for church leaders to 'rise up in the name of Christ' to support the Zimbabwean struggle for freedom and justice. In particular I called for opposition to the US purchase of chrome ore from Rhodesia in defiance of UN sanctions.

Little did I realize that my words would be heard by hundreds of thousands of Christians in the months that followed, in a film entitled 'A Child of God in Search of Freedom'. My pacifism amid persecution was extolled in that film, but my warning that bloodshed was the only alternative to a strict enforcement of economic sanctions against Rhodesia was largely forgotten.

Upon my return to Salisbury I saw how the news media can manufacture news when none is there. The *Sunday Mail,* for its largely European readership, sought to allay the fears of whites concerning the Pearce Commission verdict. It predicted that the Report had 'got round' the African rejection. I must confess that we of the ANC were also apprehensive as we awaited the result. For years we had been pleading with British officials to pave the way for justice and equality, yet we met only procrastination which left power in the hands of the white minority in Rhodesia.

Chapter 11

Buying Time

The Pearce Commission's verdict, when announced in late May, struck Rhodesia like the final flash of lightning and crash of thunder at the finale of a violent summer storm.

The conclusion was clear-cut: 'the people of Rhodesia as a whole do not regard the Proposals as an acceptable basis for independence.' The Commission felt satisfied that the Proposals had been 'fully and properly explained to all people of Rhodesia'. Apart from a small minority, the European population was in favour. So were the majority of Coloured and Asians (only 24,000 in total number). But the majority of Africans, who comprised 95 per cent of Rhodesia's population, both in public and in private, rejected the Proposals.

Europeans favoured the Proposals in the belief that 'Rhodesia will thrive economically only if there is a settlement'. They thought it would be 'the best means of preserving a familiar and pleasant way of life and of reducing the risk of violence'. Although many Europeans did not really welcome majority rule they 'realized it had to come, so that the more gradual and peaceful the road to it the better'.

As for reasons for the massive African rejection, the Commission reported that 'mistrust of the intentions and motives of the Government transcended all other considerations'. Related to this were the judgments that 'the guarantees against constitutional change were inadequate' and that the Proposals 'would not lead to majority rule quickly enough'.

Reactions to Pearce

Our people, together with a few whites, Asians and Coloureds, welcomed the Pearce Commission's verdict with wild rejoicing. For once the black majority had defeated their white masters. The sense of victory seemed to restore self-confidence, and hope for a final victory and for liberation.

Most Europeans, on the other hand, were stunned by the verdict. They had fostered the illusion that 'our loyal Africans' (employees, chiefs and headmen, civil servants, etc.) would support the Proposals. Unable to ignore the Commission's findings, the Smith regime chose to explain it away. It was said that the Pearce commissioners, having never lived before in Rhodesia, were inexperienced and inept. Others charged that 'opportunist African politicians', namely the ANC, had used intimidation and thuggery to force the African people to say 'No' instead of 'Yes'. Maintaining the myth of a silent African majority, Ian Smith said to the Rhodesian Parliament on June 8 that he was 'prepared to speak to those Africans who are now prepared to work for the reversal of the verdict'. He felt that Africans now in the post-Pearce period were beginning to understand the advantages of the Proposals.

The British Government, while accepting the Pearce Commission's report, showed its displeasure over the verdict. Sir Alec Douglas-Home announced the result to the British Parliament and promised no further British initiative. Instead he threw the problem back to the people in Rhodesia to come together and sort out their political future for themselves.

We of the ANC Executive saw the verdict as a clear-cut summons for black Zimbabweans to realize 'the essential power of unity now'. This was a victory which outshone the achievements of all the other previous black organizations. Our slogan, 'Unity is Power', had been proven right.

Anticipating the outcome, we had prepared a new initiative which I announced to more than 1,000 jubilant supporters at a press conference in Highfield Township, Salisbury, two days after the publication of the Pearce report. The 'No' response to the Proposals, I said, was not an ultimate victory. Positive steps should now be taken to arrive at a new constitution acceptable to the people of Rhodesia as a whole. I proposed the following:

First, I called for a National Convention to be attended by delegates representing all groups consulted by the Pearce Commission—all political parties, churches, business and labour interests, and African chiefs. The Convention, I stated, would have the purpose of identifying the present conflict, demonstrating the advantages of a settlement based on the interests of all the parties to the conflict, and discussing openly the fears of each racial group.

Next, a national committee formed of Convention leaders would approach the British Government, the Rhodesian regime, and the African political leaders, and urge them to set up a meeting of officials to work out an agenda for a constitutional conference. That conference would have the task of preparing a constitution which would be acceptable to the people of Rhodesia as a whole.

The call for a national convention and constitutional conference, I said, was 'a genuine, honest and democratic approach' to solve the constitutional crisis. If now the people of Rhodesia came together to sort out their problems it would be a constructive way forward.

From Mass Protest to Mass Party
Meanwhile we had to play our politics with extreme care. The ANC was too important to risk proscription. For the first time the people of Zimbabwe had an organization capable of total national unity, able to produce results, and to overcome the minority regime.

In a time of increasing guerrilla activity it was deemed essential that ANC maintain a public image of total separation from our liberation movements. We made it plain—at least in public—that we had no relations with our exiled brothers and sisters in Zambia, Tanzania and Mozambique. We tolerated and even welcomed denunciations of the ANC which were broadcast from Lusaka. From time to time I had to reject publicly any 'violent solution' to the conflict—the sort of thing the Smith regime called 'terrorism'. Meanwhile our people understood that the ANC and the liberation movements operating from bases outside were two sides of the same coin—two fronts upon which to struggle against white oppression.

'Could the mass protest by our people be transformed into mass loyalty to a disciplined political party?' we asked ourselves. We determined to try. First, we decided to open the ANC ranks to mass membership. Each member would subscribe an initial fifty cents ($.70) and receive a membership card. If present enthusiasm could find expression in regular donations, the ANC could be self-supporting. We could employ party organizers and purchase vehicles for their use. At this time only the National Organizing Secretary, Michael Mawema, was on ANC full salary. The rest of us were committed volunteers. In fact, many on the Executive gave generously from their own income to cover travel and other expenses of our work.

Persecution

From the outset the Smith regime thwarted our every effort to organize the people. In Parliament Ian Smith rejected our call for a national convention. He called the ANC leaders 'a bunch of unscrupulous politicians'. No sooner had we printed hundreds of thousands of membership cards, at a cost of more than $3,000.00 (US $5,000), than the regime prohibited the issuing of any form of membership identification.

Next the regime moved against our organizers who were raising funds through direct subscriptions. To frighten off potential ANC supporters, they arrested both fund-raisers and donors. Police closed the Mrewa district office of the ANC, sixty miles north-east of Salisbury, subjecting both collectors and donors to intensive questioning, and hauling away six, in handcuffs and leg-irons, to detention.

Then on June 6, the so-called Minister of Justice announced that the ANC, under the emergency regulations promulgated earlier, was now defined as a 'political party' and prohibited it receiving money or goods from outside Rhodesia. The reasons given were that such funds 'would be likely to interfere with public safety and the maintenance of public order'. Not only were ANC accounts brought under close scrutiny. Our United Methodist Church funds were in jeopardy if gifts from outside could be construed as 'political' donations. Gifts to me personally from friends outside the country were also suspect.

We of the ANC Executive knew that direct action against our top leadership would be taken soon, especially against those who had formerly been leaders of ZAPU and ZANU. Every stumbling block would be put in our way in an attempt to stifle our efforts without actually banning the ANC, for the Smith regime still feared world opinion.

Michael Mawema and Edson Zvobgo were obvious targets. Thus it was no surprise when Mawema confided to me that he had received reliable information about his impending detention. 'I am tired of living in detention,' he said. 'I think I can be of more use to Zimbabwe from outside than from a detention camp.'

'I totally agree with you,' I replied. 'I am one of those who believe that there is no virtue in rotting away in a prison.'

Short of telling him outright to go ahead, I agreed with him by implication. What was regrettable, however, was that the timing of his departure almost caused the cancellation of the ANC meeting which he was to chair at Margolis Hall.

Edson Zvobgo's family already lived outside Rhodesia. So when he indicated his intention to join his wife and children we appointed him Director of External Missions. What we had failed to discern, however, was that once ANC leaders were outside the country exiled nationalists pressured them to proclaim the merits of violent revolution, thereby putting into question the ANC's affirmation of 'non-violence'. Although I sent Zvobgo a telegram instructing him to 'reiterate the non-violent policy of the ANC to the Foreign and Commonwealth Offices immediately', he chose instead to say in a newspaper interview, 'My personal philosophy is that violence is justified.'

Bridge-Building

The ANC Executive knew in May 1972 that our objective of going with Smith to a constitutional convention could be achieved only if we could convince a significant number of Europeans in Rhodesia to support our proposal. We therefore engaged in a vigorous campaign to persuade the white community to enter into dialogue with the ANC.

At the same time the Rhodesian Front policy was to try to convince Africans to accept the Settlement Proposals—the very Proposals which we considered to have been rejected once and for all, and therefore defunct. Pro-settlement groups sprang up, led by Messrs. Chiota, Charambarara, Madziwa and Samson Chibi. Mr. Chad Chipunza formed the so-called 'African Progressive Party' as one such group. These stooges became rich presumably through money received from white industrialists and the Smith regime. Meanwhile whites were told that the African National Council was a small bunch of 'rabble-rousers' and 'agitators' composed of 'only Muzorewa and a few misguided individuals around him'. The ANC knew that we needed to work fast in the face of such opposition if we were to reach the white electorate.

An invitation from the Salisbury Chapter of the National Affairs Association provided a platform to launch our new campaign just two weeks after publication of the Pearce Commission report. I entitled my speech to that packed lunch-hour gathering 'Sound a Trumpet to Build a Heritage'. I began by appealing to every father with a sense of responsibility to leave behind 'a heritage secured for his children'. 'We are not yet a nation,' I said, 'but we are struggling to be recognized as one people and one nation.' I went on: 'If all of us show sufficient goodwill, and have enough mutual understanding of each other, we can become one nation for one people.' Racial insults and discrimination, as well as lack of communication and double standards, block the growth of our nation. I tried to assuage fears that African majority rule would precipitate violence towards whites and their expulsion from the country. A constitutional conference, I affirmed, is a proposal for 'lively, forthright and constructive dialogue'. I concluded: 'Let us not allow a poisonous spirit to engulf us as a nation. This could lead to bloodshed.'

The National Affairs Association speech was but the warm-up for the main event—an address to over 900 whites (and a sprinkling of other persons) on July 20, at Salisbury's largest auditorium, the Jewish community's Margolis Hall. This meeting made history, for until that day no black nationalist leader had ever addressed a political rally in the city centre of Salisbury.

The meeting almost aborted, however, due to the disappearance the day before of our Organizing Secretary, Michael Mawema. On the morning of the meeting a member of the Special Branch came to inform me that the meeting would be legal only if chaired by Mr. Mawema, who had originally submitted the permit application. 'Does it mean that we have to cancel the meeting?' I asked. Hasty enquiries brought an assurance from higher authorities that the original application could be altered to allow a different chairman.

On entering Margolis Hall I was surprised to find it filled to overflowing with whites. I observed our ANC organizers asking Africans in the audience to kindly give their seats to whites who were standing outside. Instead of rowdy heckling by Rhodesian Front extremists, customary at opposition political meetings, I found discipline and order.

White expectations that night had been heightened by banner headlines on the Sunday before, 'ANC WANTS A SETTLE-MENT . . . MUZOREWA'. In an interview I was quoted as saying: 'This impasse has to come to an end. There has to be a compromise between Europeans and Africans. And that compromise must be between 'never majority rule' and 'majority rule now'.

Speaking on the theme 'Return to Legality', I made it clear that there would be no going backward. Again I outlined the reasons why the ANC and the vast majority of Africans had rejected the Settlement Proposals. Then I spoke words which my audience found it difficult to accept: 'Let there be no misunderstanding. The last Proposals have been genuinely and spontaneously rejected, and there is no going back and accepting them.'

I affirmed the following developments among our people which I believed could ensure 'an orderly transition to democratic rule with peace and prosperity for all'—greater educational advancement by Africans than in most independent states to the north, a high level of economic development, a high understanding and commitment of our people to the Christian faith, a deep African aversion to violence, the relative absence of inter-tribal conflicts and animosities, and the presence of whites as citizens eager to build a nation. In conclusion I called for a national convention leading to a constitution conference: 'Let us come and reason together, return to legality and take our rightful place in the community of nations.'

The questions which followed showed that many Rhodesian whites wanted to hear much more. Some had expected the ANC to give up its opposition to the Proposals. Others expected me to lay out in public view the ANC's blueprint for a new constitution. This I refused to do, as this should remain part of the negotiation process.

Press reporting of the Margolis Hall meeting focused on this white disappointment. On the following weekend the *Sunday Mail* editor who had built up false hopes among whites judged the meeting a failure. He called it 'a sad waste of time'. Having found some ANC members sceptical concerning prospects for a convention he concluded that 'the ANC is divided and in disarray, and can no longer be looked to as a representative body of African opinion'. This response did not surprise the ANC Executive, however. The white-controlled press was supporting the regime's line. All along it had been giving greater prominence to the so-called 'pro-settlement groups' than to the activities of the ANC.

To West Africa

During these weeks I received a surprise letter from President

William Tolbert Jr. of Liberia. 'Come and relax from the problems you are facing and celebrate the 125th anniversary of our Independence with us,' he wrote. I was glad to accept and be able to get away for a few days from the pressures.

Upon reaching Monrovia, the Liberian capital, I learned that the celebrations were to be held some one hundred miles away. The Christian orientation of the government of President Tolbert inspired me and amid the colourful festivities of the Liberian people I did find time to relax.

On my way home I stopped in Nigeria where General Yakubu Gowon, then the head of state, received me cordially. In our discussions he impressed me by his grasp of the Rhodesian situation. It was obvious that he was deeply sympathetic with our liberation struggle. As a result of this visit the Nigerian Government offered places in Nigerian universities to Zimbabwean students. When we met next in Kingston, Jamaica, in 1975, General Gowon offered to build a technical college for Zimbabweans in response to my earlier statement that the white regime had deliberately deprived our people of opportunities for technical training.

My visit to Nigeria gave me an insight into the bitterness which is engendered by a civil war. Almost everybody I met was apologetic and remorseful that the civil war had taken place, that Nigerians had killed Nigerians. Seeing that the bitterness engendered by that conflict would take a long time to heal, I resolved to work strenuously to avoid any similar divisions among our people in Zimbabwe.

What Strategy Now?

I returned to Salisbury and was drawn into a maelstrom of debate over my Margolis Hall speech. In a press conference I denounced as 'cheap propaganda' the press reports which purported to see a split in the ANC, and which castigated me for failing to disclose ANC proposals for achieving majority rule. 'Will this genuine hand of friendship extended by moderate Africans be refused?' I asked. 'If so, one can only fear that this reasonable line of thinking, if not needed by those in power, will be replaced by a more militant one.'

The regime's response came swiftly. RF Members of Parliament denounced ANC leaders as 'hooligans, thugs, terrorists, unscrupulous rabble-rousers and agitators'. Some called for the banning of the ANC, and the detention of its leaders. The Minister of Justice, Law and Order tried to associate us with our armed brothers in Lusaka, but never succeeded in establishing an incriminating link which would justify our banning.

On September 1 the regime promulgated a Departure from Rhodesia (Control) Act and immediately served Rev. Canaan Banana, our Vice-President, with orders preventing him from leaving the country. He was about to attend a World Council of Churches' meeting in Britain to campaign against implementation of the Settlement Proposals.

A week later immigration officials arrived to confiscate my passport. They must have known of my pending departure for talks with officials of the Foreign and Commonwealth Office in London, as well as my intention to attend the meeting of the United Methodist Council of Bishops in the United States.

Stricken

There was another urgency at this time that I travel overseas. In August I entered our Nyadiri Methodist Hospital troubled with stomach pains. The doctor found an ulcer to be the cause and expressed the hope that I would seek the help of a specialist overseas as soon as I was well enough to travel.

United Methodists held their Central Conference in Malawi in August, with the selection of bishops as the principal item on the agenda. Unlike our American colleagues, bishops in Africa served a four-year term, and then were eligible for re-election. News reached me in a quiet way when Dr. Davidson Sadza pulled from his pocket a 5″ by 8″ card on which he had written '82 out of 85'. It was his way of telling me that the Central Conference had re-elected me bishop.

After several weeks in a hospital Dr. Sadza ordered me to rest at home. Knowing the constant stream of visitors which would invade my Salisbury home, I chose to spend those days at my father's farm.

My father greeted me with affection, but quickly dispelled any notion that I would be alone. 'You know,' he cautioned, 'that the Special Branch (secret police) visit here constantly. Last month one came and asked, 'Mr. Muzorewa, what do you think about what your son is doing?'

' "Which one of my sons?" I asked the policeman.

' "Your bishop son," he said.

' "Well, what about him, and what in particular do you want to know?" I asked.

'In reply the black policeman replied, "He is talking about wanting *kutora nyika* (to take the country).'

'I said to him, "How about yourself? Don't you want to be free, and have charge of your own country? Don't you want that?"

'He was silent for a long time as if tongue-tied, and then changed the subject. I decided not press him further.'

During the days which followed we did not lack visitors. First, a secret policeman came in disguise to ask if we had any problems. Next another stranger arrived to ask for a drink of water. That was not an unusual request as we lived in a hot, dry region, but we knew that he came on duty to make certain I had not slipped away to influence people in the nearby Tribal Trust Land.

When a third visitor arrived and said, 'I just wanted to pass by and see you and find out if there are any complaints you have to report such as thefts,' I replied, 'And I suppose you also wanted to be sure that I am here and not in the Tribal Trust Land.' 'Oh, oh, no,' he said, with a guilty tone.

Later, after I returned to Salisbury, the police called many people to the nearby Wedza police station for interrogation. An informer had reported that someone from the Tribal Trust Land had come to see me to talk politics. The accused, who had never met me, asked for the one who made the accusation to repeat his charges in front of them and the police officers. Seeing the informer, he shouted to the police. 'Ask *him* the question—where and when did I talk to Bishop Muzorewa?' For once a false accusation was exposed.

The days of confinement at the farm, combined with the physical discomfort of those weeks, made me question whether or not I should continue as President of the ANC. The nation needed a strong leader who could speak with courage both within and outside the country. Already I was denied access to three-fourths of our people—those who lived in the Tribal Trust Lands—and I had been denied permission to travel outside Rhodesia.

Was this the prelude to further actions against me? I wondered. While in New York City in April a friend high on the staff of The United Methodist Board of Global Ministries told me that the Smith regime planned to silence me once and for all. ANC informers in Smith's secret police had relayed the message to him.

What would silencing mean? I wondered. I recalled how Jesus had told his disciples when on the road to Jerusalem:

'the Son of man will be delivered to the chief priests and scribes, and they will condemn him to death, and deliver him to the Gentiles to be mocked and scourged and crucified.' (Matthew 20: 18-19)

I began to understand how Jesus must have felt about the impending crucifixion. It was painful to think of being silenced before I had accomplished what I felt I had been called to do.

On my return to Salisbury a friend and church leader came to warn me that I would be detained at any time, and that the ANC probably would be banned. 'If you are really a bishop,' he said, 'you should quit politics and the ANC.' I knew that he represented a considerable number of clergy and laity of our church, both black and white, who were against my involvement in politics. They felt that I was out of step by being both Bishop of the United Methodist Church and leader of the ANC in Zimbabwe. Shortly thereafter a relative who usually did not comment about my work came and said: 'I want to propose that you quit ANC. Please listen to me.' As with the church leader I allowed him to express his views.

The following day friends invited me to their home where the Moral Rearmament Group was entertaining the exiled King and Queen of Rumania. The exquisite and most charming Queen said that she wanted to share a poem with the group entitled 'Don't Quit'. I felt that she was directing it at me as she said:

'When things go wrong as they sometimes will,
When the road you're trudging seems all up hill,
When the funds are low and the debts are high
And you want to smile, but you have to sigh,
When care is pressing you down a bit,
Rest, if you must—but don't you quit.
Life is queer with its twists and turns,
As everyone of us sometimes learns,
And many a failure turns about
When he might have won had he stuck it out;
Don't give up though the pace seems slow—
You may succeed with another blow.
Success is failure turned inside out—
The silver tint of the clouds of doubt

And you never can tell how close you are,
It may be near when it seems afar;
So stick to the fight when you're hardest hit—
It's when things seem worst that you must not quit.'*

Was it coincidence that I should receive such a message only a day after I had been confronted with a suggestion to quit? The words vividly pictured the frustrations our liberation struggle felt at that time. I went home and prayed about it. Clearly I heard God saying, 'Abel, do not quit'.

The Twofold Path to Liberation

By 1973 it became increasingly apparent that two strategies would be required to wrest majority rule from Ian Smith and the Rhodesian Front. Outside the country the guerrilla attacks would need to be intensified. Within the country our stance as the ANC would need to be united opposition to white rule, coupled with an openness to negotiate for a transfer of power.

December 21, 1972, marked the opening of a new military offensive by the Zimbabwe African National Liberation Army (ZANLA). Within a month Ian Smith admitted in a press conference that there had been a 'security breakdown', especially in the Centenary District of European farms in the north-east of the country. Charging Zambian complicity in the 'terrorist attacks', the regime announced the closing of the border with Zambia. The deaths of two South African 'police' on security duty, and the wounding of five Rhodesian servicemen, were the pretext for the action. Mr. Smith said that he would not reopen the border until he received 'satisfactory assurance' from Zambia that that country would not harbour 'terrorists'. Zambia responded by cutting its trade links with Rhodesia, including the transhipment of copper to ports in Mozambique, and maintained this stand even when Rhodesia reopened its border the following month.

In the months which followed the Smith Government's actions belied their words that they had the guerrilla war 'under control'. White farms increasingly came under a state of seige. Call-ups of reserve units, including 38-year-old men, showed that the white line of defence was stretched thin. Oppression against Africans who gave support to the freedom fighters

* Anonymous, from Sourcebook of Poetry (Grand Rapids: Zondervan Publishing House, 1968), p. 618.

escalated. The maximum penalty 'for aiding terrorists or failing to report their presence' rose from five to twenty years' imprisonment. The regime began constructing in the Chiweshe TTL the so-called 'protected villages'. Government troops first destroyed rural villages and then herded the people behind barbed wire in a futile attempt to isolate the liberation forces from contact and support by the African populace.

Once again Ian Smith chose to appear more conciliatory when hard-pressed. In February he indicated to the press that he might meet me if he could be assured that such a meeting would not be a waste of time.

No sooner had the ANC Executive selected its negotiating team than the Rhodesian Front showed its ugly side. On February 26 the regime detained two senior members of our Executive. As they were both members of the ANC negotiating team we suspected that they had been dubbed 'intransigent' by some elements of the RF.

The next day, February 27, Rev. Banana and I announced at a press conference that 'The RF regime's action against leaders of the ANC without reason makes it impossible for the ANC to continue with any such plans'. Then we issued this warning: 'We fear that if the African people are denied expression of their legitimate political rights through constitutional means they will be left with no alternative but to go underground and attempt to change the present system through a violent revolution. We would hope this prophecy of doom can be avoided, but the regime is certainly not helping to avert such a threat through their thoughtless actions.'

Next Rev. Banana and I made a direct appeal to the people, both black and white, to press for constitutional talks as the only alternative to further bloodshed. I reminded Europeans in Bulawayo that acts of rudeness, unfair or segregatory practices, or repressive legislation against Africans would evoke a reverse racism by Africans 'now and for the future'. Meanwhile Rev. Banana told the ANC rally in Gwelo that the ANC has a constitutional solution to present to all the people of Rhodesia which it believes will receive sound acceptance if the Rhodesian Front can come to terms with the ANC.

Banned from the Cathedral

In May 1973 leaders of various denominations in Salisbury

invited me to preach at the Ascension Day service. My hosts
agreed that the service would be held in the Anglican Cathedral.
No sooner had the invitation been issued than the Dean of the
Cathedral banned me from preaching there 'for political reasons'.

The justification for the ban baffled not only me but many
Anglicans, including the Archbishop, who graciously sent a
telegram saying: 'Deepest apologies both personally and on
behalf of Church and Province.' Others pointed out the
inconsistency of the Dean's action. Earlier the so-called Minister
of Justice, Law and Order, Mr. Desmond Lardner-Burke, had
spoken from that same pulpit. He had misinterpreted the words
of Jesus from John 14: 2, 'In my Father's house are many rooms',
to support his doctrine of apartheid saying that even in heaven
there are different residential areas for the different races. 'If the
Dean has so rooted an objection to political preachers, why was
Mr. Lardner-Burke ever invited to preach in the Cathedral?'
one priest asked. 'Irresponsible', 'provocative', 'shameful',
'shocking', responded other Salisbury clergy, rallying to my
defence. Had the Anglican Cathedral, situated next to Smith's
Parliament Building, become prisoner of a limited gospel which
would not offend those in power? Was I banned because I was
a black politician, and therefore—by white logic—a communist?

My hosts, the Salisbury African Ministers' Fraternal, accepted
me for what I was—*both* a bishop *and* President of the African
National Council. They decided rather than cancel the service,
or change the speaker, to change the venue and move to a
Roman Catholic church. The congregation on May 31 overflowed
St Peter's in Harare, an African suburb of Salisbury. Between the
varicoloured unforms of women of different denominations I
was glad to see several white Christians who had chosen to affirm
their unity with us. I spoke on 'Christian Unity' and found it
meaningful to be doing so for the first time in a Catholic church.

This support by fellow Christians helped fill a void left by
the departure of my close colleague, Rev. Canaan Banana.
Several weeks before, the ANC Vice-President had shared with
me his desire to go abroad for studies. 'I have been offered a
place at Wesley in Washington DC, with a generous scholarship,'
he said. 'I know that I have no passport, but I have to go.'

'I don't object to your going for higher studies,' I replied,
'but this could be used against you politically.'

The next time we talked I knew his mind was made up. 'I have to go,' Canaan repeated. 'I have calculated the chances, and I will take the risks.' Still his going left our ANC without a second strong national spokesman.

Talks with Smith

From April to September 1973 the Smith regime re-affirmed its position that the Smith-Home Settlement Proposals of 1971 must continue to form the basis for any constitutional agreement. In private, however, the ANC received indications of a change in attitude. The first came in June from Sir Denis Greenhill, the permanent head of the UK Foreign Office. He arranged a meeting of some of my ANC colleagues with Mr. Lance Smith, the Internal Affairs Minister.

Next, Rhodesian Front officials, led by their chief negotiator and Secretary of the Cabinet, Mr. Jack Gaylord, and the Attorney General, E. A. T. Smith, proposed a further meeting with us. When we met I presented the ANC settlement proposals in which we demanded immediate parity of African representation in the House of Assembly as well as repeal of the hated Land Tenure Act.

Many people, including every journalist who came to Rhodesia, pressed my colleagues and me to reveal and publish our settlement proposals. As time was not ripe for such a political move we refused. To do so, we believed, would cause many whites to panic and refuse any support for a constitutional conference, which was long overdue. One must appreciate that at that time we were working from a position of weakness, rather than one of strength.

In public Smith announced that the ANC demands were 'totally and absolutely unacceptable, individually and as a whole'. He called them 'nothing less than the old parrot-cry for ' "one man, one vote" ', and called for no further concessions by whites.

It was a surprise, therefore, when Mr. Chad Chipunza came to say that the Prime Minister was eager to meet with me. Chipunza disclosed that he was in close contact with Mr. Lance Smith, and suggested that if I went to talk to Ian Smith in my capacity as President of the ANC it would be possible to reach a constitutional agreement.

Our first official meeting took place on July 17 Mr. Chipunza, who had been instrumental in arranging it, accompanied me, while Mr. Smith was supported by the same officials who had negotiated with the British Government the Smith-Home Settlement Proposals.

Mr. Smith opened the meeting by reading a prepared statement which set forth his position; he wanted acceptance of the Settlement Proposals which the African people had massively rejected. Next I presented an ANC memorandum stating our constitutional proposals. 'If these demands can be granted,' I said, 'then we can find a solution and settle the constitutional dispute.' In discussion we explored certain basic rights to be guaranteed by a new constitution: African representation in Parliament, universal franchise, removing racial discrimination, and increasing African employment in the civil service.

My colleagues were glad to hear of the open discussion held on the ANC's demands, but they were concerned that I had signed Mr. Smith's preliminary statement. The next day I determined to clarify this matter. I proposed to Mr. Smith that we insert on the signed document that I had accepted and signed it 'as a basis of discussion.' Each of us pulled out our copies, and I inserted the words 'as a basis of discussion' on mine. Jack Gaylord took Mr. Smith's copy and appeared to insert the same words on it. When later Mr. Smith released the document to the press I was astonished to read in the *Rhodesia Herald* an unaltered version. To me this was deliberate endeavour to discredit me. Mr. Smith wanted to convince the public that I had accepted the Smith-Home Proposals. The truth is that I wanted to put aside the points which the ANC had already rejected, and to build a new consensus starting with those points upon which we could agree.

I must confess that my ANC Executive became increasingly restive about the talks with Ian Smith. On July 31 the regime threw into political detention our acting Deputy President, Mr. Nason K. Ndhlovu, and Mr. John Chirisa, the acting National Organizing Secretary. The following day I announced that twenty of our ANC leaders had been arrested. Some of our leaders urged me to break off all talks with Mr. Smith. Among the most vocal was Mr. Edson Zvobgo, our ANC Director of External Mission, who resigned on September 14 to become Secretary-General of ZANU, which he said was 'waging an heroic armed struggle'. Nevertheless, the ANC Executive closed ranks and declared on October 13 their 'unshakeable support' of me as President.

Was there any point in talking further with Mr. Smith? we

wondered. In December I issued an ANC statement to let the people know of our frustration. We said that the talks were becoming 'a meaningless exercise' as the Smith regime wanted a settlement 'strictly on their own terms'.

Our discussions with Mr. Smith and his team continued sporadically in 1974. From our side the ANC Executive insisted that Mr. Chad Chipunza be dropped from the negotiating team, as he was not an ANC member. Instead our Vice-President, Dr. Elliot Gabellah, accompanied me.

Negotiations focused on African representation in Parliament. In these discussions we found Mr. Jack Gaylord to be very clever in twisting what had been said. One day he presented Mr. Smith's final offer of six additional African seats in Parliament. Dr. Gabellah and I responded that we would present this offer to the ANC National Executive as part of our progress report. For fifteen minutes Ian Smith attempted to persuade Dr. Gabellah and me to sign the statement. This time I saw through their deceit. If I did so, Smith would present to the press my agreement to six seats as if this were my proposal. The ANC Executive, of course, rejected the offer of six parliamentary seats, but re-endorsed its genuine willingness to pursue possibilities of a negotiated settlement.

While some Zimbabwean politicians doubted the rightness of our approach, the United Nations confirmed it in a dramatic way. On December 10 the UNO granted me its Human Rights Award. This honour was bestowed in a General Assembly session which marked the 25th anniversary of the Universal Declaration of Human Rights. The Assembly's President, Leopold Benites of Ecuador, opened the ceremony by deploring the cause of my absence—the Smith regime's seizure of my passport. 'Bishop Muzorewa, with complete self-abnegation and in extremely difficult circumstances,' he said, 'is working to defend human rights in Southern Rhodesia.' I felt that the award was truly to all Zimbabweans who share this struggle, and that I was being honoured as their elected spokesman.

Time Is Running Out

Since December 16, 1971, the African National Council has been led by those chosen by a nominating committee. In 1974 pressures had eased somewhat and it seemed opportune for Zimbabweans to get together to elect their leaders. To that end I called for the

Inaugural Congress of the ANC to be held at Stodart Hall in Harare Township, Salisbury, on March 2-3, 1974.

After welcoming the eight hundred delegates assembled from all corners of the land, I defined the ANC's constitutional demands as follows: a common electoral roll; a franchise qualification whereby the majority of the people of Rhodesia would obtain the vote; and representation in Parliament which would be 'a satisfactory sharing of power'. I reiterated the call for an immediate constitutional conference. 'A transfer of power to the African majority,' I declared, 'is the only way to stop the current confrontation which has brought atrocities and oppression against the black majority, and has made all white people the slaves of fear.' I assured those Africans who disliked talks between the ANC and the Smith regime that there 'would never be a sell-out'. The delegates responded by confirming me and the entire National Executive in our positions.

Intensified guerrilla activity, however, was not enough in 1974 to lead Mr. Smith to see the light. Instead, he launched an abortive 'Settler 1974' campaign to attract one million new white immigrants to Rhodesia. I joined with other churchmen in denouncing this campaign, warning that it was destroying whatever goodwill had been built up among Africans towards Europeans, as it was being conducted at the expense of the people who were already in the country.

In June 1974 the ANC publicly rejected the regime's latest constitutional proposals. We pointed out that six additional seats offered to Africans in Parliament would not break the white two-thirds majority stranglehold.

Within a week Dr. Edson Sithole, our ANC Publicity Secretary, who had announced our rejection of the constitutional proposals, was arrested and detained. 'How can we be expected to continue talks when our negotiators are being seized?' I asked reporters.

Next Mr. Smith proposed round-table conferences in which a number of African groups, including the spurious pro-settlement groups, the chiefs, and MPs, would be invited to attend along with the ANC. The ANC Executive rejected this plan, agreeing to attend only 'a full constitutional conference . . . with all genuine leaders of political parties, the detained leaders, and the British Government'.

At Sinoia, close to the war zone, I outlined on August 18 our ANC position:

'We want a conference which is capable of discussing and producing an honourable agreement which would disarm and soon stop the legal, social, political and physical violence which is now being inflicted upon the people of Rhodesia.

'We want a conference which is capable of putting our country socially and politically right-side up. Today it is upside-down because ninety-five per cent of our people are ruled without their consent and the quality of a man is measured by the colour of his skin.

'The type of conference we want should be good enough to call for a ceasefire to the present senseless and immoral civil war where our good, innocent people—black and white—are being forced to fight and be killed. We want the kind of conference which could work out a plan whereby there might be peace and harmony in the nation.'

The Church as Critic
Throughout these busy months of political activity I continued my responsibilities as United Methodist bishop. Sometimes the two roles collided with embarrasing results not only for myself, but also for others. One such occasion involved United Methodist leaders from the USA and various African countries who were scheduled to meet in Malawi in January 1974. Unfortunately, the proposed consultation coincided with the visit of Sir Alec Douglas-Home to that country. When my political rivals circulated the rumour that I would be going to Blantyre for secret meetings with Sir Alec, the Malawi Government suddenly denied permission for our church to meet there. Hastily it was agreed to hold it in Salisbury—a propaganda coup for the Smith regime which could trumpet its 'liberalism' in contrast to the policy of Dr. Banda's Malawi.

In July 1973 the United Theological College in Salisbury invited me to be guest preacher for their Epworth Day. I planned to preach on 'Turning the World Right Side Up'. As part of my message I said: "Bearing the cross of Christ means something far different from the current practice of wearing it as a piece of jewellery. It means witnessing, suffering and even dying for what we believe to be true.'

The service was held out-of-doors in front of the college chapel. A large crowd attended. In front of me was a wooden cross as part of the worship centre. On the spur of the moment, at the time when I was stressing the true meaning of bearing the cross, I was moved to seize that wooden symbol and dash it to the ground. The crowd gasped, and some, afterwards, criticized me for my indiscretion; but my point struck home that day.

I was not the only 'political parson' during these troubled months of our nation's history. The tragedy was that the issue of violence caused a rift between Christian leaders.

Certain white clergy were so vocal in their opposition to violent revolution that they approved what the Smith regime called the 'maintenance of law and order'. Fr. Arthur Lewis of the Anglican Church was their spokesman and 'The Rhodesia Christian Group' became his small coterie of supporters. Fr. Lewis viewed communism as the anti-Christ, the World Council of Churches as its ally, and 'one man-one vote' and violent revolution (called 'terrorism') as the false gospel. He credited the partnership of colonialism and Christian missions for bringing peace and the advancement of the African people in the past and believed that the same partnership would promote a 'Christian' Rhodesia. In his statements one looks in vain for a prophetic judgment on white-settler rule.

In contrast to Fr. Lewis, the Christian Council of Rhodesia continued to call for African majority rule and the end to repressive measures by the Smith regime. In its September 1972 statement the Council called for: (1) 'the swiftest possible abolition of every form of racial discrimination, including inequitable land tenure'; (2) 'giving Africans practical experience in government'; (3) 'education of all races on how to live in a multi-racial society'; and (4) 'increased opportunity for all people to meet on terms of equality.'

'Time is rapidly running out,' the Council warned. However, in the tension between white Christians who opposed guerrilla warfare for Zimbabwe's liberation and African Christians who supported it, the Council could not agree on a programme to transform vague goals into concrete objectives.

It was the Catholics who championed most effectively the cause of the oppressed. Bishop Donal Lamont of Umtali called the Smith regime with its oppressive laws 'the real terrorists'. He said: 'The Rhodesian system which keeps a whole people in subjection differs not in essence, but only in degree, from the Nazi doctrine of racial superiority.'

Rather than arrest the outspoken Bishop, the Smith regime

silenced *Moto,* the weekly newspaper of the Catholic Diocese of Gwelo, which many Africans accepted as their national voice. Fr. Albert Plangger, the editor, was sentenced to five month's imprisonment in November 1972 for publishing the Bishop's statement. In September 1974 the paper incurred the further wrath of the minority regime when it published a fiery speech I had made congratulating the people of Mozambique on their victories over colonialism. This was too much for Mr. Lardner-Burke. He banned the paper in November, quoting my speech as one of the reasons. I felt badly that my words had provoked such repression.

The Commission for Justice and Peace, composed of leading laymen and clergy, was another significant Catholic initiative. During 1974 they documented the growing evidence of atrocities by the security forces against tribesmen in north-eastern Rhodesia. Later these findings were published as *Man in the Middle,* and *Civil War in Rhodesia.* The Minister of Law and Order responded in Parliament by rejecting the call for a commission of inquiry as 'a Communist ploy'. Mr. Lardner-Burke accused the Catholic bishops of 'trying to undermine lawful authority'. He accused them of 'provoking a confrontation between Church and State'. So conclusive was the documentary evidence collected, however, that three Anglican bishops and two Methodist ministers joined with the Catholic bishops in August in presenting a dossier of ten documented cases and a call for an official inquiry.

In October 1974, speaking as President of the African National Council to a gathering in Fort Victoria, I joined in the call for a judicial inquiry. Because I had no confidence in any inquiry set up exclusively by the white ruling minority, I called for a joint ANC-RF Commission, one whose report could be accepted by all the people as truth concerning the atrocities being committed.

Persistently I continued to call for a constitutional conference. Yet it seemed that we had reached a stalemate. It was quite clear that the Rhodesian Front could not get international acceptance of any new constitutional proposals without the ANC's consent, yet every recommendation which we made was rejected. We were locked together like two wrestlers, neither of whom was strong enough to pin down the other.

Chapter 12

Fragile Unity

During the middle of 1974 a political earthquake altered the face of southern Africa. The military coup which toppled the government of Marcello Caetano in metropolitan Portugal weakened the Portuguese hold on Mozambique and other Portuguese colonies in Africa. By September 20 a transition government was in control in Lourenço Marques (now Maputo). It was led by FRELIMO's head, Samora Machel. The Mozambique liberation movement through a tenacious thirteen-year armed struggle ended 400 years of colonial rule.

These events had a profound psychological effect on Rhodesia's population, both black and white. Whites started to panic. A seven hundred mile border was now open for Zimbabwean guerrillas to intensify the liberation struggle. Rhodesia was no longer part of a solid phalanx of white-ruled states stretching across Southern Africa. Instead it now stuck out like a sore thumb thrust into black-ruled Africa.

Black leaders in Zimbabwe, however, were elated. Ultimate victory had never been doubted, but now majority rule emerged as a goal to be gained in the near future. When a journalist asked my reaction I said, 'The hand of God is at work in southern Africa.'

Detente

It was Prime Minister John Vorster of South Africa who initiated detente when he became cognizant of the new thrust upon his borders. On October 23, 1974, he announced to the South African Senate: 'Southern Africa is at the crossroads and has to choose now between peace and escalating conflict . . . The price of confrontation would be high, too high for Southern Africa.' He called upon Rhodesia and her neighbours to make sustained efforts to reduce tensions, and 'for all who have influence to bring it to bear to find a durable solution so that internal and external relations can be normalized'.

President Kenneth Kaunda of Zambia responded warmly three days later, saying, 'This, I dare say, is the voice of reason for which Africa and the rest of the world have waited.' Dr. Kaunda was facing pressing economic problems in Zambia. He wanted closer relations with the South. On October 28 Mr. Vorster was back on the air expressing appreciation for and endorsing Dr. Kaunda's stance. The detente stew was well and truly on the boil.

One morning in early November I received a telephone call from Mr. Gaylord, Secretary to the Cabinet of Mr. Ian Smith, saying, 'There is someone who would like to see you, but I can't say who over the telephone. We could arrange for a place for you to meet him.'

During those days I and the ANC Executive had become thoroughly disillusioned about further private talks with Mr. Smith and his men. They seemed a fruitless exercise. In public I had demanded that Smith release all detainees so that we might have a constitutional conference on Zimbabwe with all our leaders present. Private talks were misunderstood.

I said in reply to Mr. Gaylord: 'You can tell the person in question to come to my office or to my house, if it is after hours.'

'Let me think it over,' he replied. After some time he called again and made an appointment to meet me at my own home.

The hour arrived. With Mr. Gaylord came Mr. Derek Robinson, the head of the government's security forces.

'President Kaunda would like to see you in Lusaka,' they announced. 'You are required to come with one other person of your choosing,' continued Mr. Robinson. 'The man who wanted to see you was a messenger from Zambia, Mr. Mark Chona, but he had to catch his plane.'

I sensed that this request for talks offered something new. If President Kaunda had called and asked Smith's men to deliver the message then he must be proposing serious business.

But looking at these men many old frustrations and annoyances welled up within me. These were the people who were still confiscating my passport, even while admitting that I have a part to play in political negotiations for Zimbabwe's liberation.

'No,' I replied, 'I am not going to go, since I do not have my passport.'

'You don't need a passport,' Mr. Robinson replied. 'You will go by chartered plane.'

'I feel very strongly about the withholding of my passport.' I replied.

That night I considered the matter carefully. I realized that to refuse to go without a passport would serve as an effective protest, but it would appear that I had snubbed Dr. Kaunda and his initiative. I determined, therefore, to swallow my feelings and go.

I called Dr. Elliott Gabellah by phone in Bulawayo. All I could say was, 'Please come over, but bring enough clothes to last about seven days.'

The next day we were taken to the New Sarum Air Base at the Salisbury airport not knowing what was ahead.

Our first surprise there was to meet Mr. Joshua Nkomo and Mr. Joseph Msika who had just received a temporary release from detention. It had been almost ten years since I had first met Mr. Nkomo during my 1965 visit to Gonakudzingwa where he had been detained. During those years Mr. Msika had been detained with him as ZAPU's spokesman for foreign affairs. We learned that Rev. Ndabaningi Sithole, former leader of ZANU, was supposed to join us.

This was exciting. The ANC since December 1971 had been demanding that all detainees, including Nkomo and Sithole, be released, but to no avail. Now, apparently, it only took a word from Mr. Vorster of South Africa to bring it about.

The four of us travelled together in a small but fast jet. Lusaka is only forty-five minutes from Salisbury by air, although a day's drive by road. Within a few hours we began discussions with those who had called for us—Presidents Kenneth Kaunda of Zambia, Julius Nyerere of Tanzania, Sir Seretse Khama of Botswana, as well as Sr. Samora Machel, President of the Mozambique Liberation Front (FRELIMO).

The Presidents informed us that they hoped to help build Zimbabwean political unity. New divisions, however, aborted our discussions.

Later I learned that Dr. Kaunda originally wanted only Mr. Nkomo and the detained former ZAPU leaders to be released. When the other Presidents opposed this plan to sanction Mr. Nkomo as Zimbabwe's sole leader, Rev. Sithole was called as well. Instead of Sithole, Mr. Robert Mugabe and Mr. Morton

Malianga arrived in Lusaka, saying, 'The ZANU Executive in prison has deposed Rev. Sithole as our leader and selected Mr. Mugabe in his place.' The four Presidents questioned how Mr. Mugabe with about six of his colleagues could depose a leader who had been chosen by the entire party. Kaunda, Nyerere and others replied: 'We recognize only Mr. Sithole as President of ZANU and insist that he be released from detention and come to Lusaka.' The subject of leaders for Zimbabwe was to be discussed with him representing ZANU. However, it was to be a week before Rev. Sithole reached Lusaka, and by then the rest of us had gone home.

Dr. Kaunda proceeded to table for future discussion his unity proposal—that Mr. Nkomo should be President of a united ANC, with myself as Vice-President and Rev. Sithole as Secretary-General.

The next morning, before leaving State House in Lusaka, I chanced upon Mr. Mugabe and Mr. Malianga eating breakfast.

This was my first contact with Mr. Mugabe. He had become active in Zimbabwean politics during my years of study in the USA and was already in political detention when I returned. I had imagined him to be a tall big-shouldered man with a wide face. Perhaps that was my image of a militant Zimbabwean politician. Instead before me stood a slender figure.

There was to be no doubt, however, about the intensity of Mr. Mugabe's feelings. After exchanging greetings he suddenly said to me, 'What are your people doing there?'

'What do you mean?' I asked, not being quite sure what he was talking about.

He explained that he wanted to know what we were doing politically inside Rhodesia since he and others were put in political detention. '*Mumazuva edu, moto moto!*'—'During our time it was really fire!', he said in both Shona and English to emphasize the point.

'What did you do?' I asked. 'What do you mean, "moto, moto?"'

'We demanded one-man, one-vote,' Mr. Mugabe replied.

Two years later at the Geneva Conference I recalled this incident. At that time Mr. Mugabe pressed for quite a different position, arguing that Zimbabweans should not set up a transitional government on the basis of one-man, one-vote, whereas I would be the staunch defender of one-man, one-vote which he had advocated in Lusaka at our first meeting.

Declaration of Unity

Upon our return to Salisbury, Messrs. Nkomo, Msika, Mugabe, Malianga and Rev. Sithole were put into detention once again. We did not know whether or not the conversations initiated in Lusaka would be resumed.

The answer soon came. At the end of November an official of Smith's CID entered my office with the message, 'You are to go back to Zambia. President Kaunda and his colleagues are calling again for Zimbabwe's political leaders. You are being asked to bring with you six of your Executive men. Even if they are in detention, we will see to it that they are available.'

I almost doubted that good news. At last we were getting somewhere. It was too good to be true, that we should hear the promise of release of our detained brothers from the lips of the ones who had slapped them into detention.

'I need Dr. Edson Sithole,' I replied.

'Yes, he will be released,' came the response.

I almost said, 'Are you sure?' But I knew then that the pendulum was beginning to swing in the right direction. Great things were beginning to happen.

The following day the Special Branch phoned again—this time with the message that Dr. Edson Sithole wanted me to bring his clothes to the airport.

The following day's reunion at the New Sarum airport was a joyous celebration, as we hugged our brothers released from detention. We danced for joy as feuding brothers might be expected to do at a marriage feast. Yet we represented rival groups—six each from former ZAPU and ZANU, and six from the ANC. Six leaders from FROLIZI* would join us in Lusaka.

As we sat down together in Lusaka I knew it would be difficult to reach agreements. We faced almost a week of hard bargaining, of give and take.

All of us recognized the paramount need for unity in the Zimbabwe liberation struggle. Even the issue of what methods were to be used did not prove insurmountable. We all agreed to recognize 'the inevitability of continued armed struggle', along with diplomacy, until we achieved the total liberation of Zimbabwe.

Unfortunately the question of leadership once again divided us. When the leaders of ZANU, ZAPU, FROLIZI and the ANC agreed to unite in the African National Council (ANC) I offered

* Front for the Liberation of Zimbabwe.

142

to step down if that would advance our unity. In fact I went outside for more than three hours while the question of leadership was discussed.

First the Zimbabwean leaders considered but rejected the Presidents' proposal—tabled earlier by Dr. Kaunda—that Mr. Joshua Nkomo be President of the ANC, and that I serve as Vice-President, and Rev. Sithole serve as Secretary-General. ZANU members reacted negatively to this proposal.

Next the group considered naming Rev. Sithole as President, but it was argued that former ZAPU members could not accept his leadership.

Finally, when everybody was losing hope, I was asked to become the President of a United ANC.

'I feel the tallest man in the world!' These were the opening words of my brief speech, delivered after the historic signing of the Declaration of Unity at State House, Lusaka on December 7, 1974. On that day we announced a major breakthrough after ten years of fighting amongst ourselves.

Our Declaration of Unity committed us to unite in one African National Council (See Appendix C). Under the agreement each of the presidents of ZANU, ZAPU, and FROLIZI, together with three other persons appointed by them, would join an enlarged ANC Executive, over which I would preside as President. The enlarged Executive was to prepare for a party Congress to be held within four months. At that time the Congress would adopt a revised ANC Constitution, elect leaders for the united ANC, and adopt a statement of policy. We agreed also to rally our people behind the united ANC and to take steps to merge our respective organizations into the structure of the ANC before the impending party Congress.

No Settlement

There were two Lusaka talks, not one, going on during that week. While Zimbabwean leaders wrestled to find unity, the Presidents of Zambia, Tanzania and Botswana discussed with delegations from the Smith regime and the South African Government the question of detente. It was the non-Zimbabweans who talked about a ceasefire, the withdrawal of South African troops from Rhodesia, and the convening of a constitutional conference. No Zimbabwean was involved, at least openly.

'We can't send you back to prison again,' Mr. Mark Chona

repeatedly said to us. Only by such comments did we get an inkling of what was being discussed by the Presidents. We also learned that Ian Smith began to demand an answer as he asked from Salisbury, 'When are you going to send my people back?' Evidently the time he had agreed to permit the detainees to stay in Lusaka had expired. We felt like pawns in a game to which we had not been invited as full participants. It became obvious that Smith would re-detain, or re-imprison the Zimbabweans who had been released for the Lusaka talks unless certain conditions were met. Only an immediate and total ceasefire in the liberation war would satisfy him.

That was where the deadlock occurred. I had had enough of futile conferences with Mr. Smith about a new constitution. Stop the freedom fighters and his conversations with us would once again be empty words signifying nothing. That is why we of the united ANC said that we would not attend a constitutional conference until the Smith regime first released all political detainees, restrictees and prisoners, revoked the death sentence on political prisoners and released them, granted a general amnesty for political exiles, created conditions allowing free political activity in the country, halted political trials, and lifted the state of emergency.

We understood that President Nyerere raised another issue that resulted in the deadlock at the talks. 'We are not here to discuss majority rule in ten years or in five years time, but immediate majority rule.' Nyerere said. Later Smith charged that this demand killed a potential agreement supported by government leaders from South Africa to Zambia.

During the talks, however, Ian Smith tried to create the mirage of agreement where it did not exist. On December 11 he announced on Rhodesia radio:

'I have received assurances to the effect that terrorist activities in Rhodesia will cease immediately, and secondly, that the proposed constitutional conference will take place without any preconditions.

'Accordingly, I have agreed to release the African leaders from detention and restriction, and their followers as well. They will be permitted to engage in normal activity in terms of the laws applicable to all Rhodesians. I am taking this action on the firm understanding that everyone concerned will conduct themselves peacefully and within the law. This will, I believe, create the right atmosphere for the holding of a constitutional conference.'

What followed further confused the situation. Smith took a long time to release detainees, and when he did he freed only one-third of them. He then went on to have pamphlets dropped in the operational areas telling the combatants that the fighting was over and that all guerrillas should surrender to the nearest government officials. So infuriated were the guerrillas with the apparent betrayal by Zimbabwean leaders that they adopted the slogan, 'Down with detente'.

Theirs, however, were not the voices heard on December 12 when Mr. Nkomo, Rev. Sithole and I, with our delegations, turned toward home. First we heard the cheering thousands at Lusaka International Airport while President Kaunda and his entire cabinet bid us farewell. The jubilation surpassed even the welcomes given a few days earlier to Presidents Nyerere and Khama and President-to-be Machel of Mozambique.

In Salisbury our people surged forward to embrace us with shouts of victory, and to transport us like heroes to the African township of Highfield. For thousands of joyous supporters this was the first occasion in ten years to see Joshua Nkomo, Ndabaningi Sithole and other ex-detainees.

'The Rhodesian Front has in the past sought independence on the basis of minority rule,' I declared after the crowd had quietened to listen. 'We reject that. The independence that we have sought, and the independence that we still seek, is independence based on majority rule.'

Then, recognizing the anxiety of many whites within the country, I continued: 'We are not racists. We accept the right of white Rhodesians to live in Rhodesia and to have the same rights and obligations of citizenship as their fellow Rhodesians of the majority community, without discrimination on the grounds of race, colour, or creed.'

That was the most optimistic interpretation of the Lusaka talks that could be given. Rev. Sithole soon presented another reaction. He said, 'There is no way we can reach an accommodation because the Rhodesian Government is dedicated to minority rule, and until they change that position I cannot see how we can reach an accommodation.'

In the weeks which followed one effort and then another was made to continue the momentum of the Lusaka talks. First, Mr.

James Callaghan, the UK Foreign and Commonwealth Secretary, visited various African countries to seek for a common policy towards a constitutional settlement in Rhodesia. We of the ANC doubted that Mr. Smith wanted the liberation leaders to return to Lusaka to meet Callaghan, for the Zambian Government's plane to transport them was denied landing rights in Salisbury.

Mr. Callaghan expressed the British view that the contending parties within Rhodesia should negotiate a constitutional settlement. During February we tried to do just that. Twice I led a five-man delegation, including Mr. Nkomo and Rev. Sithole, in talks with Ian Smith. But our conversations remained procedural, not substantive.

Smith had stated repeatedly that his government was not prepared to hand over power to the African majority. On our side we said we would agree to nothing less than majority rule within one year. Smith constantly referred to the 'cessation of hostilities' as a precondition to any constitutional talks. We realized that it was the guerrilla incursions into Rhodesia (Zimbabwe) which had forced Smith to want to talk with us as political leaders. All the former ZANU members amongst us were adamant in refusing to allow our negotiations to hinge upon a 'ceasefire' or 'cessation of hostilities'.

With this gulf between white and Zimbabwean negotiators, we confined our discussions to issues of whether a constitutional conference should be held inside or outside Rhodesia, and who should be invited to chair the proceedings. To me those discussions were like a car spinning its wheels in the sand.

Midway in the Smith-ANC discussions I travelled with our top ANC leaders to Dar-es-Salaam and Lusaka to brief the Front-line Presidents, as well as Mr. James Chikerema and other ANC leaders outside Rhodesia. From Dar-es-Salaam I announced to the press our continued hope for a constitutional conference and a political settlement. 'If the talks fail,' I warned, 'then the ANC considers war in Rhodesia inevitable.'

The Difficult Reconciliation of Brothers with Guns

As ANC President, my frustration over Smith's obstinacy was eclipsed by fractious rivalries among our own members. The masses who welcomed us back from Lusaka on December 14 wept tears of joy upon seeing Joshua Nkomo, Ndabaningi Sithole, and me walking arm in arm. They hoped that at last the

The wedding, August 11, 1951.

Bishop and Mrs. Muzorewa and children. *Front, left to right:* Maggie, Charity, Chido, Abel. *Behind, left to right:* Blessing, Wesley, Philemon (1969).

The day the church voted for Bishop Muzorewa to go into the Ministry.

Graduating class, Hartzell Theological School, 1952. *From left to right*: Marshall Warne Murphree, Nason Madzinga, John Bunyan Jijita, Bishop Ralph E. Dodge, Abel Tendekai Muzorewa, Davison Mushapaidze, Jonah Benjamin Kawadza, Simon Kawo.

Bishop Dodge presiding at the consecration of Bishop Muzorewa, with Bishop S. T. Nagbe of Liberia and Bishop John Wesley Shungu of Zaire, August, 1968.

With Chief Isaiah Maranke in 1969.

Church leaders after meeting with Ian Smith to oppose the Land Tenure
Act, June, 1970. *Left to right:* Rt. Rev. Paul Burrough (Anglican), Rev.
Christopher Chikasha (African Reformed), Bishop Abel Muzorewa (United
Methodist), Rt. Rev. Donal Lamont (Catholic, partially hidden), Rev.
Andrew Ndhlela (Methodist), and Fr. Richard Randolph (Catholic).

Protest against banning of Bishop Muzorewa from Tribal Trust Lands, Salisbury, September, 1970.

Bishop Muzorewa with Chief Rekayi Tangwena, November, 1970.

Bishop Muzorewa showing gifts of spear and club presented at the ANC Inaugural Congress, Salisbury, March 2, 1974.

Bishop Muzorewa with women leaders of the United African National Council, Salisbury, August, 1977.

The United Methodist delegates from Zimbabwe at the Church's Africa Central Conference held in Kitwe, Zambia, which elected Muzorewa a life bishop, August, 1976.

Delegates at the Geneva Peace Talks, 1976.

Robert Mugabe, Leader of ZANU   Joshua Nkomo, joint Leader of the
Patriotic Front.
Rhodesia

Above left: President Kenneth Kaunda of Zambia.
Above right: Dr. Julius Nyerere, President of Tanzania.

Ian Smith arriving at the Geneva Peace Talks in 1976.

Senator Jeremiah Chirau.

Rev. Ndabaningi Sithole, co-founder of ZANU

Bishop Muzorewa talking to David Owen (Britain's Foreign Secretary) and Andrew Young (United States Ambassador to the United Nations).

Victims of the Nhazonia massacre of Zimbabwean refugees, Mozambique, August, 1976.

children of Zimbabwe who had spent ten years fighting and killing each other had come to their senses and had buried their differences. But that great hope and expectation soon faded as old rivalries emerged. The catalyst was our Lusaka agreement to hold an ANC Party Congress within four months to elect the leadership of a unified movement.

From the first the executive meetings of the 'united' ANC were characterized by open hostility between leaders of rival factions. This was in striking contrast to the peaceful and democratic procedure which we had enjoyed since the ANC began in December 1971. We of the original ANC feared that all the good work for unity which we had accomplished was now to be dashed on the rocks of the old ten-year ZAPU/ZANU rivalry. I realized that such a rivalry could not be healed overnight. There needed to be a re-orientation of all parties concerning the meaning and structures of our new unity. What I did not expect was that Zimbabwean politicians would emerge from detention and imprisonment with the same fixed attitudes and hatreds towards other Zimbabweans which they had held in 1964. Their release was like opening Pandora's box.

Some of our leaders, mostly formerly of ZAPU, referred to the united ANC as a 'unity of purpose' or 'common front'. Although outwardly co-operative, they held secret meetings. Openly they pressed for the holding of the ANC Congress, confident that they could get their way. 'Our leader, *Mudara* (the Old Man),' they boasted, 'is the traditional, automatic choice.' 'After all,' they said, 'Muzorewa is only a bishop without political experience.'

Former ZANU leaders, on the other hand, were more openly critical. They continued to hold ZANU meetings and referred to the ANC as an 'umbrella organization', implying its transient nature.

Reports circulated that some ZANU elements went from meeting to meeting, and from house to house, with guns in their pockets, declaring, 'We will use these if Muzorewa or Nkomo is elected President.'

I faced resentment and hostility from both sides. At secret ZAPU meetings they labelled me ZANU, while at ZANU meetings I was called a secret supporter of ZAPU. The ZANU men claimed that the ANC had been formed largely out of former ZAPU branches and was led by former ZAPU officials.

147

They forgot that Mr. Michael Mawema, a former ZANU leader, had been the ANC's first Organizing Secretary.

ZANU continued to broadcast from Lusaka its divisive line. One speaker said: 'If both Mr. Ian Smith and Bishop Muzorewa were put before me, I would choose to shoot Muzorewa first before I shoot Ian Smith.' It sounded like the old story of a family feud between two brothers who went hunting for lions. Upon spotting a lion near his brother the other said to himself, 'I will shoot my brother first and then shoot the lion next!'

That kind of insanity derived both from a renascent tribalism and an insatiable lust for power. It was pathetic that these leaders spent their time scheming to have those of one particular tribe rule Zimbabwe while Zimbabweans of all tribes were suffering and dying to liberate their country. I was unacceptable to them because I did not belong to their particular group. It was alleged that some had said, 'Abel Muzorewa, Joshua Nkomo, and Elliot Gabellah should be shot if the people elect them.'

I was convinced that the Zimbabwean people did not want to return to the vicious intergroup hostilities of the mid-sixties. Chief Mangwende spoke for many when he said in a public rally in Highfields: 'We are now being forced to admit that some of you people should have remained in detention because of the increasing thuggery.'

The former FROLIZI leaders were the exception. Lacking any organization within Rhodesia, they took unity more seriously than others. Although their rivals called them 'a dying party', I welcomed their support of the ANC and of the imperative need for unity at this critical time.

Rev. Sithole Redetained
All the political detainees and restrictees released by the Smith regime in December 1974 lived under the threat of redetention. At times veiled threats made them feel like pawns in the negotiations. Rev. Sithole warned in a January interview: 'Renewed detentions will not help to solve our problems, but will lead to an intensification of the guerrilla war.'

One morning early in March my secretary entered the office and said: 'There is a man who seems to be from the Special Branch who wants to see you.' With mixed feelings I agreed to talk with him.

After greetings he announced, 'I have been sent by the Minister to inform you that one of your Executive members, the Rev. Ndabaningi Sithole, has been detained. We did not want you to hear it over the radio.'

'What is the reason for his redetention?' I asked

The man replied that he did not know, neither was he the one who had served Rev. Sithole with the detention order. An hour later we heard the official announcement on the 10 o'clock news bulletin.

Immediately I called the top ANC officials in and around Salisbury to meet in my office to take appropriate action. With surprise I learned that Mr. Robert Mugabe, the former ZANU leader, had called his own ZANU press conference before I could get in touch with him.

In my press statement I expressed shock at the detention. I called on the Smith regime to prove its allegations by trying Rev. Sithole in open court with witnesses present. I announced: 'The ANC will discontinue any talks with the Government until Rev. Sithole is released.'

The charge against Rev. Sithole, according to the Attorney General's report, was that he conspired to 'assassinate certain influential African politicians'. The list included Joshua Nkomo, Dr. Elliot Gabellah, and myself. Later I went to the High Court to get the details about Rev. Sithole's case. No genuine Zimbabwean could have failed to perceive that this was another fictitious plot fabricated by the Smith regime.

Chitepo's Assassination
Clearly a dramatic move was needed if we of the ANC were to counter Smith's divide-and-rule tactics, as well as the cleavages and rivalries within our own organization. I resolved to address the people of Zimbabwe on radio and television asking them to make unity a reality. To do so I had to go to Zambia, since the Rhodesian communications media were the private preserve of Ian Smith.

Arriving in Lusaka on March 17, 1975, I found another enthusiastic welcoming party. I was glad to see standing together the former external officers of three groups now united in the ANC—Mr. Jason Z. Moyo of ZAPU, Mr. James R. D. Chikerema of FROLIZI, and Mr. Herbert Chitepo of ZANU. They had all been appointed by the ANC's National Executive as its representatives outside Zimbabwe.

At State House, where I was staying, we arranged to meet the following day at 2.00 p.m. Our agenda would be the problems and progress of unity and the liberation struggle. 'Tomorrow I want to meet with just the three of you,' I said, 'so that you can brief me about your work.' Others objected, including some who later were implicated in the crime to be committed, but my plan was accepted. That night I went to bed enthusiastic about the morrow's prospects. We needed very urgently to streamline our party and consolidate our unity.

About nine o'clock the next morning Mr. Mark Chona, President Kaunda's Special Assistant, phoned. I picked up the receiver and heard his message: 'Sir, I am very sorry to tell you that Herbert Chitepo is dead,' he said.

A long pause followed. Finally I responded, 'Mr. Chona, would you please repeat what you have just said.' The conversation continued, but I was utterly heartstricken from shock. Mr. Chona repeated the message and added that Mr. Chitepo had been killed only thirty minutes earlier by a bomb planted in his Volkswagen which went off as he tried to drive out for work.

An hour later I joined President Kaunda to go under tight security to the Chitepo home. Already a crowd of Zimbabwean and Zambian mourners had gathered—family, friends, neighbours, and even enemies of Mr. Chitepo. Slowly we threaded our way through the mourners to express our grief, not only to the Chitepo family, but also to those who were mourning the loss of Mr. Silas Shamiso, one of the bodyguards, and a Zambian neighbour's child, Sambwa Chaya, who also had been killed by the blast.

Returning to State House I prepared a press statement and a revision of my message to the people of Zimbabwe. Soon four leading former officials of ZANU came to my room. Learning that I was about to issue a press statement on behalf of the ANC, they insisted on making their own ZANU statement which they claimed was more militant. I wondered what militancy there was in announcing the tragic death of a nationalist leader. Upon reading their statement I understood why they made it. They highlighted the fact that the Smith regime was directly responsible for the murder of Chitepo in the same manner in which the Portuguese can be held responsible for the assassinations of Dr. Eduardo Mondlane of Mozambique and Amical Cabral of Guinea Bissau. Four months later I would learn that the International Commission on the Assassination of Herbert Chitepo would implicate in Chitepo's death the very men of ZANU who spoke to me that morning.

It was hard for any of us to believe that Zimbabweans could be responsible for this dastardly crime. Herbert Chitepo's dedicated and dynamic leadership in politics resulted from his selfless love of his own people. As Zimbabwe's first African lawyer he had earned the reputation of hardly ever losing cases in Rhodesia's courts. A story is told of one African police sergeant who shivered when he heard that Advocate Chitepo was defending the case in which the sergeant was involved!

But Herbert Chitepo left his successful law practice and later his lucrative post of Director of Public Prosecutions in Tanzania to spearhead the armed struggle against the Ian Smith regime. It was difficult to imagine that Herbert Chitepo had been murdered by his own Zimbabweans.

As the day of Chitepo's funeral approached, Lusaka became a beehive of activity. Mourners gathered from the four corners of Rhodesia (Zimbabwe) and many other African countries. We learned that Ian Smith refused permission for the body to be flown home to Zimbabwe for burial, but that a memorial service would be held at St. Paul's Anglican Church in Highfield, Salisbury.

The funeral itself was the most breathtaking and solemn that I have ever experienced. In recognition of Mr Chitepo's leadership and sacrifices for the liberation of Zimbabwe, the Zambian Government gave him and the two who died with him a full military funeral. President Kaunda, leaders in government, and indeed the entire people of Zambia, participated in the funeral in the same spirit in which they would honour one of their own government officials.

More than 7,000 people thronged Lusaka's Anglican Cathedral to pay their last tribute. Dr. Kaunda read the scripture lessons and I preached.

Then we joined the solemn funeral procession to the Leopards Hill Cemetery. To the slow cadence of the military band we walked to the graveside. Again President Kaunda and I spoke. Like the majority of Zimbabweans I blamed Ian Smith and his racist regime for this barbarous act of murder. Yet I doubted Smith's active hand in it. I therefore gave the benefit of the doubt in my graveside speech, saying: 'It could be a white person using another white person, or a white man using a black man, or a black enemy using a black agent.'

Within four months the Chitepo Commission would verify that my third suggestion was correct. Leaders within ZANU itself had killed Mr. Chitepo. As the grisly story of tribal jealousies unfolded, our horror increased. The murder gang mowed down more than two hundred innocent sons and daughters of Zimbabwe from other tribes. Most of these young and dedicated freedom fighters had left their homes to suffer and, if necessary, to give their blood for the liberation of Zimbabwe. Some died hideous deaths. Some were forced to dig their own graves and then were axed and buried alive. One, Edgar Madekurozwa, was brutally chopped to death with a pickaxe.

Chitepo's death saved many people from possible assassination because the members of the murder gang were arrested. The list of those scheduled for assassination included Mr. Joshua Nkomo, Dr. Elliott Gabellah, myself, and even Rev. Ndabaningi Sithole, the former President of ZANU.

I wept for Zimbabwe, not because I was one of those to be eliminated, but because it was tragic in those crucial days to have some leaders who treated people as worms or insects, to be crushed at whim. The tribal bickering and murders weakened our unity. They retarded our fight for majority rule in Zimbabwe. For a time the morale of the fighting forces sank to a low ebb.

On March 19 I broadcast to our people. I reminded them of the demon of division which divided Zimbabwe during the ZAPU/ZANU split in 1963 and how the country became hell on earth. I said, 'Remember how the demon of violence ravaged our entire country, petrol-bombing to death and maiming innocent children, men and women.' I appealed: 'In the name of Great Zimbabwe, stop all acts of enmity and disunity. The happiness, power and prosperity of Zimbabwe ultimately depend upon our love and dedication for unity, and that unity must be made real NOW.'

Returning to Salisbury, I wondered how free I would be now, and decided to make a test to determine my position. For four years the Smith regime had prohibited my entry into Tribal Trust Lands where three-fourths of our people lived. Since August 1972 I had been denied a passport to travel outside Rhodesia under a bill which implied that I would 'damage the image of Rhodesia abroad'.

Both bans were lifted suddenly. The news broke as United Methodist women leaders of Rhodesia were meeting at Old Umtali. 'Suddenly we found ourselves jumping, dancing, and weeping,' my wife Maggie reported. 'Then we joined in prayers of thanksgiving and a song of victory—*Mwari mukuru, Mwari mukuru, Baba wedu tese* (God is great, God is great, the Father of us all).' A similar outburst of joy took place at our Annual Conference as my passport was returned to me in front of the delegates from each of our churches.

Split Over Congress

Using my new freedom I hastened in May to the United States on church business. However, this was to be my shortest overseas trip due to Mr. Nkomo's desperate bid for leadership of the ANC.

On June 1, 1975, I was sitting in the home of Bishop and Mrs. Francis Kearns of Canton, Ohio, when the bishop came in to say, sadly, 'Abel, there is trouble at home. The police have shot dead eleven of your people. This news has just come over the radio.'

I hurried home to assess the situation. On arrival in Salisbury I learned that power-hungry elements on the National Executive had forced the issue of congress on the agenda. Those of former ZAPU decided to press for a meeting while Rev. Sithole was again in detention and I was overseas. They proposed that the ANC congress be held on June 21.

Meanwhile rival supporters of ZANU and ZAPU clashed outside the Highfield meeting place. ZANU activists demonstrated for *chimurenga* (liberation war) and the expulsion of whites from Rhodesia. ZAPU supporters opposed them, and even assaulted former ZANU members of the National Executive. But it was the presence of white policemen with dogs and guns which excited the people. They threw stones and bricks, and received bullets in reply.

I vetoed the plans to convene an ANC congress, although such an action went against my usual democratic practice. It was increasingly clear that the congress issue threatened the unity within ANC which it was intended to consolidate. The issue diverted us from our liberation struggle into internecine strife and power rivalries.

We had blundered. I felt an urgency to complete several steps which could make unity a reality. We needed to write a new constitution for the enlarged ANC. Existing branches needed restructuring to achieve more equitable representation among the groups now participating in the united ANC. Twenty ANC members comprised a branch in Bulawayo, the former ZAPU stronghold. Meanwhile a Salisbury branch had nearly 1,000 members, for the original ANC and former ZANU had organized only one branch in each African township. Finally, little progress had been made to achieve unification of the fighting forces. The premature holding of a congress would divide us again so that we would fight among ourselves, instead of opposing Smith and his minority regime.

When it seemed obvious that Mr. Nkomo was going all out to divide the people and organize a congress I called him to my home. We talked in my living-room. I was frank and candid. I pointed out that his pushing for a congress would be disastrous, for it would revive conditions like those in 1963-4 and destroy our acquired unity.

That same day I also called the top members of our National Executive to my home. Once again I repeated the same arguments. This time they agreed. In Mr. Nkomo's presence they pointed out that we should be united and not allow the enemy to dissuade us from the goal of majority rule.

Violence at Home

One week later I travelled with my wife to our Church's District Conference at Muchinjike, about sixty miles north-east of Salisbury. After the evening service I persuaded my brother-in-law, Alec Chibanguza, and my sister Clara to take me to their home at the Mrewa United Methodist Centre twenty miles nearer to Salisbury.

As we entered their house the phone rang. It was Maggie's sister, Phoebe Murapa, calling from our home in Salisbury, saying 'They have thrown a bomb at your house'. Fortunately, although the blast shattered most of the windows, no one among the six people sleeping inside was hurt.

We stood in silence as we took in the news. Turning to me, and shaking his head, Alec twice said softly, '*Rhodesia haidi ruponeso* (Rhodesia does not want salvation).'

It was painful to imagine, as we now know, that an African was responsible for this grenade attack on my home. It was puzzling and pathetic that the culprit had by-passed the bases of the enemy, the diabolic Special Branch police of Ian Smith, and the homes of known sell-outs and informers as he came to destroy me at my house. This did not make sense in the priorities of a liberation struggle.

Returning to the District Conference I determined to tell no one, not even my wife, what had taken place—at least until the worship service was over. That morning I preached on 'God is Commanding the World to March Forward'. At the end of the service the district superintendent broke the news to the congregation. The people overflowed with emotion—weeping, praying, and singing liberation songs.

Immediately after pronouncing the benediction I set out for Salisbury, determined to see for myself what the devil had done to my house through his agent. Fortunately the damage could be repaired.

For two weeks our home overflowed with visitors. They followed the gracious customs of our people in expressing sympathy. In fact, I felt almost as if I were attending my own funeral.

One afternoon one of the Christian workers of our church joined the crowd of well-wishers, but soon asked to see Maggie and me alone. I wondered what she was going to say. Normally she was discreet in the extreme, following that indirect approach to one's elders which we had been taught to admire. This day, however, she was different.

Speaking directly to me she said, 'Please, please, my bishop, you should now cease to be President of the ANC and stick to the Church. What you have done so far is enough. Your life is now very short. You are going to be murdered very soon. Also some people, even those in high places in the Church, are criticizing you for being in the ANC. They are saying, "We do not have a bishop". Please listen to me although I am younger and of a lower office in the Church than you are.'

I listened carefully. Looking at Maggie, I felt as if she was looking at the young lady as if to say, 'Tell him; perhaps he will listen to you because I have often told him the same thing.'

I thanked the young lady for coming to register her loving concern. But as she spoke I remembered the words of Jesus, 'Get thee behind me, Satan,'—words the Master addressed to Peter when he wanted Jesus to avoid a confrontation with his enemies.

Then I recalled another scripture passage and asked her to go home and read it each day for a week and then return to tell me what she thought. It is Matthew 16: 24-25:

'If any man would come after me, let him deny himself and take up his cross and follow me. For whoever would save his life will lose it, and whoever loses his life for my sake will find it.'

To Dar-es-Salaam

The bombing of my house was but one evidence of how serious the rift among Zimbabwean politicians had become. I firmly believed that it was inopportune to hold a congress, yet knew that I could not lead the fragile ANC by fiat. I was determined to be democratic, and also to preserve the unity as far as possible.

My next move was to approach the Frontline States through Mr. Mark Chona, Dr. Kaunda's Special Assistant, who was most deeply involved in Zimbabwean affairs. Reaching him by phone I said: 'I want to call a meeting of all the Zimbabweans who attended the Unity Talks in December 1974. Please accord us the facilities so that we can review our progress, examine where we now stand, and lay down a strategy for the future.'

The four Frontline Presidents accepted my request and arranged for us to meet with them in Dar-es-Salaam for three days in July 1975.

Assembling all our leaders was difficult, especially Rev. Sithole who had been redetained. After much diplomacy the Zambian Government advised me that I should submit a formal request for Rev. Sithole's release. They assured me that Smith would release him temporarily in time to join the Zimbabwean delegation to the OAU summit meeting.

Now it seemed as if our delegation would be complete. Next I drew up a list of the delegates who did not have passports, including Rev. Sithole and Mr. Robert Mugabe. I tried to contact Mr. Mugabe, but in vain. ANC staff members, at my request, went all the way to his rural home searching for him, but to no avail. Reluctantly we departed without him, only to learn upon reaching Dar-es-Salaam that he had crossed the border secretly into Mozambique a few days earlier.

Our new unity talks convened in Lusaka where, with President Kaunda, twelve of us discussed the unity of the ANC. Reaching

Dar-es-Salaam on July 5 we widened the consultation to include thirty Zimbabwean leaders and, once again, the Presidents of Zambia, Tanzania, Botswana and Mozambique.

It was plain that the Frontline Presidents were annoyed by our continued dissensions over leadership. They made it clear that the ANC's task was 'to liberate Zimbabwe', and not to provide a forum for the airing of internal differences.

Nevertheless, I felt it imperative to clear the air, both in private and in public, concerning Mr Nkomo's drive for power. First I called Mr. Chikerema, Rev. Sithole and Mr. Nkomo to my room for a discussion. By that time allegations were widespread that Joshua Nkomo was attempting to make a 'secret deal' with Mr. Smith. He reacted sharply when we tried to find out the facts, swore at Mr. Chikerema, banged the door, and walked out.

The open session clarified a second point of contention among us. In his bid for leadership Mr. Nkomo had claimed that he was the one who had been instrumental in forming the African National Council in December 1971. He said that he had instructed me to form the Council, and that therefore I was obligated to him, or under his command. Both Mr. Josiah Chinamano of ZAPU and Dr. Edson Sithole of ZANU stood up to refute this claim. They pointed out that they were the ones who had approached me to head the ANC, and there was no mention that I was to be a provisional leader until Mr. Nkomo gained release from detention. I was relieved to hear that I was not in any way obligated to Mr. Nkomo, and that the Consultative Meeting confirmed that the leadership of the ANC would remain in my hands.

Having clarified the leadership position, we moved on to reconsider our goals and by what strategies we could achieve them. Once again we reasserted the importance of unity among the people of Zimbabwe, and of the intensification of our armed struggle. To accomplish these ends we agreed to halt talks with Mr. Smith, and to postpone indefinitely the holding of an ANC congress. As for the planning of a constitutional conference we reiterated that the onus to hold it rested on the two parties in the dispute—namely the Smith regime and the British Government. We agreed that any constitutional conference must be held outside Rhodesia.

Once again we gave the appearance of being united. Time would tell whether this was a genuine reconciliation.

Chapter 13

Intrigues

The distractions over the holding of an ANC congress ended at the Dar-es-Salaam meeting of July 8, 1975. The most important thing agreed upon was that we were to 'de-escalate talks and escalate the armed struggle'. The Executive agreed that Messrs. Nkomo, Chikerema, Sithole and I would visit the freedom fighter training camps. We were also to reconstitute the external wing of the ANC, the Zimbabwe Liberation Council (ZLC), as had been authorized by the Executive in December following our unity agreement. Finally, we agreed to sit down in Lusaka to draft our constitution, and to formulate a military code for the united ANC army.

At last we were in a position to lay firm foundations for the effective prosecution of the armed struggle. Given honesty and dedication on the part of all concerned, I felt we were set for victory over the racists if unity and harmony could be maintained amongst ourselves. Naturally, we expected our hosts in the Frontline States to respect our desire for a liberation struggle conducted in unity.

Immediately after the Dar-es-Salaam meeting the four appointed leaders of the ANC began our tour of military camps in Tanzania, Mozambique and Zambia. I looked forward to the visits as a united delegation. After a tour of two guerrilla camps in Tanzania we left for Mozambique. But before we had visited any refugee camps there, or the thousands of recruits, President Kaunda summoned us suddenly back to Zambia.

We saw on that interrupted tour, however, some of the priority areas needing immediate attention. Our military cadres and recruits needed to understand our new unity, and to commit themselves to it, rather than to former parties and individual leaders. We lacked materials for the political consciousness-raising of the cadres—a politicization aimed at co-ordinating the internal efforts of the guerrillas and the masses alike. Our ANC external wing needed an administrative structure to give it form, channels of communication, and clear lines of authority. The military High Command, so newly established, had to be consolidated. We desperately needed a code of ethics to be strictly applied. This measure would go a long way towards correcting abuses and excesses which had burgeoned during the earlier inter-tribal fighting in the camps. Furthermore, the High Command needed to establish effective authority and control over the rank and file of the liberation army.

Travelling through Malawi, I issued the following statement to all Zimbabweans on August 5:

'The struggle for the freedom of Zimbabwe has reached a climax, and will soon be at its most dangerous and yet conclusive period. In short, we are at war and it demands our total dedication, commitment and sacrifice . . . We need our freedom now. We want to do everything in our power to end the senseless suffering, the incessant tortures and deaths through massacres our people continue to face in the war zones.'

Strengthening the Zimbabwe Liberation Council

I returned to Lusaka eager to carry out the Dar-es-Salaam mandate that we—the four leaders of the ANC—consolidate the unity of our organization. We agreed to meet for two weeks in Lusaka to work on the priority areas.

The next morning Mr. Nkomo came to my room and said: 'Bishop, I have received word that my wife is very sick. I must leave for home.'

'I am very sorry to hear that,' I responded. 'I would have liked us to work on the assignment to consolidate our party here, but we can't help it.'

'You can call J. Z. Moyo whenever you need me,' Mr. Nkomo added as he left the room.

Our colleague left abruptly for Zimbabwe. It came as a surprise, however, to learn that on arrival he went to a football match in Salisbury, instead of going directly to Bulawayo to be with his ailing wife.

In spite of Mr. Nkomo's absence, the rest of us felt compelled to carry out our responsibilities. First, a small drafting committee of three prepared the major documents. The whole Zimbabwe Liberation Council then met to finalize and approve them.

159

The Zimbabwe Liberation Council was not a different organization from the ANC-Zimbabwe, as some have alleged. It is the external wing of the enlarged ANC. Following the December 1974 Declaration of Unity, the National Executive Council met in Salisbury and authorized the formation of this external wing of the party. The tragic events culminating in the deaths of Herbert Chitepo and others had prevented its implementation earlier.

Four members each from the former ZANU, ZAPU, FROLIZI and ANC formed the initial membership of the ZLC. The National Executive gave them responsibility to meet and choose the officers and chairmen of any committees. They elected Rev. Ndabaningi Sithole as Chairman, Jason Moyo as Vice-Chairman, and James Chikerema as Executive Secretary. It looked on paper like a balanced leadership team—one each from the former parties. Dissension arose, however, when the ZLC elected chairmen for its five standing committees: Education and Welfare, Diplomatic, Finance, Publicity and Information, and Military Affairs. The four former ZAPU members—Messrs. Jason Moyo, Edward Ndhlovu, George Silundika, and Miss Jane Ngwenya—walked out in early September claiming that the ZLC was 'sectional' because they had not been elected to be chairmen of any committees.

In August, however, we appeared to be making solid progress after two weeks of hard work in Lusaka. We discussed drafts of three major documents, entitled 'Disciplinary Code', 'High Command' and 'Statement of Basic Policy'.

We all felt an urgency to form a new High Command to direct the military struggle. I believe that we sought the best leaders possible—persons committed to unity and to the effective prosecution of the liberation war. Eagerly we brought the new High Command to Lusaka for orientation and briefing—a first step towards unifying the cadres. We were engaged in this vital reconstruction when we were interrupted by a call to the Victoria Falls Conference.

Called to Victoria Falls
One evening Ndabaningi Sithole, Jason Moyo, James Chikerema and I received a summons to the Zambian State House. There Dr. Kaunda told us of an 'agreement' to have talks between Ian Smith and the Zimbabwean nationalists.

Often I have been accused of 'betraying' the liberation struggle

160

by talking with Mr. Ian Smith. In fact we of the ANC took over from the Frontline States the plan of having dual strategies for the liberation of Zimbabwe—negotiation and armed struggle.

The Lusaka Manifesto of 1969 remains the definitive statement of policy towards the Zimbabwe liberation struggle by the independent states of East and Central Africa. In it the heads of state declared:

'We would urge our brothers in the resistance movements to use peaceful methods of struggle even at the cost of some compromise on the timing of change. But while peaceful progress is blocked by actions of those at present in power in states of southern Africa, we have no choice but to give the peoples of those territories all the support of which we are capable in their struggle against their oppressors.'

This statement, I believe, supported a dual liberation strategy. While hoping for peaceful struggle, the Frontline States agreed to support armed struggle. This was the strategy I and other ANC leaders continued to follow in August 1975.

On August 6 I visited London with Dr. Elliott Gabellah, at the invitation of the United Kingdom's Foreign and Commonwealth Secretary. Mr. Callaghan wanted to continue the search for a constitutional settlement. We agreed, but stressed our commitment to intensify the armed struggle if he and others failed to persuade the Smith regime to turn over power to the Zimbabwean majority. Our joint statement reflected our mutual concern:

'It was agreed that there is an urgent need to find means of getting discussions started about constitutional changes in Rhodesia to avert the danger of a drift towards intensified armed struggle there.'

Events moved swiftly. On August 8-9 Mr. Ian Smith, with three of his cabinet ministers, met Prime Minister John Vorster of South Africa and Mr. Mark Chona, President Kaunda's special envoy, in Pretoria. Mr. Chona acted on behalf of the Governments of Botswana, Mozambique, Tanzania and Zambia in drawing up what became known as 'The Pretoria Agreement'. It declared:

(a) The Rhodesian Government through its ministerial representatives will meet not later than August 25 on the Victoria Falls Bridge in coaches to be supplied by the South African Government for a formal conference without any preconditions.

(b) The object of the formal meeting is to give the parties the opportunity to publicly express their genuine desire to negotiate an acceptable settlement.

(c) After this the conference is to adjourn to enable the parties to discuss proposals for a settlement in committee or committees within Rhodesia;

(d) Thereafter the parties will meet again in formal conference anywhere decided upon to ratify the committee proposals which have been agreed upon.

(e) The South African Government and the Governments of Botswana, Mozambique, Tanzania and Zambia, respectively, hereby express their willingness to ensure that this agreement is implemented by the two parties involved.

Note that we of the ANC were not a party to this agreement. Dr. Kaunda presented it to us at State House as a *fait accompli*. The meeting, he explained, would be held on Victoria Falls Bridge since the middle of the bridge would be considered a neutral place. He went on to stress the urgency that we agree to meet Mr. Smith there. Mr. Vorster was due to leave shortly for Latin America but was willing to twist Smith's arm to get him to participate. Mr. Mark Chona needed time to brief the other Frontline States and only two weeks remained before the appointed date of August 25.

The following day I called our ANC leaders together in Lusaka to discuss this development. Carefully we examined the 'Pretoria Agreement'. Personally, I found agreeing to participate in the talks one of the most difficult decisions I have had to take. We all felt as Zimbabwean leaders that this agreement had been reached behind our backs. It would drag us away from the armed struggle to which we were committed.

Our frank assessment was that further talks with Ian Smith had no chance of success. Nevertheless, we agreed to give peaceful change another chance.

Immediately we contacted our colleagues at home. I had to select a team to prepare documents to present at the talks. We wanted to draft a solid paper which would set forth our position.

We also needed to finalize our proposals for a constitution for Zimbabwe under African majority rule—a task which we had embarked on long before this, but had not completed.

On August 13 I confirmed our ANC agreement to go to the Falls talks, saying: 'In keeping with our policy as endorsed by our ANC Dar-es-Salaam meeting held last July, we accept the holding of a constitutional conference in order to find a solution to the problems facing Zimbabwe.'

The next day Mr. Smith went on the air giving his interpretation of the Pretoria Agreement. He treated it as a formal agreement between us, claiming that the Zambian Government's representative signed not only on behalf of the four Frontline Presidents, but also for the ANC. He said that the coming meeting at the Falls would be a purely formal declaration of intent, devoid of negotiation, or statement of political positions. In fact, he continued, it should last only thirty minutes. Furthermore, he declared that implicit in the Pretoria Agreement was an understanding that a ceasefire should take place in the border warfare between his troops and the guerrillas.

I thought Smith was up to his old tricks of deceit, and I had to expose them. On August 15 I flatly denied Smith's interpretations that the ANC was a party to the Pretoria Agreement, that we had agreed to a guerrilla war ceasefire, or that the meeting at the Falls was to be merely a brief formal expression of intent. I said, 'The ANC has no intention whatsoever to hold a serious constitutional conference for only thirty minutes!' Furthermore, I stated our rejection of one clause of the Pretoria Agreement. 'We reject completely the holding of a committee or committees within Rhodesia,' I declared. 'The committee or committees should conduct all their business pertaining to the holding of a constitutional conference in the coaches stationed on the railway bridge at Victoria Falls.'

Smith's obfuscations, however, were a minor confusion compared with the intrigues taking place within the ANC. I had warned about them in my statement to Zimbabweans on August 5 in which I called on our people not to sabotage the work of the ANC by forming 'stupid and stillborn parties'. I had ruled out the calling of an ANC congress and called upon Mr. Nkomo to join the other ANC leaders in the working party's meetings in Lusaka.

Mr. Nkomo, however, had other designs. Simultaneously he and Mr. Smith began calling for me to return home to Salisbury.

The rebel Prime Minister called the ANC a 'decapitated chicken'. 'A head without a body does not operate well and vice versa,' he said in urging me to come home.

'Why are Smith and Nkomo jointly calling for my return?' we wondered from Lusaka. Friends advised me: 'Abel, don't return to Salisbury now for Smith will lock you up and recognize Joshua Nkomo as the ANC's leader.'

These suspicions seemed to be confirmed by the manoeuvres which took place within our ANC Executive in Salisbury. There the Nkomo backers put pressure on Dr. Gabellah to appoint Nkomo leader for the delegation to the Bridge talks. That same afternoon Mr. Smith postponed making a statement on the talks because he was 'waiting to see the developments in the ANC' which were expected to take place that afternoon.

It was Dr. Gabellah who foiled Mr. Nkomo's immediate plans. Rejecting the Nkomo pressure he declared: 'If you (Nkomo) don't want to go to Lusaka to join the main delegation we will go ahead without you.'

'Wait for me,' Mr. Nkomo replied. 'I will want to contact my colleagues in Bulawayo.' The attempt to hijack the leadership of the Talks then collapsed, and Mr. Nkomo soon prepared to travel to Lusaka with the rest.

The day before our departure for Livingstone, the Zambian town at the Victoria Falls Bridge, President Kaunda called the now united ANC delegation to State House. He told us to go to the Bridge, negotiate to the best of our ability, and obtain the best result possible. This reminded me of a locker-room pep talk before some big football match, except for the grand setting of State House. Replying on behalf of our group, I thanked President Kaunda for his efforts. The following day we took a plane to Livingstone.

The Bridge Talks
Never had constitutional talks been held in a more spectacular setting. The South African Government's railway coaches were placed on the Victoria Falls Bridge so that half the train was in Zimbabwe and the other half in Zambia. In fact, the central coach bridged the boundary line so that Ian Smith, sitting at one end, could maintain that he remained in Rhodesia while the African nationalists at the opposite end, some of whom were wanted by the Rhodesian police, remained in Zambia. Before us

thundered *Musi-O-Tunya* (Victoria Falls), the world's mightiest cataract.

Journalists milled around, excited by the exotic setting of the talks, expecting dramatic events to take place. And they were not disappointed, for Prime Minister Vorster deigned to visit Zambia to eat lunch with President Kaunda and the Zimbabwean leaders, including myself.

Later we heard this funny story about what happened that day. When the Zambian Information Service van went around Livingstone's suburbs broadcasting that Mr. Vorster would be coming to Livingstone, many people ran away and hid in the bush, thinking that their country was being invaded by the South Africans. Instead, the information van was attempting to invite people to come and welcome the South African visitors to Zambia.

The relative strengths of our two delegations to the Talks reflected our conflicting aspirations there. Mr. Smith headed a small five-man delegation. We, from our side, chose twelve top ANC leaders to attend. Our support team included a three-member secretariat and thirteen political and legal advisors. Zambia and South Africa chose a low profile for the actual talks. Mark Chona, President Kaunda's personal representative, attended with Mr. Brand Fourie, the South African Secretary for Foreign Affairs. Both Dr. Kaunda and Mr. Vorster, however, addressed our opening session.

Once President Kaunda and Prime Minister Vorster gave their opening speeches to encourage us, the Talks proceeded like the attack and counter-attack of a football match.

I was glad to be able to present a united position paper on behalf of our ANC-Zimbabwe delegation. In it we proposed that our negotiations should produce a constitutional settlement that should 'transfer power from the minority to the majority—that is to say, *majority rule now*'.

Smith rejected this. He proposed instead a simple statement which read: 'Both parties took this opportunity of expressing their genuine desire to negotiate a constitutional settlement. Both parties publicly expressed their commitment to work out immediately a constitutional settlement which will be acceptable to all the people of our country.'

This we could agree upon as a minimal statement, but Ian Smith wanted us to go further to discuss and accept the details

165

of the Pretoria Agreement. When we came to the issue of cessation of the armed struggle, Smith waved the Pretoria Agreement at us, demanding that we abide by its terms. 'We were never signatories to that agreement,' I replied. Mr. Mark Chona, who had signed on behalf of the Zambian Government, supported us in that contention.

Next Smith directed the discussion to the question of continued committee talks within Rhodesia. Anticipating this issue, we countered with a demand for immunity from arrest, prosecution, detention or restriction of any person nominated by the ANC to attend such meetings. Note that when doing so we had made a significant compromise to accept negotiations within Smith's Rhodesia provided we could ensure the safety of our delegation. If Smith could not accept the Immunity Clause, we argued, then he must agree to hold further constitutional talks outside Rhodesia.

At this point Mr. Smith called for a recess. We waited at the hotel nearby, expecting to be called back after fifteen minutes, but instead waited for four hours, until past midnight.

The next day we were still waiting for a move by Mr. Smith. At 10 a.m. we learned that Smith had left, and was already in Salisbury. As expected, Smith blamed the breakdown of the Talks on us because we had introduced new conditions concerning diplomatic immunity not discussed at Pretoria.

From Livingstone I announced at a press conference our ANC reactions to the breakdown: 'If Mr. Smith cannot go with us on very small things like this (demand for immunity), ' I declared, 'we think he cannot be serious. But if he becomes serious enough —as serious as we are—then there is a ninety per cent chance we are going to succeed.'

Plainly, however, Smith was not serious. Had we been consulted as early as the Pretoria meetings we would never have wasted time and effort to attend the Bridge farce. Once again it seemed as if the only recourse was to gain majority rule through escalation of the armed struggle.

After the final collapse of the Talks, a Zambian protocol officer asked me, 'Do you wish to return to Lusaka today or tomorrow?'

'I will want to consult members of my delegation,' I replied. Upon doing so all but one opted for spending the night in Livingstone.

Joshua Nkomo was the exception. 'I have to return to Lusaka

tonight,' he said. 'I will travel with President Kaunda. My wife will be undergoing an operation tomorrow.'

'I am sorry to hear this,' I replied. 'Where is your wife?'

'In Lusaka,' Mr. Nkomo said. With other ANC delegates I expressed my sympathy and bade him a safe journey.

When we arrived in Lusaka we learned that Mrs. Nkomo had been discharged from the hospital some time back. We wondered why Mr. Nkomo had said what he had about his wife. We soon heard why he was so eager to return to Rhodesia. It was to organize an ANC congress.

Sowing Seeds of Dissension in Zimbabwe

August had seen the Bridge Talks come and go. If Mr. Smith wished to renew the constitutional discussions he knew our minimum demands.

Early in September I undertook a trip to Holland, West Germany and Switzerland to raise funds for the ANC. While there I read of Mr. Nkomo's intention to hold an ANC congress in Rhodesia.

All the evidence points to collusion between Ian Smith and Joshua Nkomo in this move. As early as June 1975, in an interview with Peter Mosley of Reuters, Mr. Smith had admitted his secret contacts with Mr. Nkomo. Ted Sutton-Pryce, the Deputy Prime Minister, subsequently told a meeting of the Catholic Justice and Peace Commission that he had had frequent contacts with Mr. Nkomo and his aides, and that he considered Mr. Nkomo to have qualities of leadership that could make it possible for him to promote a settlement. The Smith regime realized, however, that world opinion could only accept a Smith/Nkomo settlement if Mr. Nkomo were the *bona fide* President of the ANC. All the manoeuvring which ensued was designed to achieve that objective.

The July ANC Executive meeting in Dar-es-Salaam thwarted Mr. Nkomo's first attempt. In September, however, a new opportunity arose. The decisions made at Dar had never been publicized within Zimbabwe. Furthermore, the resignations from the Zimbabwe Liberation Council of four former-ZAPU members on September 1, and accusations and counter-accusations between Rev. Sithole and Mr. Nkomo, brought the split out in the open.

This became the excuse for calling an urgent meeting of the

167

ANC Executive in Salisbury. Dr. Gabellah resisted pressure to chair such a meeting on September 7, arguing that it had already been announced for September 21 when I would be back after completing my European and Zambian work.

Failing to bully Dr. Gabellah, Mr. Nkomo forced the Chairman of the National Executive, Mr. Samuel Munodawafa, to call a meeting on September 7. Dr. Gabellah quickly condemned the meeting as unconstitutional, since neither myself as President, Dr. Gabellah as Vice-President, nor Rev. Sithole as Secretary-General had authorized it.

The next day newspapers reported that 37 out of the 69 members of the ANC National Executive had met in Salisbury. Actually, only 15 out of 37 were true members of the Executive, the rest being provincial and district ANC officers rounded up for the meeting.

The bogus Executive proceeded to set September 27-28 as the date for an 'ANC' Congress. They attacked me, claiming that I had run away into 'self-exile' in Zambia, and had whittled away the authority of the National Executive by forming a junta of three. They condemned the formation of the Zimbabwe Liberation Council as unconstitutional. Finally they condemned the National Executive meeting which Dr. Gabellah had called for September 21.

Nkomo's Expulsion

I returned to Lusaka from Europe to find my colleagues in an uproar. Clearly we could not sit down and watch our comrades in disorder within Rhodesia. We owed it to our people to explain that Mr. Nkomo's action was a rebellion. What was taking place threatened to take us back ten years into the politics of division and strife.

What was the right course of action? I wondered. The need to preserve party unity was vital. I had nothing personal against Mr. Nkomo. We had never exchanged bitter words. I felt it imperative, nevertheless, to isolate Mr. Nkomo and thereby to remould the cohesive unity of our organization to which I hoped he would one day return. Such an action, I knew, could be interpreted as a struggle for power between us, but the risk had to be taken. I desired only Zimbabwean unity.

On September 11 I announced to the press that 'in order to protect the integrity, unity and security of the ANC and the future of the people of Zimbabwe', Mr. Joshua Nkomo, Mr. Samuel Mundawafa, and Mr. Killion Bhebe were 'hereby expelled from the ANC'.

My action was not popular with Zambian authorities for the long-standing friendship of Dr. Kaunda and Mr. Nkomo was well-known. In fact, the Zambian authorities forbade us to announce Mr. Nkomo's expulsion on Zambian soil. The *Zambia Daily Mail*, a Government-controlled paper, stated in banner headlines, 'Muzorewa under fire over Nkomo sacking' and quoted Mr. Nkomo's statement that the 'expulsion order is null and void'. The Frontline Presidents, when they met in Lusaka on September 13, joined in criticizing my action. President Nyerere of Tanzania spoke directly to me, saying, 'Bishop, you are not a pope. You should reconsider your decision to expel Joshua Nkomo.' I carefully considered such advice, but felt that to withdraw the expulsion order would be to vindicate Mr. Nkomo's action in breaking the unity agreement. It would only encourage further splits.

But President Nyerere, as presiding chairman of the Presidents, had words to say to our opponents as well. To the late J. Z. Moyo, Nkomo's right-hand man, he said, 'Moyo, tell Joshua that he must not hold that Congress'.

Unfortunately, that advice was not heeded. Suddenly Mr. Nkomo's helpers had fifteen Renaults and seven Peugeot station-wagons at their disposal for organizing work. To overcome the law denying permission for certain meetings to be held in the open air, the Smith regime provided tents and chairs for the Congress. Meanwhile, false reports went across much of Rhodesia that Dr. Gabellah and Enos Nkala were inviting ANC supporters to come and listen to messages from Bishop Muzorewa about the Victoria Falls Talks and other events.

On September 28 the Rhodesian press heralded Nkomo's Congress as a huge success attended by 4,000 delegates. Of these more than 2,000 came from Matabeleland, Mr. Nkomo's home area. To inflate the numbers attending, the regime instructed policemen in plain clothes, their families, and other civil servants to attend. The story spread that food for Congress delegates arrived at the meeting in a police van.

The heralded 'new elections' of leaders for the ANC were carefully stage-managed. Mr. Nkomo brought a prepared list of officers, naming himself as President and Josiah Chinamano as

Vice-President. Of the other officers, all but two were former leaders of Nkomo's People's Caretaker Council (which succeeded ZAPU) and none were former ZANU men. All these, plus the sixty-nine member Executive, were to be elected by acclamation, without a vote being taken.

ANC Consultative Meeting

To many outsiders Dr. Gabellah's rejoinder that Mr. Nkomo's congress was 'illegal, unconstitutional and unrepresentative' may have sounded like sour grapes. No leader of the ANC desired to repeat the factional strife which had weakened our liberation struggle in the mid-1960's. Instead, Dr Gabellah called for a Consultative Assembly to be held on October 26 as a properly constituted annual congress of the ANC.

Ian Smith had encouraged Joshua Nkomo to go it alone because he assumed that Mr. Nkomo still wielded mass support among the Africans of Zimbabwe. Following the same rationale he did not take steps to ban the proposed consultative meeting. On October 26 over 100,000 people overflowed Gwanzura Stadium in Highfield Township, Salisbury. So shocked were the police authorities by the huge crowds that they asked Dr. Gabellah to call off the meeting because it was over-attended! They turned away as many as 50,000 persons at hastily set up road blocks on every road leading to Salisbury.

'MUZOREWA SHALL LEAD US TO CANAAN'. 'UNITY IS STRENGTH'. 'WE SHALL ACHIEVE MAJORITY RULE'. These and many other banners waved above the enthusiastic crowd as Dr. Gabellah rose to speak. He had hoped to read the statement which I had sent from Dar-es-Salaam, but he could not be heard above the cheering and shouting. Waving clenched fists, a Zimbabwean salute, the crowd shouted, 'UNITY!' 'CHIMURENGA! (FIGHT)'. That day the people demonstrated to the world, and to Mr. Smith and Mr. Nkomo, who the vast majority supported as the leaders of Zimbabwe.

At a press conference Dr. Gabellah presented my statement. I called for increased vigilance because of the increasing viciousness of the enemy. The kidnapping of Dr. Edson Sithole, our ANC Publicity Secretary, and his private secretary, Miss Miriam Mhlanga, on October 15 exposed once again the treachery of our opponents. All available evidence, including an eye-witness account that they were taken away in a police van, indicated the

Smith regime's accountability for their disappearance. I called for unity and a rededication to the liberation struggle.

Then Dr. Gabellah concluded the press conference, saying: 'It is now clear who has the support. Smith must know who to talk to.'

The leadership dispute among Zimbabwe's leaders would continue, but the masses of the common people had voted in the only manner permitted at that time—with their feet.

Chapter 14

Righteous Violence

While the internal intrigues continued during 1975 within the ANC, the armed struggle intensified.

On September 19, the Frontline Heads of State met again in Lusaka, together with J. Chikerema, Rev. N. Sithole, the late J. Z. Moyo (representing Nkomo), and myself. This meeting was one of the most significant and unforgettable that I attended during my months in exile.

At this meeting we announced the futility of further talks with Ian Smith. His intransigence had destroyed whatever goodwill remained toward him. 'The only route to liberation in Zimbabwe,' we declared, 'is the armed struggle.' This choice was in line with the earlier decisions taken at the Dar-es-Salaam Executive meeting of the ANC.

Then President Samora Machel issued the magnanimous invitation: 'I now invite all of you Zimbabweans to come and live in Mozambique and to operate from there.' He asked us whether we wished to live in the guerrilla camps, or in the towns. We all expressed gratitude for the invitation and decided to live in the camps with our fellow Zimbabweans.

We left the meeting elated. This invitation was a major development. I wanted more than anything else to join the thousands of young ANC men and women who were offering their lives for Zimbabwe's liberation. The prospect of living in the camps in Mozambique excited us all.

The Struggle Intensifies
FRELIMO's success, and the anticipation of Mozambique's Independence on June 25, 1975, excited thousands of Zimbabwe's young people. Clearly the quickest road to independence for our country seemed to be a massive military effort. During 1975 the steady trickle of youth leaving Rhodesia to join the guerrillas became a flood.

172

The church high schools along the Mozambique border became a major source of recruits. On March 22 over one hundred slipped away by night from the United Methodist High School at Old Umtali. Others followed from St. Augustine's, Mutambara, Chikore, Mt. Silinda and other schools. In a futile effort to stem the tide, the Rhodesian authorities imposed a 6 p.m. to 5 a.m. curfew in an area 185 miles long and half a mile wide along the border with Mozambique, and around the schools affected.

Clearly, training the new recruits emerged as a top priority. The OAU Foreign Ministers decided on May 13 to offer to the ANC the Nachingwea base in Tanzania to train its revolutionary army. This was a big boost, for Nachingwea was the largest and best-equipped base in eastern Africa, and was situated well beyond the reach of the Rhodesian Air Force.

While new cadres trained to fight, guerrilla bands carried the fight to within sixty miles of Salisbury. Although Smith's troops could reach any point by road or helicopter, and hold it by force of superior arms, they could not prevent our freedom fighters from entering Zimbabwe, receiving support from the local populace, and expanding the area of the combat zone. On September 10, the Smith regime claimed they killed 629 'terrorists', but admitted the loss of 55 Rhodesian military personnel since September 1972, as well as a total white death toll of 73.

We Africans knew the despicable 'body-count' psychology of Smith's security forces—not unlike the practices of South Vietnamese and American troops halfway around the world. Smith, too, had to maintain the myth of military superiority by inflating the casualty figures of our people. To give legal justification for government 'terrorism', the white Parliament in October 1975 passed 'The Indemnity and Compensation Act'. Effective back to December 1, 1972, the Act gave the State, its employees and appointees immunity from criminal and civil court action for harm done 'in good faith' to suppress terrorism, or to maintain public order.

The Man in the Middle

Smith and his party introduced this draconian law after church leaders had exposed atrocities committed by Smith's troops—atrocities which under earlier legislation made them subject to court action.

Catholic and Anglican bishops, with outstanding Methodist

173

and Lutheran clergy, issued 'An Appeal to Conscience by Christian Leaders' on August 14, 1974. This was the first salvo. The exposé set out ten instances of assaults by police or armed forces upon innocent civilians. It indicated that the authors had received 'numerous reports of assaults upon innocent people by members of the investigating authorities of the security forces in the North-East'.

The Smith regime denied the allegations, but could not silence its critics. The Roman Catholic Commission for Justice and Peace in Rhodesia continued to accumulate evidence, especially from the so-called 'protected villages' where by 1975 more than 200,000 rural villagers were held behind barbed wire, supposedly to cut off their contact with the freedom fighters. In May it published *The Man in the Middle*, a further exposé of atrocities committed by security forces.

This report exposed the plight of many Zimbabweans who were forced to live in the 'protected villages'. It quoted a local medical officer, Dr. Hill, saying: 'The villagers nearest us are being dumped in the middle of a mealie (maize) field. There is no water, no sanitation, no shelters or poles for them to build the huts they need. It is like picking up animals and moving them from one field to another.'

The plight of the civilian in the liberation struggle was graphically pictured in the testimony of one alleged victim: 'If we report to the police, the terrorists kill us. If we do not report, the police torture us. Even if we report to the police, we are beaten all the same and accused of trying to lead the soldiers into a trap. We do not know what to do.'

In his introduction to the report, Bishop Donal Lamont of Umtali declared:

'the loyalty of the man in the middle will not be won by beating, torturing and maiming him, by shattering his home with bombs from the air, by destroying his crops and driving off his cattle, but by restoring and respecting his dignity and by jealously guarding the rule of law based on those Christian principles which Rhodesia publicly claims to respect and professes to maintain.'

Non-Violence Our Preference

I was not involved personally in the church leaders' protests

174

against the atrocities of the white racists in Rhodesia, although I agreed with their assessment of those in power. If my name had been listed, however, the exposé would have been dismissed by the whites in power as the voice of the ANC. I wanted the conscience of white church leaders in Rhodesia to be heard.

Many persons ask me: 'Bishop, how do you as a churchman explain your deep involvement in the violent liberation struggle in Zimbabwe?'

My answer may surprise you. I begin by asserting my basic personal advocacy of non-violence.

By nature I am a non-violent person. Since childhood I have recoiled at the sight of blood, and the presence of violent death. I have never been reconciled to the necessity of slaughtering animals for food. Physical suffering and pain always arouse strong emotions in me. I hold that all forms of life, even the lowliest, are sacred. Life, I believe, is God's greatest gift to the world, and should be valued as such.

I believe also in the principle of non-violence. Christianity teaches us to love and forgive our enemies. Harmony in any society is preferable to violence. Even where pressures must be brought to bear on those in power to achieve greater justice, I would prefer using non-violent direct action, as did Mahatma Gandhi and Martin Luther King, Jr.

Given a clear choice, all things being equal, I would by conviction adopt the non-violent means to settle any dispute. A settlement arrived at through peaceful negotiations, through give and take to achieve a mutual understanding, is far more stable than a settlement arising out of a test of force. The latter approach leaves a legacy of distrust on both sides, and feelings of injustice among the losers which become the seeds of future conflict. Violence breeds more violence. Violence easily becomes the precedent for settling disputes. The human consequences of injury and suffering are well-known. Knowing these facts, my preference for a non-violent approach to conflict situations is deep-seated.

At its formation in December 1971, the African National Council adopted non-violence as its principal means to reach its objective: the achievement of majority rule in Zimbabwe. I was determined as its President to help the ANC to live up to this noble intention. We declared that the ANC would wage its fight for majority rule on several fronts, political, diplomatic, and

175

constitutional. We also adopted the non-violent approach in settling disputes among ourselves. The formation of the ANC ushered in a period of peace among Zimbabweans which had been unknown before or since in periods of fractious inter-party strife.

For four years the ANC appealed to the whites in power to respond with a like spirit of goodwill, of give and take, of mutual understanding. I believed that we all needed to take risks if peace and justice were to be achieved through non-violent means.

This attempt failed. Having affirmed my preference for a non-violent approach, I must explain why today I support violence in Zimbabwe's liberation struggle. A simple analogy, all too close to reality in Rhodesia, may help in this explanation.

Imagine two families living next door to each other who affirm both the Christian faith and the virtues of African hospitality. Both abhor violence, and believe in turning the other cheek to any aggressor.

In the middle of their evening's conviviality a madman dashes into the house. He grabs one of the babies and crashes it to the floor. One mother picks up the wailing baby and remonstrates with the violent man. Next the madman turns on the other mother who is pregnant and kicks her viciously in the stomach. Before anyone can plead with him to stop he pulls out a knife and stabs a teenage daughter.

How should these Christian families react to these acts of unprovoked savagery? Should they continue to strive peacefully against brute force? And what do they do if this madman summons equally evil accomplices and begins wantonly to torture and to kill?

Here is the point where my convictions differ from those of Martin Luther King, Jr. and Mahatma Gandhi. They advocated non-violence and passive resistance without defining the intensity of the provocation. If I were in the position of the two families involved in my analogy, I would pick up the nearest weapon and strike the madman. I believe it would be gross foolishness to stand by and watch him kill my loved ones. I question whether God himself would wish me to hide behind principles of non-violence while innocent persons were being slaughtered. To act in self-defence at such times is, I believe, to use 'righteous violence'.

In Rhodesia today such madness is not fantasy, but reality. In its latest report the Catholic Commission for Justice and Peace tells of the Karima massacre. Just twenty kilometres from Mount Darwin in north-eastern Rhodesia, security forces sent some of their number into the village of Karima dressed as guerrillas. Troops then opened fire killing twenty and seriously wounding fifteen persons. Nine of those killed were children, some still babies. Four were women. The dead were then cremated—an offence against African custom. There were no casualties among the security forces, or among the supposed 'terrorists'.

It is such madness that is rampant in Rhodesia today. Our history is a long, tragic story of such unprovoked acts of violence by a small ruling minority against the African majority. We live with madmen who have spurned peaceful approaches, choosing instead to suppress us with massacres and torture.

Zimbabweans have no other recourse but to pick up weapons and fight back. The Zimbabwe war of liberation is not an aggression against white people. It is a last response, taken in self-defence, when all non-violent methods have been tried and spurned by our oppressors. This is why I am a freedom fighter. This is why I support the armed struggle. I cannot sit smugly and passively in the comfort of my home while my people are being tortured to death, shot down, or bombed.

My visits with our young men and women who are training as freedom fighters convinced me that I must support them fully. It deeply moved me when a young guerrilla said to me, 'I came (into the camp) to die for my country so that those left can live in a free Zimbabwe.' Should I have said to him, 'You should desist and revert to ordinary life in Rhodesia'? That 'ordinary life' would mean for many of them imprisonment, torture, and death as former freedom fighters. If released, it would mean unemployment, lack of educational facilities, lack of lands to plough, or opportunities for community leadership. No, I could not advocate a return to that situation for those with a complete and single-minded determination to fight and sacrifice to win liberty for our people.

Portrait of a Freedom Fighter

The true story of one young freedom fighter whom I met is typical of thousands of others. It needs telling. For reasons of security I shall call him 'Pfuti Chete'.

During his early youth in Zimbabwe, Pfuti pictured the good

177

life ahead as including a good education, an opportunity to enter a profession, and finally to marry and establish his own home. He was ambitious and determined to make good. He held his immediate family in high regard. He wanted them to feel that he was determined to serve them and society to the best of his ability.

After beginning his education in the village school, and later attending a church-sponsored high school, Pfuti gained admission to one of Rhodesia's technical colleges. There for the first time he was confronted with the reality of racist Rhodesia. One day he was driving a tractor on the training farm when a white instructor drove up furiously, and stopped him. 'You are driving far too fast, you baboon!' the white man shouted, almost choking with anger. 'That tractor is worth a great deal more than you are!'

Another day Pfuti was working at the college swimming pool, where regulations on the entry sign included the words, 'No dogs allowed inside the fence'. Along came a white woman for a leisurely swim with her well-fed dog in tow. Without regard for the rules she entered. 'Madam,' Pfuti said, 'will you please let your dog remain outside. It is against regulations to keep dogs inside the fence.' With undisguised disdain and anger she replied, 'What bloody cheek! That rule is only for African dogs, not for European dogs! I will report you for your insolence.' Stung by her insulting words, Pfuti seized a stick and chased the dog beyond the fence, while its yelps mingled with the irate screams of its mistress.

This incident led to Pfuti's immediate expulsion from the college—expulsion against which he could not appeal. It ended abruptly his aspirations and dreams. His whole future seemed in ruins. With that blot on his record Pfuti could not hope to enter another technical college, or to obtain employment. He joined the thousands of unemployed young men and women.

Next, Pfuti decided like thousands of others in his straits to escape across the border, determined to fight injustice with a gun because there seemed to be no other way to bring about change.

As Pfuti talked about life in the training camps, and his vision for a new Zimbabwe, I perceived that his training and experience as a guerrilla had not turned him into a hardened killer. He remained an idealistic young man, eager to contribute his youth and energy to the building of a new Zimbabwe. When I asked him what he wanted to do when the fighting was over he replied without hesitation, 'Farming'. He wants a small farm, and a chance to prove that he can be as good a farmer as any man. He believes that agricultural development is the key to Zimbabwe's progress. He shares his parents' and forefathers' love for the land, for cultivating it with his sweat, and persuading it to yield rich, green crops.

Next, I discovered that Pfuti, and many other young fighters, have no ambition to wield political power within a free Zimbabwe. They have sworn to chase away the enemy now oppressing their people. They are willing to fight, and even die, to gain freedom; but the selection of new political leaders Pfuti would leave to the free choice of all the people.

As he talked, I perceived that Pfuti did not hate the whites. He is not fighting against white people, but against an oppressive political system. He related several stories about military engagements in which freedom fighters, at the risk of personal safety, spared the lives of white women and children. I could see that he and others do not enjoy killing. Instead, they use the gun with discrimination against selected targets.

I found Pfuti and others to be highly disciplined. Like thousands of his fellow cadres he does not take alcohol. He told me with a smile that he would drink a toast on the day Zimbabwe is free. His high code of conduct extends to relationships with the opposite sex. Promiscuity for him is a negation of the concept of being a guerrilla. 'I will settle down and get married and raise children when things are normal,' Pfuti said. As for relations with fellow Zimbabweans in the war zone, Pfuti believes that high moral behaviour must be maintained there as well. 'You see,' he observed, 'we do not want our parents to be ashamed of us.'

It is not surprising that the Smith regime tries to discredit the guerrillas in the eyes of the people. Their vicious smear campaign presents the freedom fighter as an indiscriminate killer. The notorious Selous Scouts masquerade as freedom fighters, killing innocent people, including missionaries, while the Smith regime blames their atrocities on so-called 'terrorists'. 'We hate the Selous Scouts more than we hate any other unit in Smith's terrorist army,' Pfuti told me with a great deal of feeling. Recently defectors from the Selous Scouts have begun to verify the truth concerning their evil deeds.

I turned to go, bidding Pfuti farewell. But his last words

deeply moved me. Almost as if he were talking to himself he said softly, 'I don't expect to go back home to live. I don't expect ever to live in a free Zimbabwe. My role is to see that those at home, our fathers and mothers, brothers and sisters, will live in a free Zimbabwe.'

Building a Disciplined Army

Having met Pfuti and others like him, I determined to do my part in bringing their idealistic dreams of a liberation war, waged with consistency and integrity, to reality. As President of the united ANC, I was now 'Comrade Commander-in-Chief', as one enthusiastic young Zimbabwean often called me. I was determined to help wherever I could; and there was much, very much, to be done.

For ten years Zimbabwean freedom fighters had fought amongst themselves. Just six months earlier we lost hundreds of Zimbabweans through fighting in the former ZANU camps, then under the command of Josiah Tongogara. Zimbabweans disappeared without a trace—victims of kidnappings, or self-appointed murder squads. Such undisciplined self-seeking extended into the war zone as well, resulting in the murder of Zimbabwean civilians who refused to give instant loyalty to a particular faction. This wave of killing culminated in the violent assassination of Herbert Chitepo. After his death the armed struggle appeared to have come to a painful and bloody halt. As the sordid details emerged we saw that at least one section of the revolutionary army had been riddled with tribalism and corruption, the huge scope of which had been unimaginable. This section of our armed struggle had lost direction.

As 'Commander-in-Chief' I felt an obligation to impart to our military cadres that spirit of unity which the masses at home had achieved through the ANC. Our common dedication to the struggle for Zimbabwe's liberation could bridge our differences of tribe, or past political loyalty.

Corruption had taken a cancerous hold inside our revolutionary army. It had to be rooted out, and be replaced by a new morality giving our guerrillas nobility and respect.

The new Disciplinary Code, adopted by the Zimbabwe Liberation Council in August 1975, was a major step forward in re-imposing military discipline over the whole Zimbabwe

Liberation Army. Its tone and toughness can be grasped in the following clauses:

Any member of the Zimbabwe Liberation Army who commits any of the following shall be guilty of an offence:

7. An act of homicide involving infanticide, or manslaughter, or murder; . . .
11. Looting, forced contributions or theft from comrades or the masses; . . .
13. An act of cruelty or torture of a comrade or the masses; . . .
14. Engaging in a fight with, assault on, or disorderly conduct against, or use of insulting or bullying or swearing language to another comrade or the masses; . . .
15. Shameful conduct likely to cause indignations at, or contempt of, or the disgracing of the Party or oneself, such as taking liberties with the opposite sex; . . .
18. Drunkenness on duty; . . .
21. Taking and/or smoking dagga and other drugs.

Next we had to introduce humane punishment for infractions of this code. We of the ZLC wished to outlaw savagery like that perpetrated earlier in the name of discipline in some guerrilla camps. We banned the capital punishment of Zimbabwean fighters. No one, whatsoever, had the right to order the death of a fellow Zimbabwean who had volunteered to fight for his motherland. Concerning unarmed civilians, we ordered our fighters to attack the armed enemy only, with no attacks to be made on civilians except in self-defence.

A Just Liberation War
I began this chapter by declaring my advocacy of peace and non-violence, but then traced the realities of oppression within Rhodesia which brought me to support the armed struggle. In doing so, while seeking to remain faithful to Christian teachings, I will relate our struggle to the following criteria for a 'just war':

The war must be declared by a legitimate authority. Since November 9, 1965, when Ian Smith declared his UDI (Unilateral Declaration of Independence) from Great Britain, not a single nation has accepted his regime as the lawful (*de jure*) government of our country. At the same time Great Britain, which had claimed to be the lawful authority, has failed to reassert her control over the country. Legitimate authority, therefore, passes to the oppressed

181

themselves. It is they who have been forced to seek to control the destiny of Zimbabwe. Having tried every way possible to win majority rule through peaceful means, they now turn to a liberation war to gain their rightful inheritance.

The war must be carried out with the right intention. The intention of our people is to shake off the shackles of minority dictatorship in order to attain self-determination. The masses in Zimbabwe do not struggle against white persons, but against an oppressive and suppressive system dominated by white leadership. They fight in order to end violence—to achieve justice and racial reconciliation within a free Zimbabwe.

The war must be undertaken as a last resort. The record of our attempt to gain majority rule through negotiation is plain for all to see. Every channel for peaceful protest has been explored, but in vain. Each successive political party has been banned. Our leaders have been detained without trial. By the 'Law and Order Maintenance Act', for example, any person who 'behaves in a manner which is likely to make some other person apprehensive as to what might happen' can be imprisoned for up to ten years. By such legislation, under which Zimbabweans are to be presumed guilty unless they can prove their innocence, every peaceful effort has been crushed.

The war must be waged on a selective basis. Guerrilla warfare is not like conventional warfare. In the latter there is sometimes indiscriminate destruction of people and property. Guerrilla warfare is highly selective in its targets, seeking to destroy only those forces which maintain the oppressiveness of the enemy. For example, it is normal for Zimbabwean freedom fighters to say to missionaries, 'You are our friends; we mean no harm to you.' I know one missionary couple who live just fourteen miles from the Mozambique border deep in the war zone. The white farmers for miles around have run away to the cities, or to other countries, for fear of being killed. Meanwhile guerrillas have re-assured the missionary couple: 'You have nothing to fear. We are not plunderers. We are merely freedom fighters. You, too, are fighting for our freedom in your own way as you provide self-help and development plans for our people.' Similarly a missionary nurse visits outlying clinics without fear, driving into areas which racist soldiers dare not enter. The guerrillas have told her, 'You have nothing to fear from us. After all, you too, in your way, are a freedom fighter.'

The war must have a reasonable chance of success. In a contest in which 250,000 whites are pitted against six million Zimbabweans who believe that our country is our birthright, the final outcome is a foregone conclusion. Despite the inflow of white mercenaries from America, Belgium, Canada, Australia or New Zealand, the Zimbabwean people will win. Recent victories of the people of Angola and Mozambique demonstrated that success is attainable in the near future.

The war must be waged with all the moderation that is possible. A liberation army practises no 'scorched earth' policy, for it desires to build a new society out of the old corrupt one. It is those who have no desire to rebuild who wantonly destroy lives and property. In a war of liberation, however, some destruction must be undertaken in order to break the will of those in power who resist change. Hopefully, with the assistance of outside forces concerned for justice in Zimbabwe, destruction can be kept to a minimum.

I believe that the liberation struggle in Zimbabwe conforms to the basic criteria of a 'just war'. I also believe that this is a position which is consistent with the views of many Christian leaders who have struggled against oppressive regimes.

In an address to the Lutheran World Federation Assembly, Bishop Eivind Berggrav of Norway, who had known the tyranny of Nazism, said:

'When a government becomes lawless and acts with arbitrary despotism, the result is a demonic condition, that is to say, the government is godless. To obey such a Satanic government would be nothing short of sinful . . . In circumstances of this kind we have as a matter of principle the right to rebel in one form or another.'

Bishop Donal Lamont of Umtali, in defending his instructions to church personnel to give humanitarian aid to both sides in the civil war, asked:

'Have not those who honestly believe that they fight for the basic human rights of their people a justifiable claim on the Church for the spiritual administration of the clergy? How can one counsel loyalty and obedience to your ordinances when to do so is tantamount to giving approval to the manifold injustices you inflict? To keep silence about one reign of oppression in order the better to combat what you alone consider to be another, is wholly unacceptable.'[1]

Professor Jurgen Moltmann of West Germany very relevantly points out that 'it is not the idealistic principle of non-violence that is consonant with the Gospel, but the responsible action of love.'[2]

What does this mean? It is all too easy to hide behind the haven of non-violence and evade responsibility. Moltmann is saying that it is a demonstration of responsible love to stop the madman bent on destroying innocent people through oppression, torture, and deadly weapons.

The Church in the Liberation Struggle

I admit, however, that the destruction of life involved in any violent struggle poses a serious dilemma for anyone who would follow Christ's command to 'Love your enemy'.

Reginald Stackhouse in *Christianity and Politics* expressed it well: 'On the one hand, it is clear that the Church has a mission to the political part of the world. On the other hand, there are reasons why many Christians hesitate to undertake their mission. Obviously, the solution to the dilemma is not simply to choose between two wrongs, but, as it were, to go through the horns of the dilemma.'[3]

Zimbabwean Christians today are doing just that—going through the horns of that dilemma. We see Christians feeding the guerrillas, giving them shelter, providing military intelligence, clothes and money. All such actions are punishable by death if revealed to the whites in power. Time and time again I have heard mothers pray in church, 'Please God, be with our children in the bush.' Such prayers in the eyes of the racists are criminal acts. At least one African pastor has languished more than two years in prison without trial for uttering such prayers in church.

[1] 'Civil War in Rhodesia: a report compiled by the Catholic Commission for Justice and Peace in Rhodesia.' London: Catholic Institute for International Relations, 1976.

[2] Moltmann, 'Racism and the Right to Resist.'

[3] London: English Universities Press, 1966.

Some denominations and individual church leaders still believe that the liberation struggle in Zimbabwe is none of the Church's business. I thank God that such people are in a negligible minority. Some of these same critics do not believe in the Africaniza- of the Church.

The predominant spirit of our people, however, sees the hand of God in our liberation struggle. Reading the Bible, we find that our struggle parallels that of the children of Israel in Egypt. Sermons on the Exodus stories are received with rapt attention in Zimbabwean churches. We believe that as God led His children out of bondage in Egypt into a promised land, so He will lead his children into Zimbabwe if they are faithful to Him.

I mention 'faithfulness' because we are tempted to claim God's blessing on every aspect of our revolutionary struggle, even its excesses. I see the role of the Christian Church as vital to the re-establishment of order and peace in post-revolutionary Zimbabwe. We shall need large amounts of Christian forgiveness and charity. A new moral code must be forged—a new code to replace the old one eroded by the evils of injustice and the ravages of the liberation war.

The Zimbabwe Church, I believe, will not be found wanting in this challenge. Already the Church has established its credibility by standing with the masses against injustice and oppression. There are Christians in the world who indict us for identifying with revolutionary violence. They question the correctness of this stand taken by the Church in the Zimbabwe revolution. Little do they understand the fateful choices that are before us. Having been introduced into much of Rhodesia at the same time as white colonial rule, the Christian Church was in real danger ten years ago of being rejected by the masses of young people as foreign, Western, and part of the system of white oppression. Such attitudes persist today, especially among those separated in the struggle from the ministries of caring Christian communities—those in prisons, detention camps, and in the guerrilla camps. But by identifying itself with the fight for liberation of the people, the Church has assured itself of a place in post-revolutionary Zimbabwe.

Some of us in southern Africa who strongly believe in non-violence are prepared to support temporary righteous violence in order to eradicate the racist oppression now taking place. I believe that our cause is right, and that we have indulged in righteous violence only as a last resort.

Once committed to righteous violence, I found that the dilemma of how to make responsible choices proved to be as great, or greater, than before.

Two weeks after President Machel's invitation to live in Mozambique I took Mr. Noel Mukono, Chairman of our Military Committee, and Mr. S. Parirenyatwa, then Mukono's deputy, to Mozambique to follow up the challenge. Leaving them, as previously arranged, in the hands of the Mozambique Minister of Defence, I rushed off to Norway on an important fund-raising mission. Mr. George Nyandoro, Mr. Simpson Mutambanengwe, and Mr. Webster Mutamba accompanied me on this trip in early October, 1975.

On our return from Europe I finalized my personal arrangements to live in Mozambique with our freedom fighters. Before reaching Maputo, however, I wanted to confer with leaders in Lusaka and in Dar-es-Salaam, and to visit the guerrilla training-camps in Tanzania.

Arriving in Dar-es-Salaam I found President Nyerere away at Mwanza, but he kindly arranged for a plane to take me, with some staff members, to him. When I told him of my intention to visit our camps before proceeding to Mozambique, President Nyerere turned to Colonel Hashim Mbita, Executive Secretary of the OAU Liberation Committee, and asked, 'What is the situation in the camps?'

'The spirit is sour,' Colonel Mbita replied.

Colonel Mbita's answer was disappointing. Before reaching Dar we heard that guerrillas in one Tanzanian camp had written to the OAU Liberation Committee denouncing the political leadership of the ANC, i.e. Muzorewa, Chikerema and Sithole. At that time we were still unaware of the true situation. We assumed that our hosts desired only total unity among Zimbabweans struggling for liberation. We left for Mozambique without reaching the camps in Tanzania.

Just before leaving Dar-es-Salaam, I ordered the advance party for Mozambique to start off from Lusaka. This mission, led by Mr. J. D. Chikerema, included ten persons, among them members of the new Military High Command appointed by the Zimbabwe Liberation Council. They travelled in five large seven-ton trucks loaded with supplies for the combatants—foodstuffs, clothing, shoes, bedding, medicines, radios, watches, and various other items which we had collected. Upon reaching Mozambique in mid-November, however, the party was inexplicably arrested and detained by the FRELIMO authorities. Later some of the members were thrown into prison. As for the truckloads of supplies, they never reached their destination, nor have we been able to trace how they were used by the Mozambique authorities. No answer came despite repeated inquiries. As for our leaders, some were released, while others remained in prison. Even as I write we do not know their whereabouts, and whether or not they are still alive.

Under this cloud I continued my preparations to live in Mozambique.

Chapter 15

In Exile in Mozambique

The journey which took me into exile in Mozambique actually began in July, 1975, in Dar-es-Salaam. As I was about to depart from the ANC Consultative Meeting, President Julius Nyerere invited me for discussions on a number of issues. 'Bishop,' he said, 'I want to suggest that you do not return to Zimbabwe. You are the head of the ANC now. You are the Commander-in-Chief of the Zimbabwe cadres. There seems now to be no alternative to an intensification of the armed struggle—no hopes of a peaceful settlement. If you return to Zimbabwe the racists will detain you, or kill you.'

Taking a deep breath, I began to reflect on his advice, yet I knew I must make my own decision in this matter. 'Thank you, your Excellency,' I replied. 'I will give your words very serious thought.'

'Yes, do think about it, Bishop,' President Nyerere concluded.

A few days later, while still in Mozambique, James Chikerema suddenly said to me, 'Bishop, I have been doing some thinking. I think you should not return to Zimbabwe at this time.'

'Have you been talking with President Nyerere about this matter?' I enquired.

'No,' he replied, 'why do you ask?'

'Because President Nyerere made the same suggestion,' I explained.

'Well, you musn't go back then,' Chikerema concluded in his usual blunt way.

All this advice coming from persons genuinely concerned for my safety, and my continuing leadership, confirmed thoughts which I had been entertaining for some time. The grenades thrown at my house only the month before demonstrated that there was physical danger for myself and my family if we lived in Salisbury. But the fear of physical harm was not my major concern. My life could be in danger from political rivals, or from enemy agents, wherever I might live. My chief concern was for the effective prosecution of the armed struggle and the proper execution of my expanded responsibilities as head of the ANC.

The advice I received in this matter, however, was not unanimous. President Kaunda and Joshua Nkomo at this time were urging me to return to Zimbabwe. Getting conflicting advice from two Frontline Presidents, with whom I wanted to co-operate, made the decision more difficult.

At first I decided to reside in Zambia as my External Headquarters. Lusaka was by then the oldest and best established rear base for diplomatic, political and military activities in our struggle. The 30,000 Zimbabweans resident in Zambia were the largest concentration of our people outside their homeland. Most of the external leaders of the ANC lived in Lusaka. Furthermore, despite diplomatic tensions between Smith's Rhodesia and Kaunda's Zambia, communication links established earlier were largely intact. One could pick up the phone in Lusaka and dial directly to Salisbury or Bulawayo.

By November 1975, however, two factors made Mozambique more attractive as a base of operations. One was my desire to live as close as possible to the young people of our liberation army. Another was the embarrassment of remaining in Zambia where President Kaunda was supporting Joshua Nkomo's attempts to usurp the leadership of the ANC.

I Move to Maputo
During the third week of November 1975 I moved to Maputo, without knowing the fate of the advance mission which had left Lusaka by road several weeks earlier. About the second week of December Rev. Sithole joined me.

We expected to join our fellow Zimbabweans who were living in the guerrilla and refugee camps. This was our mission. The cadres in the camps expected us to join them to give political direction, and to help sort out the many organizational problems which they faced. They looked forward to having me with them for the first time—both as their Commander-in-Chief and as the President of the ANC Zimbabwe.

On arrival in Maputo I sought to establish the whereabouts of the Zimbabwean camps, and of our advance mission. Officials received my inquiries politely, as well as my request to visit the

189

camps as soon as possible, but they told me to await an official reply.

Two days before Christmas I exploded in frustration. Ndabaningi Sithole and I felt that we had to reach the camps. We knew we were desperately needed there, and that the donations for the guerrillas and refugees which we carried would help to meet critical needs. Again I went to the Mozambique minister responsible for Zimbabwe affairs. I announced to him that if official approval was not forthcoming I would find my own way to the camps. Out of blind desperation I had decided to hitch-hike or use any available means of public transport, although at that time I did not know for certain where the camps were located. The minister blandly told me that I would not be allowed to go 'because of the security situation'—the same excuse I had been given on previous occasions.

On Christmas Day Rev. Sithole and I sat alone in the house which President Machel had set aside for our use. Our cook served a delicious meal, but I found no appetite for it. The very sight of the meal reminded me that not far off there were thousands of Zimbabweans eking out a poor existence on one meal a day. Even sleeping on a comfortable bed was irksome when I remembered my fellow Zimbabweans sleeping on grass mats, or under the shelter of trees like wild animals of the forest.

Towards the end of January 1976 my wife Maggie and our two youngest children, Charles Scarriter Chido and Rufaro Charity, joined me in Maputo. They helped to make our house in exile more of a home. Chido, our son, was then thirteen years old, and our daughter Charity seven. They attended the only English primary school in Maputo, as all other schools taught in the Portuguese language. In February we welcomed Rev. Webster Mutamba, my Special Assistant, and his wife. Then our home became our office as well.

We liked Maputo People everywhere, every day, were talking about the Zimbabwe liberation struggle. But our seeming freedom in Mozambique to visit and talk freely did not satisfy us, for we had been denied permission to live where we wanted to be—with our Zimbabwean brothers and sisters in the camps.

Our family stay together, however, ended after a few months when Maggie left with the children for the United States. We decided to seek medical attention for our son, Chido, in the city of Nashville, Tennessee, where he had been born, and to accept an opening for Maggie to study at Scarritt College, where I had graduated with a master's degree in June 1963. We rejoiced that many friends from those days remained in Nashville to befriend our family once again.

Among the vivid memories of our all-too-brief weeks together in Maputo were our times for family prayers. Often we would sing a Shona hymn which spoke so eloquently to our needs:

In the past your people were persecuted, God;
But you saved them with your power.
GREAT GOD, GREAT GOD, FATHER OF US ALL.
They were arrested and imprisoned;
You released them and cared for them.
They were evicted from their homes and accursed;
But you comforted them and they continued to love you.
Some were laughed at and beaten up;
But you, God the Father, you strengthened them.

The Year of Great Frustration

I look back on 1976 as a year of great frustration. The people of Zimbabwe had given overwhelming support to the united ANC, and to me as its head, yet elements to the right and left sought to destroy that unity and reject my leadership. Together the ANC leaders had agreed on the priority of the armed struggle at this time as the primary strategy for achieving Zimbabwe's liberation, yet some amongst us diverted their energies into more fruitless negotiations with Ian Smith. Heads of Frontline States sought to impose leaders on us, and to dictate to Zimbabweans the path of their liberation.

Addressing the OAU's African Liberation Committee in Maputo on January 19, I sought to reaffirm the ANC's stand in our liberation struggle. 'When the ANC was formed on December 7, 1974,' I declared, 'all the people of Zimbabwe welcomed the new unity, and this position has basically not changed. Those who try to deviate from it run the risk of losing the support of the people of Zimbabwe.'

Then I outlined our basic ANC approach to the Zimbabwe liberation struggle—a double strategy. This approach has been 'that there should be negotiations for peaceful settlement and if talks fail to yield Majority Rule Now then armed struggle would be intensified.' The decision to intensify the armed

191

struggle was made unanimously by the ANC in Dar-es-Salaam in July 1975.

I went on to explain why we cannot accept any constitutional arrangement which is less than Majority Rule Now. 'Zimbabwe is unique,' I declared, 'in that of all the British colonies Rhodesia was the only colony allowed self-government and the control of an army, and security forces of its own. It is political naïvety to expect the present illegal regime which seized independence unilaterally in 1965 to preside over its own liquidation.'

Tearing Us Apart

The OAU Liberation Committee applauded my call for an intensified armed struggle, but took no action to solve the serious divisions among our Zimbabwean political or military leaders. In fact, I sensed that the resources of that Committee were being used to strengthen the position of one faction, and to isolate others from receiving international recognition.

Moves by President Kaunda and others to strengthen Joshua Nkomo's hand, served to widen the split between us. Beginning in October 1975, Mr. Nkomo talked frequently with Ian Smith, claiming that they would work out a constitutional settlement. Dr. Kaunda of Zambia threw his full resources behind these talks, sending political advisers and a secretariat to Salisbury to assist Mr. Nkomo. Clearly our unanimous ANC decision to de-escalate talks and to escalate the armed struggle was to be circumvented with the connivance of outside powers.

I learned almost by accident of another dimension of this power play when I travelled to Blantyre, Malawi, in January 1976. An official of the British High Commission in Malawi had kindly entertained me. He was on the point of leaving after our chat when he said, 'This is a strange world. Here you are, and yet we have it that Dr. Kaunda told Mr. Nkomo a few days agao that he need not worry about the possibility that Muzorewa or Sithole would get control of the guerrilla army because both of them were under house arrest in a villa in Maputo.'

Was this the explanation why for 'security reasons' Rev. Sithole and I had been forbidden to visit the guerrilla camps? If so, it implies that both Dr. Kaunda and President Machel were promoting Mr. Nkomo as a Zimbabwean leader while seeking to isolate me from the very cadres which were calling for my leadership among them. Did the house given us by President Machel mean that we were in reality in a prison—a house arrest meant to keep us away from our fellow Zimbabweans? Was this being done to prevent the consolidation of the political unity of the masses of Zimbabwe with the military unity of the cadres? Would all this explain why I had not been able to visit the camps in Tanzania as well, and why somebody appeared to be creating hostility against me in the camps? If so, such machinations seriously impaired the effectiveness of our liberation struggle and delayed the liberation of Zimbabwe. They sowed the seeds of civil war. These were the painful thoughts I wrestled with during those weeks.

I decided to bide my time, and in March the expected happened. After thirteen meetings Messrs. Nkomo and Smith announced: 'We have reached an impasse and are therefore breaking off the talks.'

On March 25 the Frontline Presidents called Mr. Nkomo and me to meet with them in Lusaka 'to plan a new, common strategy to intensify the armed struggle and to attack basically the economy of the illegal Smith regime'. For me this was not a new strategy, but one from which certain leaders had deviated during the past futile talks with Smith. But this was a time not for recriminations, but for a renewed attempt at Zimbabwean unity. From Kampala, on March 30, I issued a renewed appeal for unity in which I said:

'Now that those [Smith-Nkomo] talks have broken down, and because our belief in UNITY remains as strong as ever, I genuinely invite Mr. Joshua Nkomo to come back and join the AFRICAN NATIONAL COUNCIL—the authentic political-military organization of the preponderant majority of the people of Zimbabwe—so that together, working in organic UNITY, we can liberate our country.'

Then I went on: 'While we value UNITY, we hold FREEDOM more dear.' I explained that our people have resolved to let nothing distract them from the historic fight for their birthright. We would not again postpone our struggle for liberation while seeking to untie the knots of interpersonal rivalries among Zimbabwean nationalists. If necessary, the successful prosecution of the armed struggle itself would give birth to the unity we

193

yearn for. Once again I hoped that Mr. Nkomo might answer this call for unity, but he gave no response.

The Third Force

Another example of outside interests enhancing Zimbabwean disunity can be seen in the emergence of what was called the 'Third Force'.

In early February Mozambique Government officials conveyed to James Chikerema, Ndabaningi Sithole and me an invitation to attend another summit meeting of the Frontline Presidents—this time at Quelimane in northern Mozambique. Although we travelled with Mozambican officials we were never told what was going to be discussed, nor were we briefed upon arrival in Quelimane. This was their usual practice.

Once again we found it difficult to prepare for the meeting. Sitting in our rooms, we knew that sooner or later we would be summoned to the meeting. The normal pattern was that the chairman, President Nyerere, would inform us what decision had been taken. Sometimes he would ask for our reactions. At other times he would ask, 'Where do we go from here?' and would expect us to produce instant strategies for implementation of the decision they had imposed on us. Rarely did the Presidents inform us of the content of preceding discussions, or reveal the factors which had led them to a particular conclusion. Any dissenting opinions would be countered immediately.

On this particular occasion President Machel informed us that the guerrillas of ZAPU and ZANU had on their own decided to unit under a High Command of eighteen—nine from ZANU and nine from ZAPU. He called it 'Third Force' or ZIPA—the Zimbabwe People's Army.'

'Your people came to my place, about forty-five of them, and I addressed them,' the President continued. 'They said that they always tried to fight, but the leadership always failed them. They said that they were tired of the existing political leadership because it was divided.'

'Third Force?' my mind questioned. This was the first time we had heard the term. Later President Nyerere used it during an interview with David Martin, the British journalist, who by his writings would introduce ZIPA in the world press. Why 'Third Force?, I wondered. What then are the 'first' and 'second' forces?

My response was to ask the chairman, President Nyerere, to

allow my colleagues and I some moments alone to prepare our response. This was readily agreed to.

We decided that a forceful reply was our best approach. On return I began by expressing our judgment that this action was a serious setback to the liberation struggle. In effect it rescinded the very decision of the Frontline Presidents on September 19, 1975, to promote actively the armed struggle under the leadership of the ANC and its High Command. 'We cannot understand,' I went on, 'why a group of individual combatants would be given a hearing on matters concerning the liberation of millions of people whose direct representatives we are.' We were now convinced that the ANC's High Command had been arrested in order to destroy it, and to create another high command which would not be accountable to the leadership of the ANC, supported by the masses of Zimbabweans.

Next, I expressed our opinion that the creation of this second high command would create further hostilities, and accentuate existing divisions among the Zimbabwean cadres. Such a development would benefit only the enemy.

Turning to the points of known agreement, I said that we appreciated that the armed struggle needed to be intensified, and that this needed to be done as a united people. We admitted that Zimbabwean nationalists had a long history of divisions, but affirmed that the ANC had been formed to eradicate them. The creation of a new high command, however, was a retrogressive step which would divide further the combatants from the Zimbabwean masses.

Finally, I reminded the Presidents that the ANC had a standing policy that 'it is the Party which commands the gun and not the gun the Party'. For the soldiers to form their own party, separate from that of the masses, seemed to us to be a counter-revolutionary action.

President Nyerere appeared visibly moved as I finished our statement. He replied forcefully, 'You people seem to think that power comes from the barrel of the mouth instead of the barrel of the gun.' Defending the President's decision he went on, 'You refused to go to the camps. Samora (Machel) did what we told him to do.' This last comment referred to the action denying us permission to visit the guerrilla camps.

I suppose I could have denied that any of us had refused to visit the camps. I could have related the successive frustrations by

Mozambican officials of our attempts to visit or live in the camps, the story of our captured advance party, and other obstacles placed in our way. But these facts were known by the Presidents. Of what weight were our opinions as liberation movement leaders against those of the heads of independent nations on whom Zimbabwe depended for its operational bases in the struggle? My colleagues knew my usual response to them after such meetings, 'Countrymen, it is terrible not to have a country of your own.'

A strange paradox emerged at this meeting. On the one hand leaders of the Frontline States exhorted us to unite as Zimbabwean leaders. Meanwhile, virtually any ambitious politician or military commander who desired to break the existing unity could count on support from one Frontline State or another. Joshua Nkomo counted on Dr. Kaunda as his backer. Robert Mugabe chose President Machel and FRELIMO leaders as his sponsors. It was Colonel Hashim Mbita of the Liberation Committee who sponsored the organizing of ZIPA as a joint ZAPU-ZANU High Command, ignoring the ANC High Command which was created as part of the December 1974 unity agreement.

Frontline States Versus ANC?

We of the ANC had a clear case, as clear as a cloudless blue sky. Anybody with an open mind only had to listen. I believe that the Presidents felt no doubt about the legitimacy of our case. Of that I am certain. Nobody could doubt the sincerity of their commitment to our liberation struggle, but they had lost sight of the firm basis for our leadership within it.

Zimbabweans had decided on unity, a commitment undertaken after learning painful lessons about the consequences of disunity both within their own history and within the rest of Africa. Zimbabweans were overjoyed when their nearest neighbours endorsed their Declaration of Unity on December 7, 1974.

I humbly accepted the task as President of the united ANC, of being custodian of this unity, a unity in many ways unique in the whole of Africa. On accepting the challenge I was aware of its implications. I did not for one moment expect that it would be a bed of roses. I accepted it as the most grave and weighty responsibility that had ever come to me—taking it as a sacred trust reposed on me. I resolved to guard that unity with my life. That is why I took serious exception when anyone—Zimbabwean or foreigner, black or white, bosom friend or foe, ruler or ruled—did anything, anything at all to threaten Zimbabwean unity, let alone create a situation likely to generate future civil war in Zimbabwe.

The ANC had been created in the open—first as a movement of the masses inside Zimbabwe, and second as endorsed by Zimbabweans operating from outside our borders. It was not a clandestine movement formed by obscure individuals seeking newspaper publicity. Those who signed the Declaration of Unity had been elected representatives of the people at one time or another. The movement had the Organization of African Unity's recognition. We were making every effort to consolidate that unity.

Now it appeared that the same African leaders who had spent a week in Lusaka urging, cajoling and exhorting us into unity in December 1974 were now helping to dismantle that very unity. First Joshua Nkomo broke away with the tacit support of President Kaunda of Zambia. Now a small group of individual combatants was being recognized as an independent 'Third Force' by all the Frontline States.

I want the sources of disunity clearly understood. Do not blame the masses in Zimbabwe if civil war should break out! Do not blame the ANC which has stood resolutely for Zimbabwean unity. The onus will rest squarely on those who broke away from the Unity Agreement, and on those outside leaders who aided and abetted and financed such divisions.

'Why is this being done to you?' many persons ask. Was the ANC undesirable to some Frontline States as part of a deal with some superpower holding the purse-strings? Are some leaders supported as they break our unity because they are the 'old boys' of Zimbabwe nationalism? Do some outsiders who shout, 'You should go back to the pulpit', reject the involvement by church leaders in politics? Or could it be that the ANC was the only organization which outside forces found difficult, if not impossible, to manipulate since its leadership takes its orders from no other authority than the masses of Zimbabwe?

In each public forum outside of Zimbabwe we of the ANC have emphasized the following facts:

—That the ANC-Zimbabwe began as a grass-roots organization on December 16, 1971, in Harare, Salisbury;

—That the masses asked me to head their movement—a

197

decision which they overwhelmingly endorsed at the National Congress on March 2, 1974;

—That Zimbabwean nationalist leaders requested me to lead the enlarged ANC-Z after the Zimbabwe Declaration of Unity on December 7, 1974, at State House in Lusaka, a responsibility which I humbly accepted after offering to step down;

—That since 1971 the ANC has been engaged in a highly successful recruitment campaign which led thousands of young men and women to leave Zimbabwe for guerrilla training, inspired as they were by our new national unity and the results-oriented approach which led to the massive defeat of the Smith/Home sell-out constitutional proposal.

The logical fact is that each Zimbabwe political party has inspired its own youth to action. From 1971 to 1974 thousands of young men and women in Zimbabwe knew only one party, the ANC. They had been only young children in the early 1960's during the political activism of ZAPU and ZANU within Rhodesia. They had developed their political consciousness during the fight against the Smith/Home Settlement Proposals.

On the other hand, the older guerrilla commanders grew up as youth under ZAPU or ZANU tutelage. Having lived in exile for many years they were out of touch with the deep desire for unity of the masses within Zimbabwe. It was understandable, therefore, that there would be tensions between the older guerrilla leadership and the younger recruits. This we of the ANC were determined to overcome as in unity we would grow to tolerate, to respect, and to like one another.

The creation of the 'Third Force', like the earlier trumpeting of old ZANU and ZAPU loyalties, fomented internal strife within the guerrilla camps. Beatings, tortures, and killings took place as ZANU or ZAPU militants tried to dissuade thousands of new recruits from remaining loyal to the ANC.

Such actions could be the seeds of future civil war in Zimbabwe. We who sought to implement the people's mandate to unite all Zimbabweans in one liberation struggle watched with dismay as our brothers and sisters in Angola fought amongst themselves after independence, killing more of their own people in six months than all who had been shot by the Portuguese during the prolonged liberation war. At all costs we felt that we must avoid another Angola. But how?

198

I Appeal to the OAU

Having failed to dissuade the Frontline Presidents from supporting the 'Third Force' in February, I determined to plead our case to the full OAU Liberation Committee meeting in Dar-es-Salaam on May 31, 1976, and to the OAU Summit Meeting to be held in Mauritius in July.

In addressing the OAU I reminded the delegates of the 'divide and rule' tactics which Mr. Smith and his cohorts had used to weaken our liberation efforts over many years. While praising the material assistance given by the Frontline States to our freedom fighters, I reminded them that the efforts by the Presidents to impose leaders of their own choice on the liberation army, disregarding the wishes of the people of Zimbabwe, was playing into the hands of the enemy. They were interfering in the internal affairs of Zimbabwe. This was a hard thing to say to friends who had welcomed us into their countries, given us rear bases, taken care of us, given us security, and whose people had died in our struggle. But I felt there was no alternative to frankness, honesty and truthfulness.

I wanted Presidents Kaunda, Nyerere, Machel and Khama to give full support to Zimbabwean unity. I believed that they should bring into line and publicly castigate any Zimbabwean leader who tried to break that unity—including myself, Sithole, Chikerema, Nkomo, Mugabe or anyone else. But I wanted them to leave the whole question of who should lead Zimbabwe to the choice of the people of Zimbabwe themselves. Instead I found them forming a 'Third Force', a 'ZIPA' behind the backs of leaders chosen by the people. This, I declared, could only confuse both the freedom fighters and the people of Zimbabwe.

In conclusion I put forward the following proposals:

1. We request the OAU to respect and recognize the sovereignty of the ANC of Zimbabwe over all matters pertaining to the liberation of Zimbabwe.
2. We request immediate control of all our armed forces wherever they are.
3. All aid destined for the ANC-Z must be channelled through the ANC of Zimbabwe and not through the OAU Liberation Committee. The OAU's role is to facilitate receiving and conveyance of such aid.

4. We wish to reiterate the often repeated position of the OAU that the role of the OAU and individual member states and friends of the struggle of Zimbabwe is only to assist the Liberation Movement.

At the OAU meetings I found many delegates who took my words seriously. The Summit Meeting did not accede to the request from the 'Third Force', supported by the Frontline Presidents, that it be recognized as Zimbabwe's legitimate liberation movement in place of the ANC. Divided among themselves, the Council of Ministers chose to appoint a committee to study further the issue in true bureaucratic style. To my colleagues present I sighed and said, 'Africa still has a long way to go'.

Concerning aid for our liberation struggle, the OAU Liberation Committee won its way as the Political Committee agreed that all OAU assistance to Zimbabwe should continue to be channelled through the OAU Liberation Committee. To us this meant that whoever could curry favour with Colonel Mbita could build a power base sufficient to defy the leadership chosen by the Zimbabwean people. We feared that our unity efforts would continue to be thwarted.

Re-election as Bishop

Following the OAU Summit Meeting I took leave of the political arena to fulfil my continuing responsibilities as a United Methodist bishop. First, I travelled to the United States to speak at church 'schools of mission' in Asilomar and San Francisco, California. Interest was high as 'Nations of Southern Africa: Dilemma for Christians' was the topic designated for study in each church of the denomination during 1976.

My stay in the USA, however, had to be cut short for the Africa Central Conference of the UMC was about to convene in Kitwe, Zambia, during August. The Rhodesia (Zimbabwe) Conference was to be host, which meant that I was to prepare and deliver the keynote address.

My return journey to Africa started on August 11, our twenty-fifth wedding anniversary. Once again family needs had to take second place. I felt extremely lonely among the crowd boarding the plane that night. Once aboard I chanced to find old friends from Ohio, Dr. and Mrs. Harold Ewing, travelling with me to

London. Their words and sympathetic listening helped to ease my separation from my wife, Maggie, on this our day.

At Kitwe I bathed in the warmth of friendship with those from whom I had been separated for so many months. All present rejoiced in the return to our midst of Bishop Ralph Dodge, my predecessor, who had been assigned to represent the general Church at this important conference. We rejoiced that he had not lost the enthusiasm and passion for justice for which he had been renowned as one of our Church's most outspoken and influential bishops in Africa.

The main event of this Conference, held every four years, is the election of bishops to serve in the various countries in Africa. At this session the delegates honoured me with the election to life episcopacy on the first ballot. Once again I was assigned to the Rhodesia (Zimbabwe) area.

But in the Church, as in politics, there may be others jealous for the prestige and power of public office. After the Conference adjourned the Zimbabwe delegates gathered at the home of our fellow countryman, Mr. Ezekiel Makunike. Before separating I felt seized with the spirit of reconciliation. 'I know what was being said about me by one of our brothers in his bid to be elected bishop,' I said openly to the delegates. 'I forgive him and ask you to do so also. Let's forget the past. Let's break all forms of cliques among ourselves and go back to Zimbabwe as brothers and sisters, all of us, black and white.'

I felt it painful to part from these colleagues—painful because they were going back home and I could not join them. I was overcome with emotion as Maggie and I clasped hands and hugged each one. Then we walked silently to our room, hiding our flowing tears.

The Massacre at Nhazonia

Near the end of August, 1976, President Samora Machel called for leaders of all the Zimbabwean liberation movements to meet him in Maputo. Zambian authorities conveyed the summons to me in Lusaka. The call gave no indication of the subject of our meeting, but that was not unusual. I made my way to Maputo unaware that this was to be the one and only occasion when I would be allowed to visit a Zimbabwean camp in Mozambique— or rather the remains of one.

At a hushed meeting in Maputo, President Machel informed

us that we were to be shown the scene of the recent Nhazonia massacre, and to have a chance to meet some of the survivors. Those who went included the late Jason Moyo representing ZAPU, Robert Mugabe for ZANU, Rex Nhongo for ZIPA, Ndabaningi Sithole, James Chikerema and myself.

Our first stop was at the hospital at Chimoyo. There we met Zimbabweans with various degrees of injuries. The bullets of the racists had not killed these victims, but had left a burning hatred for the Smith regime. Almost wordless, we surveyed the results of Smith's terror. Most persons had chest or stomach injuries, indicating that they had stood unsuspecting as the guns spat out death and terror. Then, before returning to the hotel, we went to see those who had minor injuries.

The next day our Mozambican guides took us to Nhazonia. Approaching the camp they showed us the marks of the ravaging enemy. Here were the footprints of Smith's terrorists, marching on to kill an unarmed, unsuspecting people. Here was the path by which they approached the main road. Here was the spot where they cut the telephone wires. Here was the bridge over the Pungwe River, once a beautiful piece of engineering, but now an ugly ruin, blown up by the racist soldiers to cut off pursuit. At the bridge we saw the spot where the racist soldiers murdered a white priest and a white nun.

Crossing the river in a rubber dinghy, we climbed the opposite bank. Suddenly our guide stopped. Pointing at a lonely mound of earth about twenty yards away, he said, 'That is where we buried two of your comrades who were ambushed and killed in their car which was then burned.' That lone grave was our introduction to a scene of unbelievable horror.

Soon we arrived at Nhazonia. The camp took its name from a small nearby river. For Zimbabwe, it means much, much more. Nhazonia today stands as a shrine marking the oppression and misery of our people amidst their liberation struggle. It is another example of the inhumanity of the enemy.

First, we saw the remains of houses and huts gutted by fire. 'Many people burned to death in them,' our guide reported. Looking about, our eyes met a nauseating scene—the stains of blood of Zimbabweans who had tried in vain to flee from the guns which had spat out death. Scattered about were the empty cartridge shells, empty because they had done their evil work.

Here and there lay the personal belongings dropped by victims as they attempted to flee from the rain of death.

Relentlessly, our guides took us to the big earth heaps above trenches which had been filled with the broken bodies of the victims. The bodies of men, women and children had been heaped together in fourteen mass graves as follows:

Grave	Number of Bodies
No. 1	166
,, 2	25
,, 3	1
,, 4	50
,, 5	155
,, 6	140
,, 7	(unknown)
,, 8	(unknown)
,, 9	18
,, 10	24
,, 11	23
,, 12	96
,, 13	23
,, 14	(unknown)

We do not know how many bodies lie in graves 7, 8 and 14 because the enemy burned the bodies, making it difficult to know the number of victims. Altogether over 675 Zimbabweans are buried at Nhazonia.

This was the end of the road, not just for us, but for hundreds of Smith's victims. Standing there, I recalled another occasion when I arrived at a village too late for a funeral, and found a loved one already buried. It was no solace to complain about the poor telephone or mail service. I stood by the graveside in silent sorrow. It was the same for me that day at Nhazonia. There was no point in expressing openly the anger boiling up inside me. Yes, these were unarmed, innocent refugees. Nevertheless, I found myself wanting to ask officials to explain how the enemy had penetrated into Mozambique, and killed hundreds without losing a single one of their own soldiers.

Openly we comforted each other by declaring that this was war. All of us made resolutions that the enemy must be made to pay for this dastardly crime. It was galling to feel that we, the leaders of Zimbabwe, were being shown where hundreds of Zimbabweans under our charge met their death. Helpless as I was, I could only ask everybody present to observe a few moments of silence.

Then we heard a horrid postscript. In front of all of us, including the top ZAPU officials led by the late Jason Moyo, our Mozambican guide said: 'It was a ZAPU defector who led Smith's forces to Nhazonia on August 8, 1976, at 9.30 a.m.' We gasped, as he continued, 'Yes, it was a Zimbabwean who brought death to hundreds of other Zimbabweans.' I recalled pictures of the massacre which I had seen in a Beira hotel with the caption in Portuguese, 'ZAPU traitors did this'. I felt ashamed, so ashamed, that Zimbabwe had spawned people like this. And I wondered, how much money had this man been offered to be a Judas? Was his motive money? surely this tragedy could be attributed in part to those forces promoting division and disunity among Zimbabweans. I am justified in my bitterness, then and now, in laying the blame for the Nhazonia massacre on both Ian Smith and his racist oppressors, and on those external forces which delight in playing off one group of Zimbabweans against the other. What other conclusion is there to reach?

Our guides took us next to see the survivors. We found them in the process of constructing a new camp. Looking on the scene three strong impressions crossed my mind. First, it seemed as if the whole of Zimbabwe was at work there in the bush. Close to eight thousand people were there—men, women and children. Next, their industry impressed me deeply. One might have expected to see frightened people, huddled together in helplessness. Instead, everyone was busy. Some were cutting grass, others were felling trees, others were constructing new huts, while still others were preparing the evening meal. Finally, I sensed the signs of misery and suffering which even one's pride could not hide. Most of the people were dressed in rags. The children looked underfed and sickly. Nevertheless, shouting, singing, and laughing, these Zimbabweans went about the task of building a home away from home.

Within thirty minutes of our arrival, however, all work stopped as the people gathered to meet us. We greeted them and spoke a few words of comfort. At such a time words seemed out of place. We all were victims of a ruthless enemy. We could not say, 'Sorry, this tragedy has happened.' What had taken place was not an accident, but cold-blooded murder. The only assurance we could offer was that we joined with them in our resolve to destroy this rabid enemy. But we all knew that there will be more suffering before liberty is won. The survivors of this tragedy had no option but to take up the struggle left them by those whose bodies filled the mass graves nearby.

As we stood there I sensed a united determination of all present to continue the liberation struggle—to fight, yes, and to die if necessary. An odd incident, however, broke this spirit of unity as a small number of persons started heckling Rev. Sithole and myself as we spoke. '*Pasi neBeburá!*' ('Down with the Bible!') a young man shouted. Obviously, the majority in the crowd disapproved of his antics. We felt encouraged that the thousands present did not support this effort to shout down religion. Later we learned that during the night some leaders of ZIPA tried to get the refugees to repudiate Rev. Sithole and myself, but only a small group supported this effort. I learned that the one who had shouted 'Down with the Bible' was the son of an Anglican priest.

I shall never forget our parting, as the crowd burst into song, '*Zimbabwe yanetsa maihwe!*' ('O, mother, the Zimbabwe struggle has become difficult!'). It was a cry for help from the wilderness by those living widely separated from their parents and from their leaders. Slowly, almost reluctantly, the men, women and children went back to their chores, while we stood hushed and saddened.

'Can they see hope?' I wondered. 'Who keeps them informed about the progress of the struggle? Who ministers to those hungry and sick among them? Who is able to take some of the suffering from their heavily-laden shoulders?' Once again I longed to be able to live with them, to be on hand to provide them with the leadership they so desperately needed. I left with the fervent hope that they understood the true reason why I was not there, yet I carried a heavy sense of guilt.

The world which remembers the Sharpeville massacre in which sixty-nine of our brothers and sisters in South Africa were gunned down during a peaceful protest, must now add the memory of the bloodbath at Nhazonia where over 675 Zimbabweans were murdered.

Another Split During Unity Talks

From Nhazonia we went to Dar-es-Salaam for another meeting with the Frontline Presidents. They determined to make an attempt once more to unite us as Zimbabweans, perhaps feeling that seeing the horrors at Nhazonia might stiffen our resolve to unite for the intensification of the liberation struggle.

One night our hosts left all the Zimbabweans together to talk out our differences. Looking around the room, I realized how our divisions had multiplied. Just twenty months before we had signed an agreement to unite in the ANC. Now around me sat Joshua Nkomo and his ZAPU lieutenants, Robert Mugabe and those claiming ZANU leadership, and Rex Nhongo with his ZIPA officers. Rev. Ndabaningi Sithole and Rev. Max Chigwida, Publicity Secretary succeeding the kidnapped Dr. Edson Sithole, joined me in the ANC delegation.

I wish that I could report progress that night. Brother Nkomo talked a great deal, but not about unity. Instead he argued that the ANC delegation should be barred from the meeting. To my surprise the ZIPA men vigorously defended our presence. The meeting went on until 4.50 a.m., but with little headway.

Two days later, on September 9, Max Chigwida came to my room and asked, 'Bishop, do you know that Rev. Sithole is holding a press conference downstairs?'

'No, I don't,' I replied. 'What is the conference about?'

'He is pulling out of the ANC,' Chigwida replied.

'Well, I am not surprised,' I responded. 'I have heard that he has been holding secret meetings with some people. I wish, though, that he had told me first. We have never quarrelled, have we?' My question to Max could not disguise the hurt that I felt inside.

After the press conference one of Rev. Sithole's aides delivered a formal document to me declaring that he had withdrawn from the ANC. The next time I saw Rev. Sithole was in a hospital after his sudden illness.

This new development deepened our sense of frustration in our desire for Zimbabwean unity. We had come to Dar-es-Salaam, the city of peace, seeking for it, but had failed utterly in our quest. Our divisions were greater than before. Meanwhile, the drive for liberation moved forward all too slowly.

Chapter 16

Geneva

Towards the end of September 1976, it became clear that there was going to be a constitutional conference on Rhodesia. I welcomed the prospect. A constitutional conference had always been the immediate objective of our struggle during the past bitter decades. Since our decisive triumph over the Smith-Home Proposals, I had striven and prayed for a formula which would enable an effective and immediate transfer of power from the minority to the majority. The conference would be that formula.

The 'Package Deal'

Early in 1976 Dr. Henry Kissinger, the United States Secretary of State, woke up to southern Africa. Pursuing an adventurous foreign policy in an attempt to bolster Gerald Ford's re-election to the Presidency, he set out to 'solve the Rhodesian Problem'. Dr. Kissinger's chief strategy in his diplomatic shuttle between African capitals was to twist Mr. Smith's arm by winning Prime Minister Vorster of South Africa to his side. His goal was to bring Ian Smith to the constitutional conference table before November, the month of the US presidential election. In this effort Dr. Kissinger won allies for various reasons. President Kaunda of Zambia for economic reasons desperately wanted the trade routes to Zimbabwe and South Africa reopened. As for the British, they longed to dispose of Rhodesia, their last colonial thorn.

The US Secretary of State adroitly began his shuttle diplomacy by visiting independent African states. Before his departure from Washington, the US State Department informed me that Dr. Kissinger wished to see leaders of the Zimbabwean liberation movements, including those of the African National Council. I determined to seek the consensus of the Zimbabwe Liberation Council, our external wing, before replying to this invitation.

'Decline the invitation,' our members replied without much

discussion. Since the founding of the ANC, we had repeatedly asked the US Government to put economic and diplomatic pressure on Smith to accept African majority rule. Our requests fell on deaf ears as the US continued to buy chromium ore from Rhodesia in contravention of United Nations' sanctions. It continued to permit the Smith regime to operate its Information Office in Washington DC, to spread its propaganda and to lobby politicians and business leaders in support of continued white minority rule. To us Dr. Kissinger's coming to Africa just when the guerrilla war was succeeding was duplicity designed not to bring about majority rule, but to subvert the liberation war through deceitful promises. I refused to see Dr. Kissinger in Lusaka. Only Joshua Nkomo, among Zimbabwean nationalists, accepted his invitation.

Once again in September 1976 the Frontline Presidents called Zimbabwe's leaders to Dar-es-Salaam for strategy talks. Once again we agreed on the need to intensify the armed struggle. The 'militants' included all of us without exception—Joshua Nkomo, James Chikerema, Ndabaningi Sithole, Robert Mugabe and myself. Efforts by the Presidents to reconcile our differences concerning leadership, however, failed once again.

Our militancy seemed only to drive Dr. Kissinger to redouble his peace initiative. In fact, our action may have strengthened his hand with Vorster and Smith, since they both abhorred the alternative to a settlement—a prolonged guerrilla war. On September 16 the Rhodesian Front Congress gave Ian Smith a free hand to pursue his negotiations on a constitutional settlement. Eight days later he electrified the world with the announcement: 'Rhodesia agrees to majority rule within two years.'

The Rhodesia Prime Minister went on to outline the other points of Dr. Kissinger's 'Package Deal' as follows:

'Representatives of the Rhodesian Government will meet immediately at a mutually agreed place with African leaders to organize an interim Government to function until majority rule is implemented.

'The interim Government should consist of a Council of State, half of whose members will be Black and half White with a White chairman without a special vote.

'The interim Government should also have a Council of Ministers with a majority of Africans and an African First

Minister. For the period of the interim Government the Ministers of Defence and of Law and Order would be Whites. 'The United Kingdom will enact enabling legislation for the process to majority rule . . .

'Upon the establishment of the interim Government, sanctions will be lifted and all acts of war, including guerrilla warfare, will cease.

'Substantial economic support will be made available by the international community to provide assurance to Rhodesians about the economic future of the country . . .'

Within two days the Frontline Presidents met to consider the 'Package Deal'. In their statement they commended the people and fighters of Zimbabwe who by their heroic armed struggle had forced the rebel regime of Ian Smith to accept the inevitability of majority rule. They called on Great Britain to convene the proposed constitutional conference at once outside Zimbabwe. As for the proposed terms of an interim Government, the Presidents vehemently rejected them as 'tantamount to legalizing the colonialist and racist structures of power'. In conclusion, they reaffirmed their commitment to the cause of liberation in Zimbabwe and to the armed struggle. The responsibility then was Great Britain's.

The Open Door to Unity

'What will be the ANC's response?' people asked from Lusaka to Salisbury. More than at any other time in my fourteen months of exile, I longed to be back in Zimbabwe with my people to confer with them. 'Is this possible?' I wondered, 'or as the Commander-in-Chief of the freedom fighters am I also in the eyes of Ian Smith another "terrorist" to be eliminated?' Undecided, I accepted President Seretse Khama's invitation to attend the tenth anniversary celebration of Botswana's independence in her capital, Gaberone.

Upon my arrival in Gaberone, I found key leaders concerned lest Zimbabweans reach the conference table still divided politically. Having Mr. Nkomo and myself both present in the same town posed an opportunity not to be missed by well-wishers. One was Canon Burgess Carr, the General Secretary of the All Africa Conference of Churches (AACC) who chose to talk separately with Mr. Nkomo and myself. President Mobutu Sese Seko of Zaire was another catalyst in this reconciliation attempt.

I must confess that I was not optimistic about prospects for unity with Mr. Nkomo. We had made similar attempts during the year at the OAU summit meeting in Mauritius and in Lusaka during meetings of the Frontline Presidents. On returning to Salisbury Mr. Nkomo had declared that such meetings were a waste of time, and asked that I stop bothering him about unity.

His words were fresh in my mind when we met in the house of a Botswana Government official. Again, there were just the two of us. I felt that the imperative need for unity in the liberation struggle, and the requests of our well-wishers required that I meet Mr. Nkomo. Although I had been away from Rhodesia for fourteen months I did not know the feelings of my Executive members concerning such unity talks.

'I think you and I can work together,' Mr. Nkomo said after greeting me. I was taken aback by this new eagerness. Could it be that Mr. Nkomo was now fully aware of his loss of credibility in the eyes of the Zimbabwe masses? I wondered. I could sense his fear of going to a constitutional conference with so little popular support within Rhodesia.

'How do you propose that we effect this unity?' I asked soon after we met. On previous occasions his insistence that all concerned acknowledge his 'seniority' in Zimbabwe had thwarted our unity efforts. This time he hedged and attempted to evade the question.

'Exactly how do we go about working together?' I insisted.

'We can have one executive body,' Mr. Nkomo said. 'You are closer to me than the people in ZANU. I want you to strengthen my hand so that I can bring the ZANU people into the fold.' I responded that as I was on my way to Zimbabwe I would prefer to consult my Executive concerning his proposal, and then plan to meet again with him in Rhodesia. This formed the basis for our response given shortly thereafter to Mr. Edward Rowlands, British Minister of State for African Affairs, who also argued that our differences were endangering progress towards majority rule within two years.

A Tumultuous Welcome Home
I felt strongly an imperative urge that the Zimbabwean people have a say in deciding our response to these two key issues before the

ANC: the Kissinger 'Package Deal', and the new Zimbabwean unity proposals. Increasingly my advisors urged me to return home, including Mr. Musindo Chenga, Chief Representative of the ANC in London, other friends in London and Canon Burgess Carr of the AACC. In Gaberone, Mr. James Chikerema strengthened my resolve when he said, 'President, you should return home. There is a time when every leader must act alone and alone make up his mind and make a decision. This may be such a time, but no one must force you into it.'

Still seeking other opinions, I called the Alex Chibanguzas in Rhodesia, my sister and brother-in-law, and explained my intention. 'Father says you must not come back,' my sister Clara replied. Was this one of those times when even a parent has to be disobeyed in the interest of many? I wondered. My brother-in-law shared my dilemma as he responded, 'Politically, I say you should return home, Abel, but for your own safety, I am not sure it is advisable.'

The final decision was mine alone. Before making the final choice, I went down on my knees to put my doubts and fears before God, requesting His divine guidance, taking courage from His nearness and love. Arising in my Holiday Inn room, I phoned our ANC Vice-President, Dr. Gabellah, to announce my decision to return. 'I believe that the Smith regime will hesitate to act against you,' Dr. Gabellah replied, 'for they fear being accused of wrecking the prospects of a constitutional conference.'

Arrangements for my return flight to Salisbury from Gaberone, however, did not go smoothly. Dr. Chakanyuka Chikosi, ANC Secretary for External Affairs, Justin Nyoka, a freelance Zimbabwean journalist, and I failed to obtain firm reservations from Johannesburg to Salisbury. This fact only heightened our apprehension concerning the return trip. Arriving in Johannesburg we remained wait-listed on the Salisbury flight until twenty minutes before departure.

'Will there be anyone at the airport to welcome us? I wondered as the plane touched down at 2.14 p.m. on Sunday, October 3. News of my decision to return home reached Salisbury just forty-eight hours earlier. Descending the plane's stairs, I noticed a crowd of excited people on the airport balcony. Stepping inside the terminal, two police officers approached me, Dr. Gabellah, and other ANC Executive members. 'At least there will be witnesses if Smith's security forces attempt to kidnap me,' I thought to myself.

'Please hurry, Bishop,' one of the policemen said. 'There is a big crowd waiting for you at Highfield. You must only greet the people! And no political speeches, you understand,' he continued. 'We don't want any trouble.'

'Yes,' I replied, trying to puzzle out why the man appeared so ill at ease. (Later I would learn that the pre-Geneva Conference relaxation of political restrictions had indeed saved me from arrest, or worse, that day.)

In record time I completed immigration and customs formalities. 'What a contrast,' I remarked, 'to my normal treatment as an African of being made to wait until the last like an unwanted stranger in his own country.' Walking towards the exit in a kind of daze, I found myself in the arms of my mother. Someone had been thoughtful enough to arrange that she be the first to greet me. She looked as if she couldn't believe that I had come home safe and sound. The rest of the family were there also to greet me.

Suddenly, without warning, someone grabbed me and, with others, lifted me shoulder high above a mass of people who appeared from nowhere. 'HEAVY! HEAVY!' echoed through the airport building—an early slogan adopted by the ANC. As we emerged from the terminal the crowd seemed to swell in numbers and excitement. My triumphant bearers deposited me in a shiny Mercedes-Benz convertible. Later I learned the name of the supporter who loaned me that marvellous vehicle on that day, and wrote him my thanks. Soon there was a long convoy of cars filled with excited ANC supporters, who raised clenched fists in the ANC salute and sang and shouted as they passed through the crowds which thronged the roads from the airport to Highfield. All along the way people waved to me and shouted our Party slogans.

Reaching Highfield, I immediately understood the cause of the policeman's anxiety. Never before had I seen such a crowd, estimated at 500,000 by many present. Surveying the scene, trying to take it all in, I was deeply impressed by the discipline of our people, and the capability of our ANC youth leaders to maintain order. Later, many of these youth would be hauled into Smith's courts and charged by the racist police with assuming the role of the police. Every single magistrate conceded that the youth had maintained perfect order. They sentenced them, nevertheless, to varying terms of imprisonment. To have acquitted them would have been to admit that, given the chance, we Zimbabweans could run our affairs better than the white establishment.

Journalists began to ply me with questions. 'How do you feel about this reception?', one asked. How could I answer with half a million downtrodden but proud people around me shouting that they were solidly behind me? How could I explain my admiration and love for those who at forty-eight hours' notice had travelled by bus, car and on foot to see me? To be there they had braved army road-blocks, police searches, the guns of the regime eager to shoot curfew breakers, lack of money, and the scorching October heat. I felt a choking frustration at being forbidden by the police to address these brave people who had come to welcome me back after fourteen months in exile.

Later, in Geneva, I would be free to say what I felt that day— that it is the masses of Zimbabwe and no one else who are the primary factor in the so-called 'Rhodesia situation'. That day the masses by their presence told the British, the Frontline States, and the whole world that it would be futile to ignore their wishes. They convinced us that the African National Council must stand by the principle of One-Person, One-Vote.

Preparing for Geneva

That October 3 mass rally, without speeches, set in motion the ANC's preparations for the Geneva Constitutional Conference. After the rally I held a press conference and convened the ANC National Executive. We accepted the heavy agenda to be completed in three brief weeks: finalizing our official ANC delegation to the Conference, drafting our position papers, and determining our relationships with other Zimbabwean nationalists who had been invited to Geneva. Time was at a premium and the pace intense.

First, we tackled the unity issue. I briefed the Executive on my discussions with Joshua Nkomo in Gaberone and they shared with me the sentiments within the country. It became crystal clear that Mr. Nkomo had lost much of his former support by breaking away from the ANC. The people within Zimbabwe cherished their unity. They wished to safeguard it and to work together in their fight for self-determination, but considered Nkomo to be a divisive force, despite his recent unity overtures. Their response, however, did not satisfy me, for I have never turned away from unity attempts and wished to discuss this attempt further. Joshua Nkomo, however, wanted my answer immediately. Rejecting my request for more time to consider the matter, Mr. Nkomo left immediately, in a huff, for Mozambique. Within a week he and

Robert Mugabe announced in Dar-es-Salaam and Lusaka the formation of a 'Patriotic Front' which would send a joint delegation to the proposed constitutional conference.

Meanwhile, I had more than enough to consider. Selecting a balanced delegation to the Geneva Conference was a major task. We wished to include those leading in the extensive external operations of the ANC as well as those who could speak for the majority of Zimbabwe's six million blacks within the country. Our team of thirty-six included Dr. Elliott Gabellah (ANC Vice-President), Dr. Gordon Chavunduka (Secretary-General), Mr. Morton Malianga (National Chairman), Mr. George Nyandoro, the Rev. Canaan Banana whose restriction orders had recently been lifted, and the Rev. Henry Kachidza. The Rev. Max Chigwida served as Publicity Secretary and Chief Spokesman of the Delegation. From Rhodesia, Zambia, Britain and the USA we called our most talented Zimbabwean lawyers to serve as political and legal advisors. Justice R. J. H. Benjamin of Ghana agreed to assist me as Chief Legal Consultant.

Our team, however, seemed incomplete. Dr. Edson Sithole, the legal brain of the Party, was still missing, after being kidnapped, and Enos Nkala, our former Secretary-General, was still in detention. Determined that these key men should be released to join us in Geneva, I wrote a letter to Mr. Gaylord, Secretary to Smith's Cabinet, requesting their release. Concerning Dr. Sithole I wrote, 'I know that you have him, although he is at Robben Island in South Africa.' I found it revealing when Mr. Gaylord replied, 'I am going to contact the South Africans about it.' This was the first time a white official admitted that the South Africans were involved in Dr. Sithole's disappearance, and did not deny the Smith regime's involvement. No further progress took place in these cases, however, although the Rev. Henry Kachidza was released from detention and allowed to join the ANC delegation.

Barely a week before the Conference was due to start, I rushed on to Zambia to supervise the finalizing of ANC documents. In Lusaka I took up the question of the release of Dr. Edson Sithole and Mr. Enos Nkala with the British High Commissioner, who forwarded my appeal to London. Once again I received the stock reply which revealed British impotence to put pressure on Ian Smith: 'I am afraid there is very little we can do in the circumstances.'

At Geneva the ANC chose to leave two seats unoccupied, but

labelled. One was for Dr. Edson Sithole and the other for Mr. Enos Nkala. We wanted the whole world to know that the white racists had deprived our delegation of two prominent members, that our struggle was not child's play, but a matter of life and death. For me those two empty seats represented all those hundreds of young Zimbabweans who had fallen, and were falling, in the fight for liberation. They stood for the hundreds who had disappeared without a trace, and the thousands languishing in prisons and detention camps as political prisoners.

Many persons have asked me, 'If you support so strongly the liberation war, why did you go to talk with Smith again in Geneva?' I am no romantic concerning war, and the suffering and death which it entails. A liberation war is not for me an end in itself, but a means to the end of political liberation. I abhor the philosophy that prolonged war liberates the mind. This to me is inhuman. War remains a last resort, to be employed as a form of self-defence when all other means to achieve justice have been tried in vain. I went to Geneva in an honest attempt to bring an end to the untold suffering of our people, to reap the result of the sacrificial blood shed by our freedom fighters. This was my mandate from the people of Zimbabwe at Geneva.

Five Concerns

Many persons will write the factual history of our failure at Geneva to wrest African majority rule for Zimbabwe from Mr. Ian Smith and his delegation. Looking back on the Conference, I recall five issues which concerned me and the entire ANC delegation: the astronomical cost of it all, the problem of security, the image of disunity displayed by Zimbabweans, the incessant delays, and the power plays by other Zimbabweans.

First, we of the African National Council faced the problem created by the high cost of living in Geneva. We have never been an affluent body. In fact, we have not sought rich patrons for fear of being bought. Our chief backers, the six million poor of Zimbabwe, were too busy financing the liberation war inside Zimbabwe to spare huge sums for our hospitality. Thus, the very first time I met with the ANC delegation in Geneva, I raised the issue of where we should live. The British organizers assumed that we would stay at the Intercontinental Hotel. All other delegation leaders chose to stay in that posh establishment for the million-aire, rich tourist or lazy rich, while sending their delegates to

215

cheaper hotels. For my part, I chose the Continental Hotel, a homely and very unsophisticated hotel in the Rue des Alpes, and recommended that all of us from the ANC stay there together. Friendly and efficient service compensated for its lack of glitter.

Security became our second concern. Soon after our opening session Mr. Ivor Richard, the Conference Chairman, called me to one side and said: 'Bishop, I have discovered that some of the delegates are armed. I am informing every delegation leader that no delegate is to bring a gun into the Conference room.' Looking at me with a half-smile, he continued, 'Will you please let your delegation know this in case there are some carrying firearms?' I understood his concern. Many brought to this conference deep rancour towards others. Some in the past had hunted each other, gun in hand. Among Robert Mugabe's delegation were some individuals who threatened all and sundry, saying, 'We will kill you if you stand in our way,' or 'We will shoot you down if you oppose us,' or 'When we take over we are going to shoot you!'

In another respect this was an explosive situation for in the same 'neutral' city was Ian Smith and his white delegation. Back at home we formed two armed camps locked in battle. There was no assurance that violence like that which caused Dr. Edson Sithole's disappearance, and the Nhazonia massacre, would not erupt here.

A third worry was the image of Zimbabwean disunity being engraved on the world's memory by our behaviour at Geneva. Some Zimbabweans delighted in parading our disunity before the world's cameras, while our country continued to face grave, fatal difficulties. I felt like apologizing to the world for those actions by which some Zimbabweans put themselves first, and the well-being of our nation and its people second. 'Already the granting of independence to Zimbabwe has been delayed for one month,' I declared to the press on November 26, 'while some people are wining, dining, bickering and dithering in the expensive hotels of Geneva.'

The interminable delays were my fourth concern. I felt an urgency to get on with the work of planning for the transfer of power from white to black in Zimbabwe. I felt that six million Zimbabweans had mandated me to go to Geneva to obtain an honourable end to their suffering. Would the British never learn? I wondered. At Geneva Mr. Ivor Richard seemed more concerned to read the pulse of the Frontline States than to proceed with the hard negotiations leading to a transitional government. Instead of discussing substantive issues in the transfer of power, we spent three weeks arguing over a three-month difference between delegations over the proposed date for Zimbabwe's independence. The Conference dragged on and on. It seemed clear that three delegations—those of Smith, Nkomo and Mugabe —went to Geneva determined to play tricks in order to wreck the Conference. Frankly, I expected more statesmanship.

Finally, we of the ANC struggled against the power plays of other Zimbabwean delegations. Rejection by other delegations of the cardinal principle of One-Person, One-Vote was a cutting worry. My delegation placed the greatest emphasis on the involvement of the masses in the selection of an interim government on the basis of universal adult suffrage. This is what the black people of Zimbabwe had been denied for eighty-six long, oppressive years. This is what the Geneva Conference was all about—the transfer of power from the minority to the majority.

To my surprise we alone of the ANC supported One-Person, One-Vote. Ndabaningi Sithole, Joshua Nkomo, Robert Mugabe and their delegates all opposed it. Why? Each one feared rejection by their own people if universal adult suffrage came into effect. Naturally, Smith and his delegates opposed the principle. To our surprise the British did not stand with us, either, for they were too busy trying to please the Frontline States who supported the Patriotic Front, and its contention that the future leaders of Zimbabwe should be named outside the country. This rejection was a bitter pill for the ANC to swallow. We resolved to continue fighting for the adoption and application of this central, democratic principle.

Our Stand
Mr. Ivor Richard formally opened the Geneva Conference on October 28, 1976. On that day all delegations delivered their opening statements setting out their postures. At long last we Zimbabweans had the chance to tell Ian Smith to his face what the masses of Zimbabweans felt about his regime's reign of terror, without threat of immediate imprisonment or worse.

'The UANC is not here in a spirit of give and take,' I declared. 'We have come here only to take—to take our country.' Continuing, I spoke about the unity which we all affirmed as Zimbabweans regardless of our party labels:

217

'We stand solidly united in our demand for majority rule here and now. We stand solidly united in our view that Britain is the colonial power, and that the struggle for independence is an anti-colonial struggle. We stand solidly united in saying that the so-called 'Kissinger Package' is not an inviolate, sacred capsule in which is contained all the wisdom of this world. We stand solidly united when we say that in the event of an Interim Government being formed, Defence and Law and Order should not be in the hands of Mr. Ian Smith or his appointee. We stand solidly united in our resolve that in the event of this Conference not succeeding, the armed struggle will continue with relentless intensity until every inch of Zimbabwe soil is free.'

Then I went on to outline the ANC proposals for an interim government. Its mandate should be to produce a majority rule independence constitution within twelve months. As for the choice of the new Prime Minister, I affirmed that it must be done on the basis of popular election by One-Man, One-Vote. So as to permit various political groups to participate in the interim government, I proposed that cabinet posts be allocated to parties in direct proportion to the number of votes cast for each party.

In rejecting that provision of the 'Kissinger Package' which would allow the whites to retain control of the ministries of Defence and Law and Order in the interim government, I recounted the nefarious record of violence and torture of Zimbabweans perpetrated by Smith's army and police in the name of 'preserving law and order.' 'Can we allow the Ministries of Defence and of Law and Order to be headed by men who are capable of committing such brutal atrocities upon defenceless civilians?' I asked. I demanded the release of political prisoners and the revocation of death sentences imposed on such prisoners; the granting of a general amnesty; the creation of conditions conducive to free political activities and freedom of expression; the halting of all political trials; the lifting of the state of emergency together with all restrictive regulations—'in short, the immediate suspension of the present racist and oppressive constitution'.

As soon as the Chairman adjourned the session, Mr. Van der Byl, Smith's Foreign Minister, hastily called a press conference. He began: 'Ladies and gentlemen of the press, I have called you here because of what the so-called Bishop Muzorewa has said.' His method of denying the atrocities being committed by the racist soldiers against innocent African civilians was typical of Rhodesia Front tactics, as he distributed a propaganda pamphlet purporting to document atrocities committed by Zimbabwean guerrillas. Our ANC evidence revealed, however, that in reality these atrocities were the dastardly work of the Selous Scouts, the terror wing of Smith's army. The Selous Scouts are a largely black unit secretly trained in guerrilla tactics and outfitted with both uniforms and weapons captured from fallen freedom fighters. In their murderous disguise they kill civilians and white missionaries, commit atrocities against women and children, and lay traps for unsuspecting persons. They do this to discredit the freedom fighters and to drive a wedge between the guerrillas and the masses. I exposed the activities of the Selous Scouts for the first time at Geneva.

Further evidence that my exposé had stung the enemy came three days later when Mr. Mark Partridge, a member of Smith's cabinet, visited my hotel room. Representatives of Moral Rearmament had arranged our meeting. Unfortunately, one of Smith's police accompanied Mr. Partridge. His presence angered me and my three ANC colleagues because of what he represented. Mr. Partridge came to lodge a complaint about the words I had spoken in exposing the Rhodesian Front's reign of terror. 'Why don't you trust my government?' he asked. I replied that I had already given my reasons in my opening statement, and that no cajoling would cause me to change them, for they were the truth about the regime's reign of terror. Mr. Partridge sought to defend the Smith regime, but soon left, seeing that he was making no headway in the heated debate.

No Common Ground

This was not the only verbal bout, however, that went on in my presence during those first weeks in Geneva. Others took place during our ANC drive to encourage greater unity among the various Zimbabwean delegations.

Soon after reaching Geneva, our ANC delegation formed a Contacts Committee. Its aim was to contact all the other black delegations, seeking common areas of agreement and probing the prospects for a united approach. Since we were all in the one city, it would seem logical that we could establish friendship and unity if we could approach each other with good will and selflessness. I had promised Mr. Nkomo, for one, that I would return to the issue

219

of unity at an appropriate time. No time seemed more appropriate than at Geneva.

Our hopes were soon dashed on the rocks. The Nkomo group refused to talk with us, while Robert Mugabe and his delegation ridiculously suggested that the ANC should disband and join ZANU.

Undeterred, I sought another attempt at unity as the Conference turned to discuss proposals for an independence date. Surely all black groups could agree on one date. I asked Justice R. J. H. Benjamin of Ghana, legal consultant attached to my delegation, but mandated to help all groups, to contact the other Zimbabwean delegations to seek a common approach. Mr. Mugabe was about to agree with my proposal that September 12, 1977, the twentieth anniversary of the transformation of the Youth League into the new African National Congress, be accepted as Independence Day. Just then Mr. Nkomo objected. Once again the Patriotic Front became an exercise in negativeness as Mr. Mugabe withdrew his tentative agreement.

The Do-Nothing Conference

October crept into November, and November dragged on with no sign of progress. A British official said to me one day in the corridor of the Palais de Nation, 'Bishop, you will have to learn to ski going by the rate at which the Conference is moving!' I shuddered at the prospect of twiddling my thumbs in Geneva while our people were dying at home. Each Zimbabwe delegation was running into financial difficulties. One delegation leader suddenly left Geneva for an unknown destination, the story being that he was trying to round up more funds. Almost furtively, delegations moved from the Intercontinental Hotel into cheaper accommodation.

Each delay seemed to trigger off another. The Chairman began to make rather frequent visits to London 'for consultations', adjourning the sessions while doing so. For three weeks Patriotic Front leaders argued with the Chairman over the proposed date of independence without making any progress towards agreement. Only later we learned the real reason for the delay—that the Patriotic Front had not yet received instructions from its 'masters' to move on to another stage of negotiation, and so marked time.

Meanwhile Smith had become restive. Nobody appeared to be implementing the Kissinger 'Package Deal' which he declared was the only true business of the Conference. He flew back to Salisbury in a huff, leaving Mr. Van der Byl in charge of the Rhodesian Front delegation. Smith obviously feared that many whites would suspect a sell-out of white rule in Geneva unless he returned to Salisbury to bolster their morale.

An article from the *Rhodesia Herald* which reached me in Geneva epitomized the tragic consequences of Smith's intransigence. It included pictures of war victims. One was on crutches. Several were in wheel chairs because both legs had been blown off. All looked battered and shattered. Rev. Kachidza, upon seeing the photos, remarked, 'Remember, Bishop, the speech you gave five years ago in which you asked, "Are we waiting to go to a constitutional conference in wheel chairs and tucked-in-sleeves?" Now here we are at the Conference and there (pointing to the photos) are the wheel chairs and tucked-in sleeves being paraded at home.'

Finally, on November 15, after consultations in London, Mr. Ivor Richard announced that the Conference would 'move on to something else' since it lacked agreement on the independence date. I responded favourably to his desire for forward progress, saying, 'For the sake of Zimbabwe's liberation and freedom my delegation desires that the conference should now move to discuss substantial matters, and, in particular, the structure of the interim Government.'

Mr. Richard responded, and put forward a British-US proposal for a two-tier interim Government consisting of a small legislature responsible for drafting a new constitution, and a council of ministers to formulate and implement policies for the transitional Government.

We of the ANC opposed the proposal to have a non-elected legislature. 'For us it is basic and essential that even the transitional Government be a representative Government,' I said, 'and this can only be created by an election on a One-Man, One-Vote basis. We are adamant in this respect.' Other proposals which I introduced included the formation of a National Security Council as part of the interim Government, with a Governor as Chairman appointed by Her Majesty the Queen on the advice of the Prime Minister. The Council would be responsible for national security, and would 'transform the present guerrilla forces into a national Army'.

While realizing that our proposal for the national army would cause Smith to reject it, we expected our fellow Zimbabweans to find it attractive. Instead the Patriotic Front rejected our initiative, principally because they wanted leaders of an interim Government to be chosen by outside nomination rather than by popular election. Evidently the Frontline States had instructed them to react in this way to protect their own survival. They estimated that Joshua Nkomo and Robert Mugabe would win little support in a popular election within Zimbabwe.

It was the Patriotic Front, together with the Rhodesian Front, who wrecked the Geneva Conference. Together they formed what I call an 'undemocratic front' as they united to oppose universal adult suffrage.

Our Popular Mandate

With the Conference deadlocked, I decided to return to Salisbury on December 12. Once again I discovered a huge crowd waiting to welcome me. Again there were nervous policemen, saying, 'Please hurry up, Bishop, and talk to the people before they get out of hand!' Once again I found myself rushed through immigration and customs formalities and out to the waiting crowd. As on October 3 I found the streets lined with cheering crowds as the long motorcade wound its way to Highfield in Salisbury.

The response of the masses astounded me. Only a few weeks previously hundreds of thousands had turned out to welcome Dr. Gabellah upon his return from Geneva. Here again were an estimated 500,000 to welcome me back. Standing on a roof top, I failed to see the far edge of the assembled crowd.

I attempted to tell all the people assembled about my desire for a new mandate, but the police forbid use of a public address system. The megaphone which I used seemed hopelessly inadequate, yet somehow the issue at hand got through to the monstrous crowd. With one voice they roared 'WE WANT ONE-MAN ONE-VOTE ONLY!' A forest of placards waving in the air carried the same message. The people would accept nothing short of One-Person One-Vote.

Then the miracle of October 3 occurred again as the multitude responded to my request to disperse peacefully. The hundreds of thousands simply melted away, giving the clenched fist ANC salute, shouting 'Heavy!' and singing our ANC victory songs.

Once again I called a press conference to outline in clearer terms than was possible in a political rally the position of the ANC. Our mandate at Geneva, I declared, was '(1) to demand for an interim Government elected on the basis of One-Man One-Vote, and (2) for independence within the shortest possible time after a general election, conducted on the principle of One-Man One-Vote.' I described how other delegations had opposed this principle, some arguing that the people of Zimbabwe do not have sufficient 'political education' at this stage to be able to elect a Prime Minister. 'What a load of rubbish and insult to our people,' I went on. In conclusion I appealed to everyone 'to bring into the grass-roots ANC all, regardless of colour, religion or race, who accept to be free Zimbabweans and are willing to join us in rebuilding Zimbabwe and creating a democratic, non-racial and prosperous society.' I called upon Ian Smith and the white Rhodesians to accept the nationalist demands and thus to end the suffering and bitterness amongst all our people.

It was now time to brief the National Executive of the ANC, the National Assembly, and provincial delegations on the Geneva Conference proceedings. This we did at St. Mark's United Methodist Hall in Highfield. Again the leaders unanimously endorsed our stands taken at Geneva and reaffirmed that we must stand firm on the principle of One-Man One-Vote.

The Geneva Conference was a bankrupt institution, however. It could post signs saying, 'To be reopened shortly', but they could not gloss over the stark reality of failure. Officially, Ivor Richard 'adjourned' the Conference until January 17, 1977, but it never reopened again.

Morton Malianga, ANC National Chairman, spoke for all of us at the adjournment on December 14, 1976, as he declared at a press conference that 'the central issue in this Conference is the granting of rights, freedoms and independence to the people of Zimbabwe on the basis of One-Man One-Vote.' Although disappointed with other African delegations for their failure to allow our people to have the right to elect an interim Government, he announced that we would press on toward that goal.

Our clear statement and advocacy of the following positions will remain our chief accomplishment at Geneva:

We used the setting of the Conference 'to make the whole world aware that Zimbabwe's independence is long overdue and must be granted NOW.'

We proved that Zimbabwe's people are well-equipped and educated to rule themselves and to rule a modern democratic state NOW.

We argued that an interim Government must and can be elected within fourteen days provided Britain will ensure peaceful conditions for its execution.

We defended vigorously the right of the people of Zimbabwe to elect their leaders through One-Man One-Vote.

We sought to achieve a common front with other Zimbabwean delegations in fighting for the inalienable rights of the Zimbabwe people.

Then Mr. Malianga concluded: 'Finally, we call upon Britain to decolonize Zimbabwe speedily. We also call upon all Zimbabweans, and all the freedom fighters, to remain united and to continue to demand and fight for majority rule and independence on the basis of One-Man One-Vote.'

Our position seemed clear and straightforward, awaiting the time when men of vision and determination, both black and white, would rally to our cause.

Chapter 17

I Enter into Negotiations with Mr. Ian Smith

One afternoon in mid-November 1977, Mr. Solomon Nenguwo, my Permanent Secretary, received a call from Mr. Derek Robinson, one of Mr. Smith's most senior security chiefs. The message from Mr. Robinson was simply that he, Mr. Robinson, wished to see me. On receiving this message, a score of guesses came into my mind. My reader should appreciate that in mid-November 1977 it was unthinkable that I could have a casual discussion with somebody from Mr. Smith's office. We were still going by the idea that it was considered political suicide to do so. One guess which came into my mind was that some drastic action was being planned against the UANC. Another thought which occurred was that I was to be given some warning, some caution about measures being planned against me. One thing certain was that Mr. Robinson was acting on instructions and I could well guess the source of those instructions. I was seriously tempted not to respond or to turn down the request for a meeting with Mr. Robinson. However, such a meeting might possibly give me an opportunity to raise matters about UANC people in death cells.

The upshot of my soul searching was that I agreed to meet Mr. Robinson. Accompanied by a colleague, Mr. Robinson duly came to my office. His message turned out to be brief and to the point. 'The PM wants to have a meeting with you together with Rev. Sithole and Chief Chirau. And he suggests 8.30 p.m. tonight.' Mr. Robinson waited for my answer.

My reaction was quick and immediate, 'A meeting together with Rev. Sithole and Chief Chirau?' My mind was racing. This could only mean one thing. This could only mean that Mr. Smith was going ahead with his already planned and announced intentions to form a broad-based government. Earlier during the year, Mr. Smith had given this broad-based government as a possible

225

line of action. The UANC had consistently refused to entertain the idea of this broad-based government. As defined then, it meant that black leaders would be co-opted into Mr. Smith's Government while token changes were made to the constitution. Mr. Smith's arrogant assertion that there would not be majority rule in 'a thousand years' was still ringing in our ears. During that same election campaign, Mr. Smith had declared that majority rule, if ever conceded, would not mean black majority rule. This idea of being tricked into a broad-based government was anathema to me and the UANC.

Another horrid thought kept on nagging at me. It was this mention of Rev. Sithole and Chief Chirau in conjunction with the UANC. The very idea was repugnant. The masses of the UANC could not and would not stomach any collusion with those two leaders. To be seen to be working together under the prevailing circumstances would have had very grave repercussions within the rank and file of the UANC. For a UANC to be seen talking with a ZUPO person or Sithole person was a crime in the eyes of UANC people. When Mr. Robinson mentioned Rev. Sithole and Chief Chirau, my response was, therefore, a reflex action.

Mr. Robinson confirmed that Rev. Sithole and Chief Chirau were to be included.

'I am sorry,' I told him. 'It is not possible for me to attend a meeting together with Rev. Sithole and Chief Chirau.' In putting it this way, I was not rejecting the approach out of hand. For one thing, I wanted time to think the thing out. For another, I wanted to keep our options open. A third reason was that I wanted to make it absolutely clear that the UANC would act independently and maintain an independent status so that our policies and principles would remain intact.

Having received my answer, Mr. Robinson left, saying he would report accordingly to Mr. Smith.

I knew he would come back. Meanwhile I had to take a major decision, probably one of the most grave decisions in the whole of my political career. This was one decision I had to take alone. There was no question of going to my colleagues and involving them in such a dangerous matter. Everything was still obscure. For any nationalists to flirt with Mr. Smith meant political suicide. On the other hand, there did not appear to be alternatives. The war was raging, taking scores of lives every week. Our people were a pathetic sight. There was massive unemployment. Hundreds of thousands of the people were living in camps, virtually refugees in their own country. The economy of the country was on the brink of collapse. What frightened me most and worried me sick was that the whole black population looked to me to do something about the situation. The faith of the people in me was one of the heaviest crosses I have ever carried. I had to keep on trying and striving and my worries were torture.

There appeared to be no viable alternative. The most recent Anglo-American Proposals were all but dead, having been rejected by virtually all the parties involved. It would be criminal for me to sit around and wait for somebody to come up with a new set of proposals. The overtures from Mr. Smith were in themselves an opening but what did they in fact mean? Mr. Smith had consistently and insistently refused to accept majority rule, let alone One Person One Vote. He had made it clear that he would not entertain the idea of power being transferred to the black majority. My tortured mind weighed this factor until I took a bold decision.

On the same day, as I expected, Mr. Robinson was back to me. This time, his message was, 'Number one man will see you without the other two parties at his residence at 8.30 p.m.' I told him I would go because that was the decision I had taken.

That evening, at the appointed time, my First Vice-President, Mr James Chikerema, and my Permanent Secretary, Mr. Solomon Nenguwo and I were at Mr. Smith's residence. We found Mr. Smith all by himself. I told him that we had come to listen to what he had to say. He then introduced the subject.

'The Anglo-American Proposals appear to be heading nowhere. It only means that more precious time is being wasted,' he started. 'It is time we all get down together and see what can be done. We have all sat down doing nothing for a long time while the people and the country are suffering. I have information from my security people that close to 200 people of all races are dying every week. Business people tell me that the economy will not survive much longer.

'Meanwhile, the British Government continues to pander to the Patriotic Front, wanting to impose them on to this country. That is what the Anglo-American Proposals are all about. The British are collaborating with the Frontline States in all this.'

Mr. Smith went on to say that the British idea was to exclude those nationalist leaders within the country as they had attempted over the Malta Conference to which he, Mr. Smith, had refused to go.

He went on to say that from his sources, the Patriotic Front had no support inside the country. He went on and on in the same vein. I remember observing how tired Mr. Smith looked that evening. That tiredness appeared to underline the sincerity of the man. His whole personality was appealing to me as genuine, unlike the past. He continued: 'People inside this country should all sit down and sort things out. We can all sit round a table or we can discuss separately but we must do something.'

We sat and listened, trying to come to terms with serious doubts in our minds. My most grave worry, the thing which solidly held me back from responding to Mr. Smith's strong appeal, was the question of confidence and trust. Could I trust Mr. Smith? Was he being sincere? Could his sincerity be proved? I did not fear negotiating with him but the number one thing I feared was that he was not being sincere.

Mr. Smith seemed to divine the trend of my thoughts and repeatedly sought to assure me of his sincerity. 'I have sincerely and honestly declared for majority rule,' he said. 'I love this country above all else and it breaks my heart to see it falling apart. I know I could retire to my farm if people think I am in the way of a settlement but I can't just throw my country up in the air and hope somebody will catch it. I want to hand over this country to somebody responsible.'

I asked Mr. Smith if he had any concrete proposals to put to me. 'We have learnt from past experience that it is futile to talk about talks. We are not prepared to take part in time-buying exercises. On the other hand, if you are now prepared to accept universal adult suffrage, not in principle but in practice, then we are in business,' I told him. I was now giving voice to my suspicions. To me, this was the acid test. I fully expected Mr. Smith to hedge, prevaricate and to dodge the issue.

Yet, I was in for a surprise. Mr. Smith's answer was as completely unexpected as it was revolutionary. Its dramatic effect was made the more poignant by the flat and almost casual tone in which it was delivered. 'Well, Bishop, I would accept such a commitment provided of course that I received, in return, guarantees for the whites under majority rule. I believe that whites must have guarantees in order to give them confidence if they are to remain in the country and build up the economy. I believe that white confidence is absolutely essential.'

I exchanged glances with my colleagues. It was difficult to hide the shattering amazement we felt. For my part, I began to see a glimmer of light in our whole situation. But I did not show a flicker of emotion. I told Mr. Smith that we would go away and think about what he had said. We agreed that we would meet again on the following day at the same time and place. We also agreed to broaden out the discussions and involve more of our colleagues.

After an almost sleepless night in which I tossed and turned, plagued with mixed feelings, I was back at the Prime Minister's residence on the following day at 8.30 p.m. This time, I was accompanied by Mr. Chikerema, my First Vice-President, Mr. Bulle, my Second Vice-President, Mr. Mazaiwana, my Secretary General and Mr. S. Nenguwo, my Permanent Secretary. Mr. Smith had with him Mr. David Smith, his Deputy, Mr. Hilary Squires and Mr. Gaylord.

'Well, Bishop,' Mr. Smith started.

We talked again, going through much the same ground as we had covered on the previous day. Mr. David Smith came into the discussion now and again; Mr. Squires was largely silent. He is a person who seemed to me to be mad with everybody all the time. The Prime Minister sounded less persuasive, less tired, than on the previous day. But even in front of his colleagues, he declared his sincerity and seriousness.

I took an opportune moment to put Mr. Smith's sincerity to yet another test. 'Would you be prepared to announce in public that you accept the transfer of power on the basis of One Person One Vote?'

Despite Mr. Smith's previous declarations, his answer came as a major surprise. 'Well, if the statement also stated that universal adult suffrage was in exchange for safeguards for whites, yes, I would'.

I was shocked. If this man was pulling wool over my eyes, then he was a veritable magician. In any case, I could not very well storm out of the meeting in anger in the light of such sweet reasonableness. I sought from Mr. Smith absolute guarantees that he was not having me on, that he was not proposing a doomed venture. Paramount in my mind was the need to avoid failure. Mr. Smith reaffirmed his sincerity in such a way as to almost put me to shame. None the less, I was determined that we both be agreed on what we were talking about. I informed Mr. Smith that I would give the UANC's basic demands as a basis for further discussions.

229

I received a frank response. 'Fair comment. I will of course also put down my basic conditions. Let me be quite frank, I will insist on guarantees for the whites because I have to carry the white people with me, otherwise the whole exercise would be futile. There is not much time to lose, Bishop, time is fast running out.'

I sought to establish in some detail what guarantees Mr. Smith had in mind.

'I have not given detailed thought to the matter, Bishop. You must realize that I did not expect such an encouraging response from you. None the less, the sort of guarantees I have in mind are the sort of guarantees we sought in the Anglo-American negotiations. I have talked about this before; justiciable Bill of Rights, independence of the Judiciary, that sort of thing,' he said.

I want my reader to note that this is all Mr. Smith mentioned about white guarantees at that stage of the negotiations. It later transpired that he discussed the question of guarantees in much greater detail with the other two black parties. The content of these early discussions was to become a thorny subject during the full-scale negotiations.

We ended the meeting with a discussion of the statement Mr. Smith was to make. We agreed that he would make a draft and submit it to us for our approval. At the very end of the meeting, Mr. Smith said, 'This has been a very successful meeting. In fact, this has been one of the most constructive meetings I have had in this room for very many years. I now feel we are getting somewhere. I want you to know, Bishop, that the whole thing depends on you. My information is that you command the majority following in this country and my sources are normally very reliable.'

When he raised the question of support, I reminded him that it was our wish that those nationalist leaders who were outside the country should also be invited for the talks. We left that particular problem with him.

I have given much space to this phase of the negotiations because it was then that we discussed the fundamental issues, the question of the franchise and the issue of minority safeguards. We had agreed on One Person One Vote. We had agreed to talk about safeguards for whites. But the really significant thing was that we had actually started talking to each other. A few days before, this would have been totally unthinkable. This was the major breakthrough. This was a near miracle. The UANC had started talking to Smith.

To me, what followed became almost routine. Mr. Smith made his statement on the 'peace initiative'. He publicly, in Bulawayo, conceded universal adult suffrage in exchange for guarantees for whites.

On November 26, 1977, I issued the UANC's Final Demand for Freedom at Highfield. I delivered the Declaration at a National Youth Rally of the UANC in Gwanzura Stadium. I informed the nation that I had accepted the challenge issued by Mr. Smith that we go in o negotiations on the basis of One Person One Vote. The UANC youth assembled gave me a standing ovation and asked me to go into negotiations. It was at that rally that a new slogan was coined. '*Zvikaramba tinoyedza zvimwe*' (If this fails we will do something else). The youth also shouted another new slogan, '*Wasara wasara*' (One man for himself). This was in reference to other parties, notably the Patriotic Front. I felt enthralled when the youth of Zimbabwe endorsed my decision. The youth were the group most likely to oppose any of my actions. I could now move ahead with confidence.

And yet, that very weekend, the whole initiative was jeopardized by the Rhodesian raid on to Chimoio and Tembe in Mozambique. That tragic and unfortunate raid killed, according to my sources, over 3,000 Zimbabweans, guerrillas and refugees alike. I was shattered. The UANC was shocked. My people sent messages to me to forget about the projected negotiations. In protest, I wrote a letter to Mr. Smith telling him that I would not talk to him until I had received an explanation. At the same time, I announced a week of national mourning during which I suspended all political activities including any negotiations. I was livid when Sithole and Chirau virtually condoned, by silence on the issue, the raid and went on with the talks as if nothing had happened. I was disgusted when Sithole and Chirau actually held a meeting with Mr. Smith during the week of national mourning. My only consolation was that virtually the whole world applauded my decision and there was overwhelming support inside Zimbabwe. Even the Dean of the Anglican Cathedral to my happy surprise held a memorial service in Salisbury in commemoration of the event.

Mr. Smith wrote to me trying to explain the raid. I knew he could never explain it. But I was not going to be small and risk the UANC's pragmatism. My delegation and I joined the constitutional negotiations on December 9, 1977.

And so I entered the talks, but on a note of protest. It was only

231

pragmatism which impelled me. Many in my Central Committee had advocated that we stay out of the talks all together. In my opening statement, I made it clear that the UANC expected the conference to work out the mechanics for the transfer of power from the minority to the majority. 'Because we want to end here and now the misery and suffering of our people, we have come here. Our message is a simple one. It, in fact, reverberates day in and day out, throughout the length and breadth of this country. It is, simply: *Gogogoyi vaSmith, tauya kuzotora nyika yedu*. (Allow us to enter, Mr. Smith, we have come to take our country.)'

The actual progress of the talks will be familiar to many people. Although we had all undertaken to keep the proceedings in absolute confidence, leakage started right from the very beginning. The leakages continued right through until we all discovered their source. There was a delegation amongst us which deliberately took notes for the purpose of propagating the proceedings, not in the public interest but in the interest of the particular Party. This delegation even published jaundiced verbatim reports. They went to the press with details of our secret negotiations after each meeting. A reporter at *Rhodesia Herald* met a certain person each day. I was disgusted. It was all I could do to resist intense pressure from my Central Committee to do likewise. All I could say was that we were men and women of integrity. Even at the time of writing, I shudder when I think that the leader of this particular delegation might release to the public all the proceedings of the new Executive Council.

However, we were in the talks. At the very first meeting attended by the UANC, it was agreed that we would end negotiations in two to three weeks. As everybody knows, the negotiations went on for three months.

Thereafter, the UANC negotiating machinery went into action. I regenerated the negotiating team which had performed so brilliantly at Geneva. Enoch Dumbutshena had come back from Zambia. Professor Samkange had come all the way from the United States. Dr. Arne Palley was again on hand. So was Advocate Sandura. The team also included Mr. Chikerema, Mr. Bulle, Mr. Mazaiwana, Mr. Zindoga and Mr. Nenguwo. My negotiating team and I worked day and night. Before each session, the team and I worked out our position. We would prepare our position paper and we would work out negotiating strategy. Each day there was a negotiating session; each and every single day we would have a meeting of the UANC Central Committee to review the progress of the day and map out the broad strategy for the following day.

I was proud of the teamwork involved. I was proud that my officials were daily and intimately involved in the negotiations. This systematic and methodical approach gained us as much advantage in these negotiations as it had done in Geneva. We soon became a model delegation in much the same way as we had become a model delegation at Geneva. My greatest pride to this day is that no other delegation involved in the negotiations could rival us in terms of efficiency, thoroughness, preparedness and dignity. It was soon clear that I could not count on an alliance with Rev. Sithole and Chief Chirau. It was obvious that I would be fighting not only Mr. Smith but the other two black delegations as well. But I was not daunted. I had behind me the might of the UANC. I had with me a team of seasoned negotiators, veterans of the Geneva campaign.

The negotiating styles of the other delegations were intriguing. Mr. Smith's style, which he himself confessed, was to put his minimum demands on the table and then sit tight. That is what he did when he presented the eight safeguards he was asking for the retention of white confidence. All he wanted was for us to accept all the eight as they stood. I found this style frustrating and at times infuriating. I will credit him with this. He was a shrewd negotiator and a most persuasive debater. He was also a master at playing one group off another. I felt very strongly that ZUPO was being used by Smith to manipulate the whole exercise to his favour. And to a certain extent he succeeded in that he got some concessions he would have never got if ZUPO had been out of negotiations. Rev. Sithole tended to give long dissertations whenever he got the floor. I found the Sithole people lacking in consistency. At one meeting, for example, they were advocating a voting age of 21 years. At the next, they had changed to 18 in line with the UANC, and this was adopted. Chief Chirau negotiated through an interpreter, which was a novelty. And yet he demonstrated a profound basic intelligence and a great deal of common sense.

The negotiations centred on Point No. 8 on Mr. Smith's proposed safeguards. We found little to quarrel about with seven of the demands because we had already accepted them in the Anglo-American Proposals. But we were stuck on Point No. 8 which read: 'to retain the confidence of the whites in regard to the

233

entrenched safeguards in the Constitution, one third of the seats in Parliament should be reserved for direct election by white voters.'

'I am quite convinced that a blocking third represents the absolute minimum white representation necessary in order to retain white confidence,' Mr. Smith repeatedly argued.

On December 12, the UANC made its response to Mr. Smith's eight points. We accepted the Bill of Rights. We accepted the independence of the Judicature. We accepted the need for efficiency of the public service but insisted that the defence forces be the subject of separate treatment. We won that point too. We soon conceded the need to guarantee pensions reluctantly and we accepted the principle of dual citizenship. These were all relatively non-controversial issues.

In the same response, I issued our first challenge on the contentious Point No. 8. I voiced our rejection of separate rolls for whites. I demanded the common roll for all voters, black, white and brown.

Chief Chirau accepted the Smith position as it stood. Rev. Sithole accepted separated rolls but rejected the demand for one-third white representation.

The UANC's initial position on the whole issue was given as a package deal. We conceded a one-third white representation provided the one-third was elected on the common roll, that is, by black and white voters. In support of this position, I stated, 'We have openly and publicly stated that any system which compromises the principle of one person one vote is unacceptable to the UANC . . .' The system of election advocated by the UANC represents a positive step towards non-racialism, being a compromise between the existing racially-dominated machinery and the requirements of majority rule.

In response, Mr. Smith launched a concentrated attack on the UANC position. He was absolutely livid and again called us devious. He claimed that any whites elected by the common roll would be nothing less than 'stooges' of the blacks.

We argued and haggled and quibbled. It was a complicated debate because Rev. Sithole was also pushing his own position in which he wanted one-fifth white representation, but elected on separate rolls.

On December 21, we submitted a new and compromise position. We conceded separate rolls but insisted that white representation be reduced to one-fifth. In making this concession, I made it clear that we had not, in principle, shifted from our original position. 'I . . . want this to be specifically noted and recorded that the very major concession we now make . . . in no way represents a change in our position to separate voters' rolls. We believe that separate voters' rolls are wrong in principle . . . But we are at the negotiating table and we have avoided the sin of intransigence in the greater interest of our people . . .'

On December 28, Mr. Smith took the UANC by surprise when he introduced a new suggestion. He still wanted one-third white representation. But he now proposed that there be a system of primary elections involving white voters. Any white candidate who failed to obtain fifty per cent. or more of the votes cast would have to face election on the common roll. Any candidate who obtained fifty per cent. or more of the votes cast would be declared elected to Parliament.

On the following day, the UANC accused Mr. Smith of wanting to obtain his one-third through the back door. 'Indeed,' I said, 'the UANC wishes to register an objection to the deviousness of the Government delegation. In their bid to secure one-third white Rhodesian Front representation in Parliament, they have deliberately twisted two UANC positions.'

The talks were deadlocked. Nobody was agreeing with anybody else except that the ZUPO people were largely in agreement with Mr. Smith and Rev. Sithole agreed with Mr. Smith on separate rolls. The UANC had now rejected Mr. Smith's demand for one-third white representation. We now wanted this special representation to be limited to one-fifth.

The conference changed its normal procedure and we resorted to meetings of heads of delegations and their deputies. At these calm meetings, our differences were hammered out. It was at one of these sessions that I suggested another approach. I called for a meeting of the black delegations on their own. I said 'Gentlemen, I know we are different Parties but we are negotiating a settlement for the nation. So let us try to take a joint position to strengthen ourselves.' I tried to obtain a common approach from the blacks. I was pleased when this worked out. As a result, we were able to force Mr. Smith from his demand for a third white representation and we agreed on twenty-eight per cent. This was a major breakthrough. We also agreed that entrenched clauses would last for the life of two Parliaments or 10 years, whichever was the longer. The life of two Parliaments was what the British had proposed in the Anglo-American Proposals except that in Rhodesia the life of Parliament was 5 years and not 4. I repeatedly made the point that there was still need to determine the method of election of the twenty-eight per cent whites since the UANC still insisted that only twenty per cent be elected on separate rolls.

On January 27, back in plenary sessions, the debates centred on the method of election of the twenty-eight per cent seats. The UANC and I were the odd man out. Mr. Smith, Rev. Sithole and Chief Chirau all wanted the 28 seats to be elected on separate rolls. Tempers ran high when the three delegations tried to induce me to accept Mr. Smith's position. Tempers ran so high that Mr. David Smith, deputy of Mr. Ian Smith, although the most reasonable friendly one of them all, made allegations of untruthfulness on the part of the UANC. He said, referring to us, the UANC, 'I have never heard lies such as I have heard this afternoon. And, if this is a reflection of what the Government of this country will be, God help us.'

One of the most meek members of my delegation wanted to reply to Mr. David Smith's provocative remarks when he, Mr. Smith, stood up and started putting his jacket on saying, 'I don't want to hear anything more from that side.' It was then that I jumped up on my seat saying, 'If you are going to call us liars and walk out, then we are going out ourselves before you.' I stood up simultaneously with my delegation and walked out. Our walk-out was followed by intensive behind-the-scenes activity to bring us back into the talks. Everybody, particularly the other three delegations, knew that the talks would amount to nothing without the participation of the UANC. Eventually, a meeting was arranged between the UANC 1st Vice-President, Mr. J. R. D. Chikerema, and Mr. David Smith. Our differences were mutually patched up and we went back into the talks.

On February 7, the UANC came up with a compromise proposal. We conceded that 20 of the special seats be elected on separate rolls but we demanded that eight seats be elected on the common roll. Mr. Smith rejected this new proposal, bringing in the old argument of 'stooges'. We were back in another deadlock and heated debates followed. On February 8, Mr. Smith unwittingly revealed that there had been prior agreements between him and other two black delegations on the question of separate rolls. On the following day, I told the conference that this admission created a totally new situation as far as the UANC was concerned. I want to be clear on this. This admission by Mr. Smith that there had been prior agreement between him and Rev. Sithole and Chief Chirau and that I had not been apprised of such agreements really made me angry. My Central Committee shared my anger and some asked me to walk out of the negotiations altogether. I gave a strongly worded statement to the conference. I told the conference that all along the UANC had been negotiating in good faith. I told them I could now understand why three delegations had ganged up against the UANC on the method of election of the twenty-eight per cent special seats. I again attacked the whole concept of separate rolls. 'We have been told that separate rolls are tolerable on a temporary basis. We strongly dispute this. Separate rolls are absolutely intolerable and undefendable . . . All through this impasse, the UANC has been extremely puzzled why black delegations have been vociferously advocating separate rolls. We got the answer at yesterday's session . . . The UANC is now left with no choice. If we stay in these negotiations it will be to rubberstamp what has already been made . . . We now ask ourselves whether there was a prior agreement on the issue of the Security Forces or the composition of the Transitional Government.' I thereupon asked for an adjournment in order to seek a fresh mandate from the masses of the UANC. The conference gave me time to consult the masses.

On February 12, I met a consultative meeting of the UANC. On the following day, I was back in the conference room and I gave the delegates the answer from the masses. The masses had simply endorsed the UANC's stand and declared the UANC's independence from any other delegation in the talks. The deadlock continued.

On February 14, a decision was taken to revert to meetings of heads of delegations and their deputies. The aim, as usual, was to try to break the deadlock in a calm manner. The meeting was duly held and a compromise was duly suggested. On February 15, the UANC responded to the compromise. I stipulated that we would accept that eight of the special seats be elected on the common roll from candidates chosen by whites. We also stipulated that all of the special seats would not be allowed to form a coalition with a minority party in order to form a government. As the majority party, the UANC was

237

particularly worried that the whites might combine with some minority party and form a government. Agreement was reached on this basis and a major breakthrough had been achieved.

Mr. Smith wanted us to sign an agreement there and then. He was supported by the other two delegations. I told all of them that the UANC would not sign any document until the issue of the Defence Forces and the composition of the Transitional Government had been agreed upon. We were heading for yet another crisis but the other delegations gave in to the UANC and we went on to discuss the remaining issues.

The next hurdle was the composition of the future army. Early in the negotiations, I had indicated that this was an issue of particular concern to the UANC. The masses of the UANC were playing a significant role in the war. The masses regarded the guerrillas as their children, children to be fed and sheltered and cherished. The UANC itself was playing a direct, support role in the war. I was in contact with the fighters. The whole matter was very close to the hearts of the UANC.

When the subject was broached at the negotiating table, there was surprisingly little resistance from Mr. Smith. The UANC wanted the integration of the nationalist forces with Mr. Smith's forces. I was supported by the Sithole delegation on this stand, much to my relief. The ZUPO delegation did not play much of a role in this aspect of the negotiations. I was thankful that at least they did not oppose us. Agreement was reached on the principle of integration of forces and the rehabilitation of the other guerrillas.

The negotiations then moved to the thorny subject of the structure and composition of the Transitional Government. The UANC had already worked out a position on this and I sold this position to the other two black delegations.

The black delegations held several joint meetings with the result that on February 22 we agreed on a joint position which was in reality the original position of the UANC. We demanded a neutral Chairman to the Executive Council. We demanded a black majority on both the Executive Council and the Ministerial Council. We demanded that the existing Parliament be dissolved. Mr. Smith wanted parity between black and white on both Councils and he wanted Parliament to remain as it was. We were soon deadlocked, so deadlocked that Mr. Smith actually suggested that we do without a Transitional Government at all.

238

Following what was by then an established custom in the face of deadlocks, the conference resorted to meetings of heads of delegations and their deputies only. Blacks also continued to meet separately from the whites. It was at one of such meetings that both the Sithole delegation and the ZUPO people came up with a compromise proposal and began to sell it to the UANC. We did not want to but we were faced with the dilemma that if we continued to hold on to our position, we would be accused of moral intransigence. In any event, we would be facing three delegations ranged against us. Crisis day was March 2. By this time, I was certain that Mr Smith would accept the compromise proposal suggested by the Sithole and ZUPO delegations. Mr. Smith committed himself to a definite date of independence but this was not enough for the UANC. Mr. Smith gave in on the question of Chairmanship, moving from his demand that the Chairman be himself and accepting that we have a rotating Chairman, but it was still not enough to satisfy the UANC.

There was only one thing to do. The country would never have forgiven me if I had broken up the conference at that stage. It was also out of the question to accept that we dispense with a Transitional Government. The UANC and I decided to express our reservations. Our position paper of March 2 listed our reservations on black to white parity on the Ministerial Council. 'We sincerely believe that this Council should have reflected a black majority so that all organs of the Transitional Government are set on the path to majority rule.'

I expressed reservations on the continued existence of Parliament. I expressed reservations on the continued existence of the post of Prime Minister. We wanted all these reservations on record and the conference duly recorded them. The conference had no alternative because it was unthinkable that there could be an agreement without the signature of the UANC.

On the following day, March 3, 1978, we signed the agreement in front of a whole barrage of press paraphenalia. It was an emotional moment. It was the culmination of a hard fight.

On the same day, March 3, 1978, at the invitation of Dr. Owen, I left for the United Kingdom. When I got to Britain it was necessary to proceed to the USA. I took this trip of my own volition. I had signed an agreement and I was duty bound to sell this agreement. I had discussions with Dr. Owen. I met the leaders of the British Conservative and Liberal Parties. I had meetings with Mr. Vance and Mr. Young. I put Zimbabwe's case before a sceptical world and the world listened but reserved judgment. The number one question I was repeatedly asked was whether the Agreement to which I had put my signature would work since Smith could not be trusted, they said. I decided to answer this questions in my own way. Smith had conceded majority rule and the date to hand over and that was enough for us.

On Tuesday, March 14, 1978, I rang my Party Office from New York and I asked my officials to organize a national rally to coincide with my arrival back in Salisbury on Sunday, March 19, 1978, as a demonstration of Zimbabwean support for the Salisbury Agreement. I knew that this gave the Party a bare four days in which to organize the rally but the world wanted an answer. I duly arrived in Salisbury on the 19th. The UANC rally which had been organized in four days turned out to be one of the 'largest gatherings ever held in the history of Africa'. It was certainly a larger gathering than any ever held in Zimbabwe. Almost a million people, representing a third of a one-person one-vote electorate, attended. The world had received the answer it wanted.

On Wednesday, March 22, 1978, I was sworn in as a member of the new Executive Council together with Rev. Sithole and Chief Chirau. In keeping with the express wishes of the UANC we were sworn in by a black churchman, the late Bishop Murindagomo of the Anglican Church.

Looking back on the three months of negotiations, I cannot help but feel that a mammoth task had been achieved. We achieved a settlement out of the jaws of tragedy. We created hope where there was despair. It was nothing less than a miracle that we had lasted at the conference table and that we struck success where so many had failed. I am glad that I played a hand and helped to usher in a new era. I have few regrets and I am full of hope for the future.

Chapter 18

Will a Free Zimbabwe be Truly Free?

I have already referred to the Sunday of February 13, 1972, when I stood in Trafalgar Square, London, in front of a colourful crowd of well over 10,000 people. At that meeting, I called on the great crowd to be witnesses to my complete belief that Zimbabwe will be free. Together we sang, 'Free, Free, Free; Zimbabwe shall be free!' My unequivocal belief in the inevitability of majority rule was as strong then as it is today. Majority rule will come as surely as the sun will rise. The question has now become, 'How, in what manner, will national liberation be achieved in Zimbabwe?'

At the time I was singing my faith in Trafalgar Square I believed it was still possible for majority rule to come to Zimbabwe through classical peaceful negotiations. Since that time the situation has changed radically. A hot liberation war rages, claiming the lives of soldier and civilian, young and old, black and white. Some outside powers would prolong that conflict so as to enhance their power and prestige or to install their chosen favourites as Zimbabwe's first rulers. As I write, the question of Zimbabwe's independence is like a cold-war football, tossed here and there to the dictates of the strains between East and West. At the same time those of us within the country desire African majority rule with the free choice of Zimbabwe's political leaders through one-person one-vote election. We seek for a transfer of power from the small white minority to the African majority which will enable persons of all races to live in peace and dignity one with another.

'Will a free Zimbabwe be truly free?'

Will future generations accuse us of delivering to them a country whose independence is a fraud, a sham, a hollow shell? Will ours be called a 'free state', but in fact be mortgaged heavily to external international interests? Will we of Zimbabwe stand in danger of being satisfied, yes even thrilled, with the mere

241

trappings of independence—a brand new flag fluttering in the breeze, sleek and shiny limousines, and black faces in Parliament, State House, the OAU and the United Nations—while those in power are not accountable to the governed for their actions?

We who are directly involved in the struggle for Zimbabwe's independence owe it to future generations to keep on asking these questions. We must dedicate ourselves to achieve for Zimbabwe a genuine independence.

I am not sounding a false alarm in expressing these doubts. We have watched and observed some of the new states in Africa and elsewhere in the Third World. As one of the last few countries in Africa still to achieve sovereignty, we have been given a golden opportunity to study Africa's progress after independence. It will be our fault if we do not utilize this opportunity to try to learn from the pitfalls into which other states have fallen.

What have we seen? We have seen states emerging as happy, prosperous dominions at independence only to fall into the grip of local tyrants who treat the state as their own fiefdoms. We have seen states emerge as 'independent' but owing their independence to some external country which then proceeds to hold them to ransom—the former ally overstaying her welcome and exploiting the people's wealth. We have seen states emerge at independence as rich, self-sufficient entities but later become poverty-stricken 'banana republics' through frivolous spending, laziness, and maladministration. I have come across independent peoples who rue the day they obtained political freedom, who furtively wish that the former colonizer were back.

There are a host of cancerous growths which can enter the body politic of an independent state and chew up the inside. Many states in Africa have achieved only formal independence. They still have to achieve true national freedom and majority rule.

What type of freedom do we wish for Zimbabwe? Naturally we want Zimbabwe to have the very best available. Zimbabweans want no counterfeit freedom, no second-rate independence, no worn-out ideologies. We want the genuine article.

Genuine freedom involves three essential qualities of political life: freedom from outside control, the sovereignty of the people, and self-determination of the nation's political and economic destiny.

In this chapter I propose to outline first those economic realities and policies which will affect the extent of true freedom in

Zimbabwe. Then I shall refer briefly to those political realities and policies which influence Zimbabwean political freedom.

Zimbabwe at independence will inherit a dual economic system based on racial discrimination. On the one hand one sees an impressive, modern and affluent economy. By world standards it is judged to be technologically advanced. By design, however, it was created to benefit Europeans only. By the Land Tenure Act the most fertile and productive lands have been reserved for white farmers only. An array of racially discriminatory laws ensures the welfare, security and prosperity of the white population.

By nature Zimbabwe has been endowed with abundant natural resources, making possible a diversified economy. Much of the land is fertile and graced with sufficient rainfall for intensive crop production and ranching. Rich deposits of copper, coal, gold, nickel, chromium, asbestos, iron ore, platinum, tin and other minerals attract extensive foreign investment and mining production. A highly-developed transport and communications network contributes to the efficient development of these resources. This infra-structure makes possible the growth of manufacturing industries. Since 1965 the international imposition of economic sanctions against Smith's white regime in Rhodesia has stimulated import substitution. Today local industries produce most of the manufactured goods required in the country.

On the other hand the Africans have been restricted through legislative and other means to live in an underdeveloped rural economy. The fifty per cent. of the land reserved for the 6.4 million Africans contains the poorest soils and receives uncertain rainfall. Our African farmers cannot rise above the grinding poverty of subsistence agriculture, being limited to six to eight acres of land to plough and five head of cattle, while 6,000 European agricultural enterprises flourish owning half the country and averaging at least 5,000 acres of the most fertile land in Zimbabwe. Desperate conditions in African Tribal Trust Lands, now aggravated by the ravages of war, by dislocations and political restrictions, have forced masses of people to migrate to the towns. There their availability as cheap, unskilled labourers allows employers to exploit them, paying wages far below the poverty line. Unemployment is high among urban Africans. Almost all who find work are restricted to unskilled and semi-skilled levels.

In almost every sector of the economy salaries of white workers average more than ten times those of Africans.

Our people have suffered from economic oppression and exploitation for more than eighty years. The first priority of Zimbabwe under majority rule will therefore have to be the establishment of a just and viable economic order for all its people and particularly the African population which has endured so much deprivation under the present system. Exploitation and oppression of one citizen by another, or of one group in society by another, must be rooted out.

Every Zimbabwean must be given an opportunity to contribute fully to the development of the country. I believe that this right should be extended to every Zimbabwe citizen regardless of race, ethnic origin, culture, sex or religion. All will be needed to build up a strong and new Zimbabwe.

The economy of the new Zimbabwe must be designed to meet the basic needs of all its citizens. The quality of our life together should be judged by the diet, shelter, education and health care provided for the poorest and weakest of our citizens. To provide opportunities for all to have gainful employment, and to guarantee minimum living standards for all will require disciplined effort and sacrifice by us all.

A New National Ideology

Zimbabwe must develop her national resources along the lines of her own national ideology. An ideology, to be progressive and constructive, must be the product of the circumstances of a particular people and society. It arises out of a people's material conditions of life, their heritage, their culture, and their attainments. It has always been my belief and conviction that the social and economic system under which any society must live ought to be rooted in that society's own history, culture, traditions, its orientation and the general make-up of its people.

I therefore strongly oppose any attempt to reproduce in Zimbabwe a carbon copy of any other foreign economic system or ideology.

I do not favour the wholesale importation of free-enterprise capitalism from the West. Could Zimbabwe choose a capitalist system with its built-in profit motives and inherent exploitation of man by man? Could such a system still hope for justice in the distribution of national wealth? I doubt it. And I don't believe that economic injustice would be an incentive to hard work and efficiency.

On the other hand, it would be an equal mistake to try to import and reproduce a communist blueprint of state socialism in Zimbabwe. Such a system would fail to harness sufficiently that individual initiative and potential which has already been demonstrated by our people.

The economic system I favour will be based on the realities of the economic, social, political and cultural setup of the people of Zimbabwe. As no economic system exists in isolation, our own chosen system would draw upon the experiences and economic developments in various other societies with which of necessity we will interact. As Zimbabweans we shall adapt for our own use those constructive elements from other economic systems that are consonant with our own economic realities. The result, I believe, will be a mixed economy in which we shall emphasize (a) those aspects of initiative and incentives which have been the mainstay of western economic growth and efficiency as well as (b) those aspects of selective state control of essential activities where such state control shall be deemed to be in the public interest, national welfare and in particular national security, in order to ensure the basic welfare of all. I would choose to call it *Zimbabwean Socialism*.

There are strong cultural roots in Zimbabwe for the type of economic system which I am proposing.

In traditional society all land was held in common and allocated to persons or family units according to their requirements as well as their capability to utilize it constructively. Land which lay fallow reverted to the community for reallocation as others had need.

There existed numerous opportunities for individual initiative so long as it was neither exploitive nor harmful to the personal growth of others. Ours was a nation of family farmers, of family craftsmen and of small shopkeepers.

Any increase in family wealth, however, carried with it a corresponding increase in social responsibility. He who acquired a large herd of cattle was expected to share them with relatives, neighbours or friends who had less or none. Through gifts and rewards for services rendered the poorer members of the community were able through their initiative, hard work and efficiency to obtain cattle from their rich neighbours and eventually accumulated their own wealth. They, in turn, subsequently accepted the same social responsibility and so the system went on.

Our fathers knew the dignity of manual work. Too often people in Africa equate independence with freedom from hard work. Laziness creeps in, closely followed by hunger. Production in factories falls. Everybody wants a white collar job as manual work is considered to be too menial. Our people need to recover the dignity of labour of their forefathers.

When I returned from the United States in 1963, I took a few weeks to spend with my father at our village farm. There I found a whole lot of chores needed to be done. I borrowed some old clothes from my father, and was soon busy digging cattle manure from the kraal. Unknown to me, I had become the subject of discussion and some disapproval. The men who were working for my father did not approve of my manual exertions. After a debate amongst themselves, they approached my father and stated their case. They were, they said, puzzled and concerned that his son, just back from overseas with degrees, where he was living with Europeans, should indulge himself in such 'dirty work'. 'Is it right that your son should undertake such work while we are here?' they asked. 'Besides his degrees, is he not the highest African at Old Umtali? Is he not also a minister?'

My father patiently explained that there was nothing the matter with me. I had always done this kind of work. Education and a five-year stay abroad had not changed me. I do not believe that my father fully satisfied the men. The colonialists have rammed it into our people's minds that hard work is 'dirty'. They knew from experience that education in racist Rhodesia was the gateway to a white collar, supervisory job.

Zimbabweans need to reaffirm the value of hard work and manual labour in building a new nation. One of the greatest joys of independence is that one is putting one's efforts into the development of one's own country. It is through hard work that people contribute to the stability and peace and freedom we all want. Poverty and hunger are the biggest invitation cards to neo-colonialism, foreign domination and loss of freedom. Some countries in Africa have hectare upon hectare of rich, virgin soil, plenty of rainfall and lots of sunshine. Yet the people are starving. They consider farming too menial. They consider agricultural extension officers as 'colonialists' bent on forcing them to work.

246

In contrast, other countries encourage development and utilization of the land for the full benefit of the people. This is a country where they crushed big stones to make fields for sugar and other crops.

Together with the dignity of manual labour, our forefathers bequeathed us a noble heritage of working together to promote the welfare of the whole society. To work for private, *individual* gain was unthinkable. Each person found meaning and joy in life in being part of an extended family to which each person contributed and through which each person's physical, emotional and social needs were met. At other times the entire community, led by their political leaders, joined in communal work parties to bring in the harvest or build a new home for one of their members. These values also should be reaffirmed in Zimbabwean socialism.

Opportunities for initiative, joy in manual work, co-operative effort, and sharing with those in need—these traditional economic values of the Zimbabwean people can remain cornerstones of our new economic ideology.

First, we must guarantee a more equitable distribution of wealth and of opportunity to all the citizens of Zimbabwe. To achieve this the Government will have to assume a major leadership role on behalf of and in the interest of the people. A carefully designed system of personal and corporate taxation will be required to provide revenues so as to ensure that such basic services as education, health, social security, etc. are available to all. A vigorous programme of manpower training will need to be implemented in order to prepare and enable Zimbabweans to acquire the technical, administrative and managerial skills necessary for efficient and effective development of all the various aspects of the economy and government.

All the citizens of Zimbabwe are greatly concerned about the present imbalance in national land allocation and utilization. The redress of this imbalance must be a top priority of the new majority rule government, bearing in mind the goal of making the most effective use of all available land. To this end I believe that a land bank should be established to facilitate equitable acquisition of land by groups previously deprived under the old system and to promote more efficient productive utilization of the land resources of the nation for all its peoples.

The majority rule government of Zimbabwe shall need to take

urgent and very bold decisions on the distribution of the nation's land resources. I stress urgency because of the existence of land hunger amongst the majority of the population, a hunger which has accumulated over decade after decade of minority rule. Nothing short of bold decisions will suffice in a situation where 280 000 whites held fifty per cent of the available land while 6½ million blacks were confined to the other fifty per cent. Indeed, the gross imbalance in land distribution was one of the fundamental and original evils of minority rule. It was the basis of social discrimination, whites objecting to having black neighbours. It was the basis of economic discrimination, blacks being denied land resources for individual development while whites allocated to themselves the choice stretches of land. It was the basis of statutory discrimination, giving rise as it did to the Land Apportionment Act and its successor, the Land Tenure Act.

The imbalance of land distribution was a serious restraint on economic development. The economic potential of the black farmer remained unexploited. A restrictive ceiling was imposed on the development of his land utilization skills. The over-crowded, over-grazed and over-cultivated land allocated to blacks was rapidly turning into sandy wastes while some whites hoarded stretch upon stretch of unutilized and under-utilized land.

It was a similar situation which caused the bloody Mau Mau explosion in Kenya and in our situation, the frustrations and injustices inherent in the land problem were major contributors to the war which broke out in the early seventies.

That there must be land redistribution, to me, is unquestionable. Land is the major resource in Zimbabwe and must be made available to the people on an equitable basis. I accept that land is too valuable a resource for its distribution to be determined by purely political considerations. I accept that land distribution or redistribution must be largely guided by economic considerations because I subscribe to the view that land is primarily for production and must continue to be a viable and not a wasting resource.

Having argued for land redistribution, a need for which, incidentally, most of the country's leading white farmers accept, it must be emphasized that such a redistribution must be exhaustively planned and programmed. For example, the first step must be a comprehensive and scientific survey of all land resources with a view to determining their potential in terms of suitability for specific utilization. It must be insisted upon that all projected land reforms be based on the results of such a survey. And now, what land reforms do I view as necessary and pertinent to our situation in Zimbabwe?

Firstly, all idle and under-utilized land must be progressively turned to production. There is, for example, land held by absentee landlords and land held by speculators. There are also land-owners who hold land which is far in excess of their ability to develop or exploit. The state must acquire such land and make it available to those with the capability of turning it to production and those facing land starvation. Having said this, it needs to be emphasized that such transactions should be on the basis of justice and sound economic sense. For instance, adequate compensation must be paid to the holders of land so acquired and re-allocation must be to persons with the proven ability to produce and to conserve.

Secondly, there must be a deliberate and progressive and programmed movement of farmers from the overcrowded and so-called Tribal Trust Lands, not only in order to relieve the excessive pressure on these areas but also in order to expand farming opportunities to the thousands of land-starved but highly motivated black farmers. We have, in Zimbabwe, a class of black farmers confined by law to miserable six to eight acre plots in a country where the white farmer holds anything up to 50 000 acres of rich soils. It needs no economist to advocate a policy of standard farm holdings of, say, one or two thousand acres, depending on the nature of farming activities. It is sheer commonsense to insist that a farmer should hold only as much land as he can handle, surrendering the rest to the land-hungry and to the needs of future generations. I have no quarrel with private ownership of land but I cannot accept that an individual should buy up the whole state if he so wishes and if he has the financial capabilities.

Thirdly, it would be futile and negative to make more land available to the black population without a corresponding availability of capital and development funds. The land reforms I am proposing as being essential for stability and economic progress will only succeed through considerable capitalization of the black or any would-be commercial farmer. The State will need to establish loan facilities in the form of a development bank. It will be incumbent on the State to make absolutely certain that the transactions of such a bank are based on sound economic practice. One cannot over-emphasize this aspect.

Fourthly, the strength of the cultural values of our society makes it absolutely necessary that we preserve the concept of communal land tenure, at least for the foreseeable future. It is inherent in traditional Zimbabwean culture that the chief holds land in trust for his people, that land belongs to the ancestors and to the unborn generations, that land utilization cements the social values of society. The Zimbabwean peasant farmer holds to this concept and only a massive social revolution will shift him from it. Until he does shift from it, there shall be need for a provision for communal land tenure. It is, nonetheless, my conviction that the majority rule government of Zimbabwe must progressively move away from the concept of communal land tenure. Meanwhile, there shall be need to make the so-called Tribal Trust Lands more viable, more economic and more productive.

Fifthly, it remains for me to affirm my conviction that the State must maintain a reservoir of land resources or land-based resources in the form of national or state land. We must make provision for the conservation of wild life. We must make provision for recreation requirements. In other words, Zimbabwe must have its game reserves and its parks and its sporting facilities. Besides, there are forest reserves which must be maintained. To this end, a land bank must be established to cater for the needs of future generations.

In essence, we must, in Zimbabwe, take stock of our land resources, delimit them into commercial, urban, industrial, communal and state segments, make them available on a non-racial basis, make financial provisions for their more equitable exploitation, and plan for their continued economic viability.

Utilizing the energies of all our citizens will naturally require a great deal of planning and constructive effort. In some sectors of the economy private initiative will need to be encouraged since certain areas of the economy are best suited to be run with minimum government involvement. Other sectors of the economy can best be developed by government in consultation and association with both private and public enterprise responsible for the functioning and management of the national welfare. Our goal should be to create a national economic system that will contribute to the reconstruction of the nation.

National economic reconstruction in Zimbabwe will not be

easy. Around the world we have witnessed too many illustrations of people starving, states faced with economic collapse, and national leaders living in luxury and seeming disinterest in the plight of their people. We are determined that Zimbabwe shall not go down a similar path to destruction.

The rebuilding of Zimbabwe will require hard work and sacrifice, but will bring the reward of a new prosperity and sense of community as well as joy in building together a new nation. Will Europeans and Asians be willing to give up their economic and social privileges in order to find a new acceptance and appreciation of their initiative and skills? We shall continue to encourage our white and Asian minorities to stay in the country and to join in the rebuilding of Zimbabwe. Will Africans resist the temptation to exploit their fellow man from new seats of power? I hope so. A rapid strengthening of labour unions, of co-operatives, and of associations of small farmers and business-men, together with governmental vigilance, will protect the rights of the common people so that exploitation of one person by another can be rooted out from our society. The crux of the matter is that political independence under majority rule will have to be the occasion for uprooting the old socio-economic system and for transforming structures and attitudes which work against the construction of a new and truly independent economic order.

Another difficult problem will be how to achieve rapid economic development without a new dependency on foreign governments, banks and corporations. I believe whole-heartedly in the adage that he who pays the piper calls the tune. If Zimbabwe fails to grow enough to feed her people, then she has sabotaged her sovereignty. The international 'Good Samaritan' who comes along with bags of maize and wheat and other left-over grain becomes a shareholder in the state. If large chunks of Zimbabwe's land are owned by absentee landlords, then we shall need to beg the landlord for permission to develop and exploit our own natural resources. If Zimbabwe is to depend heavily on borrowed capital, then outside financiers will determine the use of their money. The State may be forced to buy goods almost exclusively from a country which helped it with a large 'interest free' loan. Zimbabwe must depend on her own hard work and sweat to produce goods so as to generate her own capital and feed her own people. An independent relationship with other countries, including the big powers, must be created but maintained on a wholesome and non-subservient level. Aid will be needed for Zimbabwe's development but we would prefer to receive it through international agencies.

Sovereignty to the People

Let us turn now to the second aspect of true freedom in Zimbabwe—the quest for true political freedom.

Throughout this book the odyssey of my own struggle for personal freedom and dignity has been intertwined with that of our nation—Zimbabwe. Although our hearts throb with excitement over promises of majority rule now, we continue to suffer from the legacies of prolonged white oppression. The power of control over the means of security, over the army and police, has remained too long in white hands. The European colonialists were so convinced that they would rule indefinitely that they allowed only a handful of Zimbabweans, and those principally in African education, to gain administrative experience in Government. The result is that we approach Independence with a tragic shortage of experienced administrators, although some Zimbabweans have, through grit and determination, gained experience outside the country.

Another legacy of white settler rule is the continued suspicion by Zimbabweans of the intentions of whites in power. Many whose parents were evicted from their lands to make way for white settlers, and whose sons have been denied technical posts after higher education because of the colour of their skins, continue to doubt that whites will voluntarily give up their power and privileges.

A third political reality standing in the way of true freedom is the lack of political unity among Zimbabwe's political leaders. In large measure the dissensions, bitterness and hatred among us are the bitter fruits of Smith's divide and rule tactics in the past.

In Lusaka

I have already stated that in December 1974, the leaders of the main Zimbabwean National Groupings converged on Lusaka, Zambia. The objective was to extend the national unity established by the UANC at home to Zimbabwean nationalist groupings operating from abroad. Thus, ZAPU was represented. So was ZANU and FROLIZI. The UANC, then ANC, being the unity movement, was of course there. We went to Lusaka in search of national unity in the face of a common enemy. We were seeking to bury our differences and to establish a purpose centred in our total struggle. To me, the prospects of the meeting were exciting and represented one of the most significant developments in our struggle. At long and cherished last, petty little personal differences amongst the Zimbabwean leadership were to be sunk in the greater interest of the masses and the struggle.

My enthusiasm was considerably dented when, after the very first round of talks, it became clear that our hosts, the Frontline Presidents, wanted us to be united on their own terms. President Kaunda of Zambia and his colleagues had, unprompted by us, drawn up a written blue print for Zimbabwean unity. The scheme was presented to us by our smiling host and was couched in altruistic terms. I could hardly believe the brazenness of it. Predictably, Mr. Joshua Nkomo was to be President of the new unity movement. I was to be Mr. Nkomo's Vice-President while Rev. Sithole was to be Secretary-General. My mind went numb with righteous wrath. These exponents of democracy, assuming powers which by right belonged to the people of Zimbabwe, were trying to dictate to us how we should order our affairs. I was indignant.

Our reaction to this piece of devious and gross interference must have been as shocking to our hosts as their nefarious proposals were to us. We literally threw the scheme back into their patronizing faces. We made our rejection so clear that the talks were bogged down to such a point that they were contemplating walking out and going back home. Students of Zimbabwean history will know how much we, in Zimbabwe, loathe paternalistic attitudes.

It is to our credit that we, the Zimbabweans, saved these talks from collapse. Briefly, and eventually, we said to our hosts, 'Let us be alone. Leave us and allow us to discuss these matters amongst ourselves. Give us the opportunity to solve our problem.' Our proposal was accepted. Indeed, there was no choice, no alternative. Our hosts having retired, we the Zimbabweans spent the next four or five hours seeking a unity formula. My reader will already know the outcome of our efforts.

The Frontline States dearly wished to see the emergence of a Zimbabwe subservient to their wishes, a Zimbabwe whose leadership could be manipulated.

253

There have been numerous attempts by the Frontline States to impose a leadership on Zimbabwe. Let me give another example. Immediately we reached the unity accord of December 7, 1974, President Kaunda assumed responsibility for the success of the talks and in tones of self-righteousness, declared that any one of us who broke away from the new unity would receive no sympathy or help from him or from Africa as a whole. That is what Dr. Kaunda said in December 1974. A bare eight months later, Mr. Nkomo broke away from the unity accord. We waited with bated breath to see what Dr. Kaunda was going to say and do. We waited in vain. Instead, Dr. Kaunda lavished attentions on Mr. Nkomo. Dr. Kaunda showered Mr. Nkomo with his blessings in the form of advisors, transport, and unlimited material aid, especially supporting him in his internal talks with Mr. Smith which took place towards the end of 1975 and lasted three months ending early in 1976.

A truly independent Zimbabwe will need to be run by a leadership freely chosen by the people—not by some puppet imposed on the people by external interests to whom he gives obedience.

Too many African states are ruled by small élite cliques who monopolize all state power in their own hands and direct the affairs of the state primarily for their own welfare. Such an oligarchy determines who shall go into Parliament, who shall run the major industries, who shall be appointed to what post. In such states the people become mere spectators—receivers of crumbs dropped by the oligarchic octopus.

It is for fear of this frightful development that I wish to see Zimbabweans freely choosing their political leaders.

Second, the people should choose their political system.

They should be free to choose a multi-party system if they so desire. Zimbabweans, by and large, are extremely individualistic in their approach to problems. It would be difficult to lump them together under one party. Many would desire freedom to support different parties, some of which would form the political opposition. I believe that the majority of Zimbabweans are mature enough to handle the potentially explosive nature of an opposition.

On the other hand, Zimbabweans may find that a one-party system serves them better. The one-party state can be democratic and dynamic. Rooted in the African past, it is a system which is close to African tradition. The people themselves should decide by democratic means whether there should be a one-party system or not.

Rarely has this happened in independent African states. More often the ruling parties have decided on a change to 'one-party democracy' either because they have lost touch with the masses or because they were afraid of the opposition. They did so either because they were in danger of becoming unpopular or because the opposition was gaining ground.

Other African states have been plagued by *coups d'état*. Such events are not political accidents. They are a product of the unpopularity of the ruling cliques. All too often these *coups* have not succeeded in installing rulers who governed more efficiently or more justly than those whom they toppled from power. *Coups* look like mere power struggles within the ruling class, which result in the massacre of innocent people rather than better government.

I wish that the people of Africa could concentrate on developing their societies—their communications, economics, education, and health systems—rather than spending year after year having governments rise and fall by *coups*. Invariably this happens because the people are not allowed to exercise freely their democratic rights.

Leadership

Another crucial issue for an independent Zimbabwe will be the quality of its leadership.

Will Zimbabwe's leaders be at one and in harmony with the masses? Will they be committed to the total welfare of the people? Will they be persons of principle, of integrity? Or will they be opportunists, bent on self-aggrandisement at the expense of the masses?

These are vital questions for Zimbabwe, a state which has been at the receiving end of colonialism and racism and minority rule for almost one hundred years. Zimbabwe has suffered the ravages of a bitter war which has resulted in the impoverishment of most of the population. Zimbabwe deserves a leadership which is beyond reproach. It is for this reason also that a less restricted system of elections will probably be the best. The voice of the suffering masses will need to be heard very loudly in Zimbabwe.

255

If Zimbabwe is to be truly free and liberated, the head of state must be a liberated person himself. He must be free from the shackles of evil deeds or an evil past which would catch up with him. He must be liberated from the constraints of tribalism and racism. He must be an ordinary person—not one infatuated by his own sense of self-importance. Zimbabwe needs as a political head a man or woman capable of love, for the nation is going to need a great deal of loving after 100 years of burning hate.

He will need to be a mature person—mature enough to know that he is not God and that he is frail and human. The Zimbabwe head of state must be a man humble enough to accept criticism and to accommodate critics and friends alike. He must be confident in his ability to lead. An insecure person almost always sees plots behind every bush, plots for which he invents plotters to execute or harrass. Zimbabwe will need a statesman for her head of state. It is only statesmanship which will raise the country from the mire of racism and suspicion which has become second nature to many of our people. Harmony will need to be created, almost from scratch. Blacks, Whites, Asians, Coloureds— all these groups will need to be welded into one, homogeneous society based on mutual trust, mutual respect and healthy inter-dependence. Finally, Zimbabwe's first servant must be an able administrator and manager. We have referred to the erosion of a country's wealth through bad management. An inefficient leader will surround himself with fools—people who will not show off his inability. An inefficient leader will try to reduce the whole nation to the level of his own inefficiency, will frown upon ability and will discourage innovation. Zimbabwe must avoid being saddled with this type of leader. It must have a person with planning ability and sound administration at the top.

Can Zimbabwe find a workable formula of succession—a system whereby the people can constitutionally remove a head of state and replace him with another of their choice without going through a process of bloodshed or a coup? I hope so. After all, if a people cannot freely remove a head of state, can they be called free?

I must confess, however, that looking around in black Africa today, I cannot see a retired head of state living freely in his own country. Former heads of state are inevitably dead from assassination, or in exile or prison. We appear to have fallen victim to the old African custom where a chief stays in office until his death. But even in traditional politics there were ways of replacing a sick or incapacitated chief without bloodshed.

I want to see the day when Zimbabwe will remove a head of state democratically. I want to see an elder statesman gracefully step down and settle down to private life or to some other public office without becoming the focal point for a rebellion against the new leadership. I want to see such persons guiding the young with their wisdom and experience, following the example of the traditional African elder whose main role was to counsel the young. One of the most respected persons in traditional life is the grandfather. He is also one of the most loved. As soon as he hands over control to his heir, he sits back, contented, offering advice when asked, taking the young under his wing. This tradition has not died. We must cultivate it in our politics.

Guarantees of Freedom
Next, I believe that Zimbabwe will achieve genuine freedom and independence only if the judiciary is independent of manipulation and control by the powerful. The greatest guarantor of freedom is the rule of law.

Government must respect the independence of the judiciary. Too often we have seen the judiciary dragged into the errors of the government in power. I have seen governments force the judiciary to return verdicts favourable to them and not to the welfare of the people. Such governments slowly but surely turn into dictatorships. For Zimbabwe, I want to see a judiciary free from political influence, manned by men and women of the highest integrity—persons of experience and ability, not some political appointees.

The judge, however, remains an interpreter of the law of the land. To protect the basic freedom and rights of all Zimbabweans we need a constitution which contains a clear declaration of rights. It should contain precise statements of the following basic freedoms for which we have fought a long and bitter war.

First, there must be freedom of speech and expression. Hundreds of Zimbabweans during our liberation struggle languished in jails because they had dared to exercise this freedom under the existing minority dictatorships. Many independent African states likewise overtly abuse this fundamental freedom.

and freedom in our economic life, in our culture, and in our religion. We must accept the principle that freedom includes the responsibility to be held accountable for our own actions and not to be found wanting.

One day soon the people of Zimbabwe will proclaim their independence. Some will shout, 'Heavy! Heavy! Our struggle is over. Our victory has been won!' But that will be a day fraught with great danger if we think that the struggle to win freedom is over. Major battles remain to be won. We must ascend and accelerate in development to self-sufficiency. We must build one nation and stamp out racism and tribalism. We must create a land of happiness, reconciliation and harmony. Then and only then can we say, 'Yes, Zimbabwe is truly free!'

Postscript

During April and May 1978 the Executive Council in Salisbury proceeded to implement many of the terms of the Agreement for Majority Rule (Appendix C). On March 28 Bishop Muzorewa, the Rev. Sithole and Chief Chirau each nominated three black ministers to serve in the new Ministerial Council as counterparts to those whites already in office. Next, the Executive Council ordered a halt to executions of political prisoners, including nationalist guerrillas. Their release of an initial 461 political detainees received public acclaim. By May 2 over 700 detainees had been freed, with the cases of the remainder, a little over 200 in number, under review.

With the intention to restore free political activity in the country, the Council lifted on May 2 the banning of ZAPU and ZANU. Under an amnesty agreement, all Zimbabweans in exile were guaranteed safe return through 'free entry zones' along the borders provided they came in peace.

Many political leaders outside Zimbabwe, however, continued to oppose the settlement and to argue that only a settlement endorsed by all Zimbabwean political groups would bring lasting peace. Dr. David Owen, Foreign Secretary of Great Britain, and Mr. Cyrus Vance of the USA visited Africa in April to promote the Anglo-American proposals and the convening of an all-party conference on Zimbabwe. Meeting in Dar es Salaam with leaders of Frontline States and of the Patriotic Front, they urged acceptance of key elements of the proposals, including a UN peacekeeping force and a British residential commissioner during a transitional period. Mr. Mugabe, however, remained adamant that the guerrilla army should form the new army for Zimbabwe and that the Patriotic Front should hold predominant leadership in the council of any interim government acceptable to the Front.

The Executive Council of the Transitional Government in Salisbury also rejected the Anglo-American initiative following a meeting with Dr. Owen and Mr. Vance on April 17. 'The objective

261

of the nationalist parties, namely majority rule on the basis of universal suffrage, is enshrined in the Salisbury agreement,' they argued. They called for the Patriotic Front's return and full participation in the Transitional Government, and for the immediate lifting of sanctions. They rejected the proposed plan for an all-party conference as one serving no purpose, and found within a month that all concerned parties within southern Africa had come to the same conclusion.

In the absence of political agreement, the guerrilla war continued unbated. Civilians-suffered the heaviest casualties. Government troops killed 94 blacks attending a political meeting in the Gutu District near Fort Victoria on May 14. While dozens of Africans were dying weekly, the world press headlined killings of whites by guerrillas, including tourists, missionaries, and Red Cross workers. Mr. Mugabe of ZANU voted to intensify what he called 'a people's war', while Mr. Nkomo of ZAPU claimed that he possessed a 6,000-man army based in Zambia, supplied with arms by the Soviet Union, and trained by Cuban instructors.

The dismissal of Byron Hove, the UANC-appointed co-minister of Justice and Law and Order, on April 28 brought to the surface the key issue of future control over police and army within the country. Mr. Hove had criticized the absence of black leaders in the police and army and had advocated 'positive discrimination in favour of the African policeman' in future promotions. The Executive Council first reprimanded Mr. Hove and then dismissed him, but without Bishop Muzorewa's knowledge or consent. Africans, particularly of the UANC, angrily objected to this action. After three weeks of intense debate, however, the UANC's National Executive voted to remain in the interim government, fearing that its withdrawal would result in the immediate collapse of the coalition. To demonstrate its continued anger and disgust over Mr. Hove's dismissal, the UANC Executive determined that Bishop Muzorewa would not join with Messrs. Smith, Sithole and Chirau in public meetings to promote the internal settlement. Mr. Hove from London continued to support Bishop Muzorewa's leadership and remained the UANC's Deputy Secretary for Foreign Affairs.

During June the transitional administration worked on the machinery for the general elections projected for November. The plan included election by party, with each voter to indicate party preference only. Following the election, party leaders would select Members of Parliament at party congresses in numbers proportional to the popular vote received by each party. Discussions continued concerning the removal of discriminatory laws, including the Land Tenure Act, and the drafting of a new constitution, in expectation that power would pass to the black majority on Independence Day, December 31, 1978.

Historical Notes

1890 September 12	First European settlers, the 'pioneer column', raised the British flag at what was named Fort Salisbury; the beginning of 33 years of rule by the British South Africa Company in Rhodesia.
1893 October	A force of British South Africa Company volunteers invaded Matabeleland, destroying Bulawayo, the capital of Lobengula, King of the Ndebele.
1896–1897	Ndebele and Shona people rebelled against white settler rule.
1922 October 27	White settlers voted to become a self-governing colony of Great Britain, gaining control over their own army and police force. Britain retained the legal right to intervene in protection of African majority rights but in succeeding years did not exercise these powers. ·
1923 October 1	The new constitution of Southern Rhodesia with white settler rule came into effect.
1930	By the Land Apportionment Act, the white settler government further allocated the best land to exclusive white ownership relegating the marginal lands to Africans in communal tenure ('Reserves') or small family farms ('African Purchase Areas').
1934	ANC—the first African National Congress—was formed in Bulawayo as a voluntary association to petition for greater justice for Africans.
1946	A second wave of European immigrants into Rhodesia began after World War II. Three-fourths of the present white population of Rhodesia have settled since 1946.
1947	The African Voice Association, led by Benjamin Burombo, was organized to link rural and urban Africans in active protest against racial injustice.

1948	A general strike of African workers in Bulawayo and Salisbury was held for the first time.
1953	Southern Rhodesia joined with the British colonies of Northern Rhodesia and Nyasaland to form The Federation of Rhodesia and Nyasaland. White settlers extended their political power northward under a slogan of 'racial partnership'. Garfield Todd became Prime Minister of Southern Rhodesia.
1955 August	The Southern Rhodesia National Youth League was established with James Chikerema and George Nyandoro as leaders. Civil disobedience was introduced as a tactic to press for social change.
1957	ANC—The Southern Rhodesia African National Congress—was formed by the amalgamation of the Salisbury-based Youth League and the Bulawayo branch of the African National Congress. Joshua Nkomo was named President and James Chikerema Vice-President.
1959	Prime Minister Edgar Whitehead declared a state of emergency and banned the African National Congress, which had grown to become a national force demanding justice and African majority rule. More than 500 ANC leaders were arrested with Chikerema and Nyandoro and others kept in prison for four years.
1960 January 1	NDP—the National Democratic Party—was founded with Michael Mawema as Interim President. (Joshua Nkomo was elected President in November 1960). In July a raid on NDP headquarters in Highfields, Salisbury, led to a mass demonstration and strike by 25,000 to 40,000 Africans. The Government reacted by passing the Law and Order (Maintenance) Amendment Act making illegal all mass protests.
1961	New constitutional proposals included African direct representation in Parliament (15 out of 65 seats) for the first time. NDP leaders opposed the new constitution as inadequate and organized an unofficial constitutional referendum with 372,546 voting 'No' and only 471 voting 'Yes'. White

officials countered with mass arrests and the banning of the NDP on December 9, 1961.

December 18 ZAPU—the Zimbabwe African Peoples Union—was founded with Joshua Nkomo as President and the Rev. Ndabaningi Sithole as National Chairman.

1962
September 20 ZAPU was banned following demonstrations of its mass support in political rallies. A wave of violence swept the country with attacks on schools and government buildings and the burning of forests. About 2,000 African leaders were arrested.

December 14 In national elections white voters supported the conservative Dominion Party headed by Winston Field and rejected Whitehead's United Federal Party with its slogans of 'multi-racialism'.

1963
July ZAPU split when Nkomo suspended Ndabaningi Sithole (National Chairman), Leopold Takawira (Secretary for External Affairs), Robert Mugabe (Publicity Secretary) and Marton Malianga (Secretary General).

August 8 ZANU—the Zimbabwe African National Union —was formed and Ndabaningi Sithole elected President.

August 10 PCC—the People's Caretaker Council—was chosen as the new name for the banned ZAPU by 5,000 supporters at the Cold Comfort Conference.

1964
April 13 RF—the Rhodesian Front Party—the most conservative white party, won new elections and Ian Smith became Prime Minister. Within a month more than 2,000 Africans were placed in political detention, including Joshua Nkomo and Ndabaningi Sithole who were to be held for ten years.

1965
November 11 UDI—the Unilateral Declaration of Independence from Great Britain—was declared by Ian Smith.

1966 While the UN Security Council imposed economic sanctions against the Smith regime, African nationalists began the armed struggle for liberation and African majority rule.

1971
October FROLIZI—the Front for the Liberation of Zimbabwe—was formed among Zimbabweans in

	Zambia led by James Chikerema and George Nyandoro. It failed to reunite ZAPU and ZANU and became instead a third movement.
November	Sir Alec Douglas-Home, British Foreign Secretary, and Ian Smith agreed on amendments to the 1969 Rhodesia Constitution as Proposals for a settlement of the constitutional dispute.
December	ANC—the African National Council—was organized with Bishop Abel Tendekai Muzorewa as President to oppose the Smith-Home Settlement Proposals.
1972 January- March	The Pearce Commission tested public opinion within Rhodesia concerning the Settlement Proposals and found massive African rejection of the Proposals.
December 21	ZANLA—the Zimbabwe African National Liberation Army—the military wing of ZANU, began its military offensive in the north-eastern section of the country.
1973 January	The Rhodesian and Zambian Governments closed their common border.
1974	The Frontline States (Botswana, Tanzania, Zambia, Mozambique and Angola) supported Zimbabwean political unity and simultaneous strategies of negotiations with the white rulers of South Africa and Rhodesia and an intensified armed struggle.
December 7	By the Lusaka Agreement, Joshua Nkomo for ZAPU, Ndabaningi Sithole for ZANU, James Chikerema for FROLIZI, and Abel Muzorewa for ANC agreed to unite in the African National Council with Muzorewa as President.
1975 March 18	Herbert Chitepo, Chairman of ZANU since 1963, was assassinated in Lusaka, Zambia. President Kaunda of Zambia appointed an international commission, which investigated and disclosed a serious leadership split within ZANU which resulted in this and other murders.
July	ZLC—the Zimbabwe Liberation Council—was formally organized as the external organization of the African National Council.

August 26	The Victoria Falls Bridge talks were held between a Rhodesian white delegation led by Ian Smith and the Zimbabwean ANC delegation led by Abel Muzorewa. Talks quickly broke down, but the visit of Prime Minister Vorster of South Africa and President Kaunda of Zambia spotlighted the new drive for '*détente*'.
September	Bishop Muzorewa expelled Joshua Nkomo from the ANC for secret collaboration with Ian Smith· Nkomo held a bogus ANC Congress in Highfields and claimed election as President of the ANC.
1976 March	ZIPA—the Zimbabwe People's Army—was formed in an attempt to unite guerrilla forces of ZANU and ZAPU. In political negotiations they chose to be called the 'Third Force', with Robert Mugabe of ZANU as their spokesman.
September	UANC-Zimbabwe—the United African National Council of Zimbabwe—the official ANC led by Bishop Muzorewa chose to use this name since both Ndabaningi Sithole and Joshua Nkomo had broken away but continued to use the name 'ANC' in hopes of gaining some popular support.
October	The Patriotic Front—a unity move between former ZAPU and ZANU elements—was formed under the joint leadership of Joshua Nkomo (ZAPU) and Robert Mugabe (ZANU).
October 25	The Geneva Constitutional Conference on Zimbabwe (Rhodesia) Independence opened in Switzerland to discuss proposals for a peaceful transfer of power within Zimbabwe (Rhodesia) to the African majority. It adjourned on December 15 without agreement on a new constitution.
1977 January 24	Ian Smith rejected proposals presented by Mr. Ivor Richard for the United Kingdom calling for British leadership in an interim government.
April	Dr. David Owen of Great Britain visited eight African countries to present new proposals for majority rule.
August	New Anglo-American 'Proposals for a Settlement in Rhodesia' presented by Dr. David Owen and

Mr. Andrew Young, US Permanent Secretary at the United Nations, to all parties concerned.

September 21 Catholic Commission for Justice and Peace in Zimbabwe published *Rhodesia: The Propaganda War*, which documented brutality and torture of civilians by the Rhodesian army.

November 24 Ian Smith announced acceptance of the principle of majority rule based on one man one vote as a starting point for negotiations with black nationalist leaders living in Rhodesia.

1978
March 3 Agreement for Majority Rule signed in Salisbury by Bishop Abel Muzorewa, the Reverend Ndabaningi Sithole, Senator Jeremiah Chirau and Ian D. Smith of Rhodesia.

March 28 Ministerial Council of Interim Government formed, composed of equal numbers of black and white ministers.

April Dr. David Owen of Great Britain and Mr. Cyrus Vance of the United States, attempted unsuccessfully to gain acceptance of an Anglo-American plan for an all-party conference and transitional government including all Zimbabwean political groups.

April 28 Dismissal of Byron Hove (UANC-appointed co-minister of Justice and Law and Order).

June The civil war continued with increased killing of civilians, including white missionaries.

The ANC Manifesto

Are African Nationalists People?
Brothers and sisters, we welcome you here on this occasion, although we are the ones who should be really welcomed by you, for it is because of your cry, petitions and demands that we responded by setting the African National Council (ANC) in a viable structure. This new organization, like the old ones, will be referred to, by outsiders, as an African nationalist organization. The very term 'African nationalists' has unpleasant connotations to many people with closed minds.

We want to affirm that we are nothing but normal human beings who have an innate desire for freedom and justice to all people. We have organized ourselves so that with a common voice our cry can be heard and our aspirations can be reached.

This cry, to many, will have an undesirable sound. They will regard us as 'dangerous creatures' who should be watched and prevented from acting freely. We here declare that we are simply creatures made in the image of God and, therefore, His children who need to be liberated; nothing more, nothing less.

Only as we are fully liberated can we fulfill the purpose for which we were created.

Dedication
On this tenth day of March, 1972, at Highfield, Salisbury, we are here assembled, claiming no more than to be heirs to the People's Struggle which has ceaselessly been waged since the imposition of alien rule in 1890. In the name of Almighty God, who, in His love and mercy, created all people and races in His image, we do hereby proclaim, constitute and declare the African National Council to be the one sole voice and instrument of the African masses of Zimbabwe and all people of goodwill, in their just and normal struggle for national emancipation from the yoke of a racist and oppressive minority rule.

Accordingly, the African National Council is born today as a result of the need and demands of primarily the African people and other racial groups of this country. And we here and now summon every African in this land, young or old, rich or poor, educated or uneducated, chief or subject, and those members of other races dedicated to the establishment of human brotherhood, to recognize the trumpet we here sound and to rally around us, so that together, we continue our arduous journey to Zimbabwe in a Christian and non-violent manner.

Beliefs

1. This Council believes in the power of the unity of the African masses in the imperative need for the opposition of those elements or forces which seek to sow the seeds of division among our people. Divided, we will remain slaves and strangers in the land of our birth. United, though we may suffer, we shall toil, but with dignity, until we are free. We should, therefore, be warned that our worst enemies are those who seek to divide us and those who labour to keep us in perpetual oppression, be they black or white.
2. *We* believe in the invincibility of numbers of the masses of men and women of goodwill in Rhodesia and that the African National Council is truly a grass-roots organization in its very scope, membership and spirit.
3. *We* believe in a government that will establish and promote the sanctity and practice of the essential human freedoms of conscience, of expression, association, religion, assembly and movement of all people irrespective of colour, race or creed.
4. *We* believe in non-racialism, the universal brotherhood of man under the Fatherhood of God. This means forced segregation and integration violate the principle of free choice of association.
5. *We* believe in a non-violent, peaceful, orderly but permanent and continuing struggle to be waged within the Law and for the establishment of a constitutional government.
6. *We* believe that true peace and harmony among all people and economic stability of this country can only be assured for all time by the establishment of 'the government of the people, by the people and for the people.'
7. *We* believe that the rights and property of the minority should be protected; we do not, however, believe in the minority's amassing of social, political and economic privileges at the expense of the freedom of the majority.

Declaration

The African National Council solemnly dedicates itself to strive for the realization of those universal human rights conceded to the citizens in all democratic and just societies. This being so—

1. *We* shall not waiver or prevaricate in our demand for the creation, in this country, of a just social order; but shall strive to achieve this justice which is long overdue;
2. *We* shall not deviate from our just demand for universal adult suffrage;
3. *We* shall never concede to the fallacy that there is any justification for racial and other forms of discrimination as between one human being against another. Thus, we shall continue to oppose racial bigotry, religious intolerance, class arrogance, the idiocy of tribalism and undeserved economic privileges, and we shall strive to create a nation where black and white can live as children of the One Almighty God;
4. *We* shall never compromise with the sin of greed which is the main characteristic of a minority-controlled economy; but will continue to promote a fair and free participation of each and every citizen of this our motherland—rich in natural resources;
5. *We* shall for ever abhor the continued denial, under the pretext of 'preservation of Western Christian civilization', of the masses' demand for legitimate self-determination;
6. *We* shall never support nor respect a system which lays emphasis on Law and Order at the expense of charity, justice and human dignity; but will continue to call upon the conscience of this country to influence the establishment of Law and Order with justice;
7. *We* shall require and desire nothing less than self-determination.

External Relations

We declare our solidarity with those international organizations dedicated to the peaceful creation and preservation of the basic universal human rights and the brotherhood of man under the Fatherhood of God.

Challenge to the Nation

Having stated our beliefs and declarations, we now challenge all people of this country—Africans, Asians, Coloured and Europeans—who sincerely and honestly seek a genuine peace and mutual understanding to join us.

272

Only as we work together can we bring our country out of its present political deadlock.

We challenge the people of this country to come out of the current political dream-world by realizing that what has been called 'peace' and 'happiness' and 'good race relations' are, in fact, repressed fear, restless silence, forced tolerance and hidden hatred of one another.

We call, and call again, to make people aware that our race relations are deteriorating and that they will continue to do so until all discriminatory legislation in this land has been removed.

We challenge our Rhodesian whites to realize the simple socio-psychological fact that no one should expect love from a person he hates; or expect respect from a person he disrespects; or expect admiration from a person he despises, nor loyalty from a person whom he does not love.

We finally and particularly direct this challenge to the Europeans of Rhodesia, that now is the day to sit down with us and, in peaceful negotiations, try and find a mutually agreeable formula for achieving racial harmony. This is absolutely necessary for social stability, economic growth and a secure future for all of us and our children.

Time for such negotiations is fast running out. Believe it! This is the day that circumstance and fate or, as we want to express it, God, has led us all.

If we want to be blessed and not cursed by our children and children's children, we have no time to lose.

We challengingly remind our African people that whatever position we hold, or status we enjoy, we are all condemned as *black people* in this country. All are treated as second-class, if not third-class, citizens. We therefore feel very sad when we see some of our people and hear about their behaviour which points to the fact that they have lost the purpose and goal and are living and fighting for their own stomachs and self-interests instead of liberation for all, which should be every sane person's goal.

We have seen signs of these kinds of people, who are bought to work out division, to work out frustration, to work out embarrassment, and to work out perpetual slavery of the Africans. Shame!

We challenge our African people to stop fulfilling the accusation that 'The worst enemies of Africans are Africans themselves,' and instead become our own liberators by stopping all sorts of traitorous actions against the African united fronts for liberation and labour for the common goal of independence.

We call our African people to praise and congratulate our fathers—the chiefs—for their courageous stand and true representation of their people which they displayed during the test of acceptability of the Anglo-Rhodesian Settlement Proposals. We trust this is the beginning of a new day in Rhodesia for Africans.

We challenge the clergy of this country to stop preaching the useless and archaic doctrine of 'pie in the sky' and start vigorously to preach a 'whole gospel for the whole man'; to teach our people that politics is not a 'dirty game', but that what makes politics dirty is the kind of people who play politics and how they participate in it; that the definition of politics is 'the science and art of governing people' and that there can never be any evil in that kind of science or art. There is no virtue in participating or not participating in politics, but Christians must be involved when the political system disturbs people and churches such as in the case of the Land Tenure Act.

We challenge our African people to be purpose-centred rather than personality-centred.

We challenge our African people to realize that while we have chosen a peaceful and loving method of approach, in *unity* we have more than a bomb can achieve. Therefore, be *united*, be *united* until *unity* is *strength* and *strength* becomes *power*.

Zimbabwe Declaration of Unity at Lusaka, Republic of Zambia, on December 7, 1974

1. ZANU, ZAPU, FROLIZI and ANC hereby agree to unite in the ANC.

2. The Parties recognize the ANC as the unifying force of the people of Zimbabwe.

3. (a) They agree to consolidate the leadership of the ANC by the inclusion into it of the Presidents of ZANU, ZAPU and FROLIZI, under the chairmanship of the President of ANC.

   (b) ZAPU, ZANU and FROLIZI shall each appoint three other persons to join the enlarged ANC Executive.

4. The enlarged ANC Executive shall have the following functions:
   (a) To prepare for any Conference for the transfer of power to the majority that might be called.

   (b) To prepare for the holding of a Congress within four months at which (i) a Revised ANC Constitution shall be adopted; (ii) the leadership of the united people of Zimbabwe shall be elected; (iii) a statement of policy for the new ANC shall be considered.

   (c) To organize the people for such a Conference and Congress.

5. The leaders of the ZAPU, ZANU and FROLIZI call upon their supporters and all Zimbabweans to rally behind the ANC under its enlarged Executive.

6. ZAPU, ZANU and FROLIZI will take steps to merge their respective organs and structures into the ANC before the Congress to be held within four months.

7. The leaders recognize the inevitability of continued armed struggle and all other forms of struggle until the total liberation of Zimbabwe.

Abel Tendekai Muzorewa
PRESIDENT OF ANC

Joshua Mqabuko Nkomo
PRESIDENT OF ZAPU

Ndabaningi Sithole
PRESIDENT OF ZANU

James Robert Dambaza
Chikerema
PRESIDENT OF FROLIZI

STATE HOUSE, LUSAKA.

Statement Issued in Salisbury by the Newly Formed African National Council at 1600 Hours on Thursday, 12 December, 1974.

Recognizing the paramount need for unity in the Zimbabwe liberation struggle, the Executive Committees of ZAPU, ZANU, FROLIZI and ANC have met in Lusaka to discuss the aims, objectives and methods to be pursued. Full agreement was reached on the following points:

1. We have agreed to unite under one organization with immediate effect. We have agreed further, that this organization shall be the African National Council.

2. We shall be working for the independence of our country. We assume that on this demand for independence there is no difference among Rhodesians of all races. But there has until now been a difference on the kind of independence which Zimbabwe must have. The Rhodesia Front has, in the past, sought independence on the basis of minority rule. We reject that. The independence we have always sought, and the independence we still seek, is independence on the basis of majority rule.

3. For the purpose of achieving that objective we have always

276

been ready to enter into negotiations with others concerned. Now that some of us have been released from detention, we believe that the time is ripe for us to repeat this offer. Without pre-conditions on both sides, we are ready to enter into immediate and meaningful negotiations with the leaders of the Rhodesia Front, and with the British Government in Britain, on the steps to be taken to achieve independence on the basis of majority rule.

4. As a demonstration of our sincerity, all Freedom Fighters will be instructed, as soon as the date for negotiations has been fixed, to suspend fighting.

5. We are not racialists. We accept the right of White Rhodesians to live in Rhodesia and share the same rights and obligations of citizenship as their fellow Rhodesians of the majority community, without any discrimination on the grounds of race, colour or creed.

6. We call upon all Zimbabweans, wherever they are, to remain united behind the demand for independence on the basis of majority rule, and to give full support to the African National Council.

7. We call upon all Rhodesians who reside in Rhodesia, to remain calm, maintain peace and go about their normal business, while these matters are being considered and while any negotiations are proceeding.

8. We appeal to all friends in Africa and abroad to continue their support for our struggle until independence is achieved on the basis of majority rule.

Signed:

Abel Tendekai Muzorewa
PRESIDENT OF ANC

Joshua Mqabuko Nkomo
FORMER PRESIDENT OF
ZAPU

Ndabaningi Sithole
FORMER PRESIDENT
ZANU

James Robert Dambaza
Chikerema
FORMER PRESIDENT OF
FROLIZI

Agreement for Majority Rule, March 3, 1978

WHEREAS the present constitutional situation in Rhodesia has led to the imposition of economic and other sanctions by the international community against Rhodesia and to armed conflict within Rhodesia and from neighbouring territories;

AND WHEREAS it is necessary in the interests of our country that an agreement should be reached that would lead to the termination of such sanctions and the cessation of the armed conflict;

AND WHEREAS, in an endeavour to reach such an agreement, delegates from the Rhodesian Government, African National Council (Sithole), United African National Council and Zimbabwe United People's Organization have met during the last two months in Salisbury and, having discussed fully the proposals put forward by the various delegations, have reached agreement on certain fundamental principles to be embodied in a new constitution that will lead to the termination of the aforementioned sanctions and the cessation of the armed conflict.

NOW, THEREFORE:

A

It is hereby agreed that a constitution will be drafted and enacted which will provide for majority rule on the basis of universal adult suffrage on the following terms:

(1)

There will be a legislative assembly consisting of 100 members and the following provisions will apply thereto:

(a) There will be a common voters' roll, with all citizens of 18 years and over being eligible for registration as voters, subject to certain recognized disqualifications.

(b) 72 of the seats in the legislative assembly will be reserved for blacks who will be elected by voters who are enrolled on the common roll.

(c) 28 of the seats in the legislative assembly will be reserved for whites (i.e., Europeans as defined in the 1969 Constitution) who will be elected as follows:

(i) 20 will be elected on a preferential voting system by white voters who are enrolled on the common roll.

(ii) Eight will be elected by voters who are enrolled on the common roll from 16 candidates who will be nominated, in the case of the first parliament, by an electoral college composed of the white members of the present House of Assembly and, in the case of any subsequent parliament, by an electoral college composed of the 28 whites who are members of the parliament dissolved immediately prior to the general election.

(d) The reserved seats referred to in (c) above shall be retained for a period of at least 10 years or of two parliaments, whichever is the longer, and shall be reviewed at the expiration of that period, at which time a commission shall be appointed, the chairman of which shall be a judge of the High Court, to undertake this review. If that commission recommends that the arrangements regarding the said reserved seats should be changed:

(i) An amendment to the constitution to effect such change may be made by a bill which receives the affirmative votes of not less than 51 members.

(ii) The said bill shall also provide that the 72 seats referred to in (b) above shall not be reserved for blacks.

(e) The members filling the seats referred to in (c) above will be prohibited from forming a coalition with any single minority party for the purpose of forming a government.

(2)

There will be a just declaration of rights which will protect the rights and freedoms of individuals and, *inter alia,* will provide for protection from deprivation of property unless adequate compensation is paid promptly, and for protection of pension rights of persons who are members of pension funds.

(3)

The independence and qualifications of the judiciary will be entrenched and judges will have security of tenure.

(4)

There will be an independent public services board, the members of which will have security of tenure. The board will be responsible for appointments to, promotions in and discharges from the public service.

(5)

The public service, police force, defence forces and prison service will be maintained in a high state of efficiency and free from political interference.

(6)

Pensions which are payable from the consolidated revenue fund will be guaranteed and charged on the consolidated revenue fund and will be remittable outside the country.

(7)

Citizens who at present are entitled to dual citizenship will not be deprived of their present entitlement.

(8)

The above-mentioned provisions will be set out or provided for in the constitution and will be regarded as specially entrenched provisions which may only be amended by a bill which receives the affirmative votes of not less than 78 members.

B

It is hereby also agreed that, following the agreement set out above, the next step will be the setting up of a transitional government. The prime function of the transitional government will be:

(a) To bring about a cease fire, and

(b) To deal with related matters such as:

(i) The composition of the future military forces, including those members of the nationalist forces who wish to take up a military career, and the rehabilitation of others;

(ii) The rehabilitation of those affected by the war.

C

It is also hereby agreed that it will be the duty of the transitional government to determine and deal with the following matters:

(a) The release of detainees;

(b) The review of sentences for offences of a political character;

(c) The further removal of discrimination;

(d) The creation of a climate conducive to the holding of free and democratic elections;

(e) The drafting of the new constitution in terms of this agreement;

(f) Procedures for registration of voters with a view to the holding of a general election at the earliest possible date.

D

It is also hereby agreed that the transitional government will comprise an executive council and a ministerial council, and the following provisions will apply thereto:

(1)
EXECUTIVE COUNCIL

(a) Composition:

The executive council will be composed of the Prime Minister and three black ministers, being the heads of those delegations engaged in the negotiations. The members will take turns in presiding as chairman of the executive council in such sequence and for such period as that council may determine. Decision of the executive council will be by consensus.

(b) Functions:

(i) The executive council will be responsible for insuring that the functions given to and the duties imposed on the transitional government by the constitutional agreement are dealt with as expeditiously as possible. It will take policy decisions in connection with the preparation and drafting of the new constitution and the other matters set out in sections B and C of this agreement and with any other matters which may arise.

(ii) The executive council may refer the matters set out in sections B and C of this agreement, or any other matter, to the ministerial council for examination and recommendation.

(iii) The executive council will review decisions or recommendations of the ministerial council and may confirm such decisions or recommendations or refer them back to the ministerial council for further consideration.

(2)
MINISTERIAL COUNCIL

(a) Composition:

The ministerial council will be composed of equal numbers of black and white ministers. The black ministers will be nominated in equal proportions by the heads of those delegations engaged in the negotiations. The white ministers will be nominated by the Prime Minister. The chairmanship of the ministerial council will alternate between black and white ministers. The Prime Minister will nominate which white minister shall take the chair, and the heads of those delegations engaged in the negotiations will nominate which of the black ministers shall take the chair in the sequence and for the period determined by the ministerial council.

  (b) Functions:

    (i) The ministerial council will operate on the cabinet system. For each portfolio, or group of portfolios, there will be a black and a white minister who will share responsibility.

    (ii) The ministerial council will be responsible for initiating legislation and for supervising the preparation of such legislation as may be directed by the executive council.

    (iii) The ministerial council will make recommendations to the executive council on all matters referred to it by the executive council and on any other matter it thinks fit.

    (iv) Decisions of the ministerial council will be by majority vote and subject to review by the executive council.

(3)

PARLIAMENT

  (a) Parliament will continue to function during the life of the transitional government and will meet for the following purposes as and when the executive council considers it should be summoned:

    (i) To pass a constitution amendment act enabling ministers who have not been elected to parliament to serve for periods in excess of four months;

    (ii) To pass legislation for the registration of voters;

    (iii) To pass the 1978-79 budget;

    (iv) To enact any legislation or deal with any other matter brought forward by the transitional government (e.g. for the further removal of discrimination).

    (v) To enact the new constitution;

    (vi) To nominate 16 whites for election by voters on the common roll to eight of the seats reserved for whites.

  (b) The work of the various select committees and of the Senate Legal Committee will proceed as normal.

E

It is also hereby agreed that Independence Day shall be Dec. 31, 1978.

> signed at Salisbury,
> this third day of March 1978.
> Prime Minister Ian D. Smith
> Rev. Ndabaningi Sithole
> Bishop Abel Muzorewa
> Senator Jeremiah Chirau

Index

287